With the hope that you
will enjoy this story of
Mr. Sam and grass roots
politics in Northeast
Texas.

Anthony Champagne

Congressman

SAM
Rayburn

"Showing the City Folks How It Is Done."
*Rayburn was proud of his farm origins. At a social
event in Maryland, he showed that he knew
how to mow alfalfa, 1938.
Courtesy of Sam Rayburn Library.*

Congressman

SAM
Rayburn

Anthony Champagne

Rutgers University Press
New Brunswick, New Jersey

Library of Congress Cataloging in Publication Data

Champagne, Anthony, 1949–
    Congressman Sam Rayburn.

    Bibliography: p.
    Includes index.
    1. Rayburn, Sam, 1882–1961. 2. Texas—
Politics and government—1865–1950. 3. Texas—
Politics and government—1951–   . 4. Legis-
lators—United States—Biography. 5. United
States. Congress. House—Biography. I. Title
E748.R24C47 1984   328.73'092'4   83–4454
ISBN 0-8135-1012-0

This book is dedicated to
the memory of
my father

Contents

Photographs follow page 21

Foreword

HE CONSTITUENCY CONNECTION IN THE CA-
reer of Sam Rayburn has been neglected by
political writers. Thus a significant gap has existed in Rayburn literature.

I was born and reared in the Oklahoma congressional district that borders his on the north,
extending to within fifteen miles of his hometown of Bonham. I represented this district in Congress for
thirty years, serving with him during the first half of this period
and working daily with him as majority whip for almost seven
years. I have visited with Mr. Rayburn in his home, have campaigned with him in his district, and he with me in mine. I have
known many of his friends, some of whom long ago became
good friends of mine as well. I knew Mr. Rayburn well enough
to be certain that no one can understand him without grasping
the nature of his district and his vibrant, ever-present relationship to it and its citizens.

Professor Anthony Champagne in his book, *Congressman Sam
Rayburn,* has done a masterful job of filling the constituency
gap. His research has been exhaustive. He has meticulously examined published materials, periodicals, and correspondence.
More important, he has interviewed a large number of Mr.
Rayburn's friends and associates both in his district and in Congress. He has made a splendid case study based on these irre-
placeable interviews obtained while those with firsthand knowledge were still around and thus saved for posterity this vital part
of the Rayburn story.

Mr. Rayburn was an extraordinary human being, warm,
humble, and friendly, while projecting the very essence of
greatness. His background was made to order for his district.
He was a poor farm boy who attended a three-room country
school and worked his way through a small college in his district. He knew the hard toil of the cotton farmer. He had seen
his family suffer from the ravages of the boll weevil and the gy-
rations of the cotton market. He came up the hard way. He

ix

never forgot. This was his image when he entered politics; it remained his image as long as he lived.

I believe Mr. Rayburn had the best judgment of anybody I ever knew, and as he liked to say: "It doesn't make any difference how much sense a man has if he doesn't have judgment." He also had rare political instincts. His ability to anticipate was unbelievable. The man never lived who could put him in a corner and keep him there. He could walk a political tightrope through almost any situation. He loved his district and watched it like a hawk. He could put out most fires before they started burning. I am not certain that anyone ever fully understood him.

From his earliest years Mr. Rayburn dreamed of climbing to the top in national politics. He was modest but never self-effacing, and deep down he had a burning desire for fame. He knew what he wanted, and he set out to get it. He had almost infinite patience, but when he moved he moved with all his might. In 1911, while Speaker of the Texas House of Representatives, he set up the five-county congressional district that he wanted to represent, and he nurtured it until he died. Except for the addition of two relatively small counties in a redistricting act after the 1930 census, he had the same district in 1961 that he had in 1913. From the beginning he knew he did not want to be simply a one-district congressman forever. He had his eye on the Speaker's chair long before he ever saw it. But Mr. Rayburn never forgot for a moment, even after he was elected Speaker, that he could not be Speaker nor a congressman of any kind if he were defeated in his own district.

He was a master at orchestrating his politics between Washington and Bonham. The way he did it was typical of the Rayburn genius. First of all, he continually courted his district. While Congress was in session he always stayed in Washington and worked. When Congress adjourned he went home to Bonham and stayed there. He visited all the counties of his district every year. He did favors for any and all constituents. As he once wrote, "I make myself available to the people I represent so they can see me at any time." He cultivated people and made friends young and old. He built an informal and loosely knit organization of able and dependable supporters in every section of his district. I have known many of his friends and leaders, all of them well informed in their own areas and respected in their communities. They were all perfectly loyal to Mr. Rayburn. They watched for him and kept him advised of anything significant that happened at home while he was in Washington. They campaigned for him whenever he had opposition.

Mr. Rayburn took care of his district. He brought major projects into all areas. His handiwork can be seen even today in almost every precinct. These are things that help win elections.

With solid accomplishments for his district, steady loyalty to his people, and slowly growing prestige, he established a political base that gave him the elbow room he needed to operate as a national leader in Washington. But in doing so he never neglected his home people. He accomplished one of the rarest and least understood achievements in American politics, that of acting dynamically while holding the balance between the interests of his district and the broader ones of the nation as a whole. He weighed every issue in terms of its effect on his career in the district and in Washington. He knew when he could be completely parochial in Congress, on such issues as tidelands oil and the oil depletion allowance, even though opposed by a majority of Democrats in Congress. He also knew when he could be a national leader, on such issues as foreign aid and reciprocal trade. And he knew when he could be a liberal on such issues as social security. He tried to please his constituents and his colleagues at the same time. He would go as far as he thought his colleagues would let him in his efforts to please his people. He would also go as far as he thought his constituents would permit on unpopular national issues. Only one time during my service in Congress did I see Mr. Rayburn lean further toward his district than he first said he would go. The civil rights issue became so hot during his 1948 campaign that, upon the insistence of his friends, he came out in opposition to nearly all civil rights bills and proclaimed his support for racial segregation. He told me after the campaign that had he not done so he would have been defeated. I am not sure of that, but failure to do so would have given him problems.

Mr. Champagne takes readers right through the Rayburn career, step by step. He gives case studies showing how Rayburn built his strength in his district. In my judgment *Congressman Sam Rayburn* will become a classic.

Carl Albert
Member of the House of
Representatives (Democrat),
1947 to 1977
Speaker of the House,
1971 to 1977

Preface

THIS BOOK IS NOT A BIOGRAPHY; TWO EXCEL-
lent book-length biographies and a collection of
Sam Rayburn's writings are already available.[1]
Nor does this book focus on Rayburn in Washington, the topic covered by most Rayburn research. Instead, it is an effort at understanding
Sam Rayburn and his success within his home
district. It is a study of Rayburn's political longevity, a topic ig-
nored or only briefly mentioned in most Rayburn research. This
book flows from a belief that the role of a congressman in his
district deserves treatment just as much as his Washington role.[2]
It has as a premise that congressional politics cannot be understood without examining that district role and its relation to the
congressman's Washington behavior.

Because Rayburn's district behavior was not under the scru-
tiny of the press like his Washington life and because Rayburn's
files are incomplete, much of this study relies on interviews with
his associates, listed in Appendix A. The book is divided into six
chapters. Chapter 1 examines the characteristics of the Fourth
District, for it was the Fourth that elected and reelected Rayburn for twenty-five terms in Congress. The chapter suggests
that the stability of both the Fourth's boundaries and its population had much to do with Rayburn's political longevity. Chapter
2 examines the Rayburn style. The chapter points out that Rayburn, that most professional of national policy makers, also had
a surprisingly strong district orientation. The nature of the political organization so central to Rayburn's electoral successes is
examined in Chapter 3. Chapter 4 studies Rayburn on the campaign trail. It analyzes his campaign strategy in five primary
elections along with the nature of Rayburn's opposition. Chapter 5 discusses the linkages between Rayburn's district behavior
and his national leadership. Finally, Chapter 6 offers some concluding remarks about Rayburn's leadership and political longevity. It also suggests some possible explanations for his
lengthy and successful political career.

A book such as this needs the assistance and cooperation of many people. I was especially fortunate to have the aid of H. G. Dulaney, the Director of the Sam Rayburn Library and an assistant to Sam Rayburn. H. G. provided invaluable help in locating materials at the Rayburn Library and in arranging meetings with associates of Sam Rayburn. He also allowed me to probe his memory. H. G. was one of the small number of persons who was very close to Rayburn, and the formal and informal interviews he provided were especially important in giving me an understanding of Rayburn and the district.

I am also indebted to the people listed in Appendix A for their kindness in talking to me about Sam Rayburn. The Sam Rayburn Foundation and The University of Texas at Dallas Organized Research Grants provided partial funding for this research. I am also so grateful for the aid and encouragement provided by the staff of the Sam Rayburn Library, University of Texas Vice Chancellor Bryce Jordan, Professor John Sommer, Professor Brantley Womack, Center for Policy Studies Assistant Sunny Johnston, and graduate students Dottie Anderson, Rick Collis, and Ruth Willis. I am indebted to Mary Fae Kamm, who aided me with many of my interviews in Washington, D.C. Thanks also to Cynthia Keheley for her work in preparing the manuscript. Naturally, responsibility for errors or misinterpretations rests with me alone.

Unless otherwise noted, interviews, news articles, and correspondence are from the Sam Rayburn Library. The Sam Rayburn Library materials were supplemented by materials from the Lyndon Baines Johnson Library, the Harry S Truman Library, the Dwight D. Eisenhower Library, and the North Texas State University Oral History Collection. The oral history collections of these libraries proved especially useful. The Dallas Historical Society holds the Joseph Welden Bailey papers and the Hatton Sumners papers. I am indebted to the society for allowing use of some of their papers. Thanks are also due to the East Texas Historical Association for allowing me to reprint my article, "The Two Roles of Sam Rayburn," which appeared in volume 20 of the *East Texas Historical Journal*. Chapter 5 includes this article.

Congressman

SAM
Rayburn

1. The District

IN HIS LONG CAREER AS A REPRESENTATIVE, Sam Rayburn had served three terms in the Texas legislature, the last term as its Speaker, and had then gone to the U.S. House of Representatives, where he served for nearly forty-nine years. During that time, he had worked closely with fellow Texan John Nance Garner, played a major role in the creation of the Roosevelt-Garner ticket in 1932, served as the workhorse of the New Deal during his chairmanship of the Interstate and Foreign Commerce Committee, served as majority leader, and finally, as the most powerful and effective Speaker since Joseph Cannon early in this century. Rayburn had been considered for presidential nomination and more seriously for the vice presidency. He played a key role in such legislation as rural electrification, soil conservation, antimonopoly laws, the regulation of railroads and securities, the oil depletion allowance, and the 1957 Civil Rights Act. He was a strong defender of the Democratic party, attacking Texas's pro-Eisenhower governor with a ferocity not found in other major Texas politicians, yet also attacking Texas's liberal, loyal Democrats who, he was convinced, had strayed too far from the mainstream of the Texas Democratic party. Rayburn was both loved and hated, but for years he was unquestionably one of the most powerful figures in American politics.

Born in 1882 in Tennessee, the son of small farmers, Rayburn, at the age of five, had moved with his family to a farming community near Bonham. There his parents raised their eleven children and worked a cotton farm, on which young Sam acquired experience with poverty and the difficulties of rural life at the turn of the century. But he was a boy with ambition. He heard Joe Bailey orate and was inspired to enter politics. First he completed his education, limited though the offerings were in the tiny country schools he attended, then went to Mayo College in Commerce, Texas, where he worked his way through. He taught briefly, but his childhood political ambitions drew him to seek office.

Bailey, one of the most influential and controversial figures in Texas politics and then senator from Texas, combined populism,

1

conservatism, greed, and vindictiveness. The Rayburn family were among his most loyal followers. Young Sam ran for the Texas House of Representatives in 1906, won, and with Bailey's help was elected Speaker in 1911. During his tenure in Austin, he attended a brief law school program at The University of Texas and was admitted to the Texas bar. The next step was Congress. Rayburn was elected after a close Democratic primary and began his exceptional congressional career in 1913.

The poor cotton farmer's son had indeed done well, but in late 1961 he was dying of cancer of the pancreas, which had spread throughout his body. At home in Bonham he lay in great pain in the day room. He would never return to Washington. Roland Boyd, one of his closest friends and for years his campaign manager in Collin County, was with him. Boyd tried to tell Rayburn how much he had helped the people of the Fourth Congressional District and how grateful they were for his service. But Rayburn demurred: "No, when a man dies, it is just like pulling your finger out of a bucket of water. Every man is the same way."[1]

Rayburn died shortly after that conversation, and was wrong about his impact. In Washington, his name is still synonymous with strong leadership. Most people do not know the name of their congressman, but twenty years after Rayburn's death, constituents still call upon one of Rayburn's aides, who resides in Bonham, with every manner of problem, and they still get help. Bonham still celebrates Rayburn's birthday every January 6. There is an annual banquet sponsored by the Friends of Sam Rayburn and a barbeque at Rayburn's house, now a state museum. During the course of my research in the old Rayburn congressional district, people would come to me and tell me stories of favors Rayburn had done for them or their relatives or friends. Few politicians have won such respect and admiration from constituents. Fewer still have been able to retain the voters' favor for so long.

To understand how Sam Rayburn maintained political power for half a century, it is necessary to understand his congressional district, for a district's characteristics are sources of a congressman's political strengths or weaknesses. Some districts require undivided attention; others allow a congressman great flexibility. Some districts have boundaries that are frequently changed and populations that are highly mobile; others have stable district boundaries and stable populations. Some districts reflect uniformity of interests; others, very diverse interests. As this chapter suggests, Rayburn's district, though quite parochial, was one that was stable, reflected uniform interests over long periods, and allowed him great flexibility in Washington.

The Counties

The Fourth Congressional District in Rayburn's time was a compact, agricultural district primarily composed of small farmers and small businessmen. Great Texas fortunes were not made there; even now, oil and gas are not found there in great quantities. The finance and insurance fortunes were just outside the district, to the south in Dallas. The great cattle ranches were to the west.

Rayburn's district was initially composed of just five counties: Grayson, Fannin, Hunt, Collin, and Rains. In 1934 congressional redistricting led to the addition of two more counties, Kaufman and Rockwall (see map). It was never again redistricted. Pressure for redistricting came primarily from the federal courts, and the judiciary was not pressuring state legislatures to redistrict until after Rayburn's death. Compared to today's congressional districts, Rayburn's district had remarkably stable boundaries.

The Fourth District had a large agricultural economic base (see App. B, Table 1) with heavy emphasis on cotton cultivation. Wheat, hay, oats, and sorghum were the other main crops. Much of the land was rolling prairie with a rich, black soil, although by the early part of this century, much of the land was "cottoned out," eroded through one-crop agriculture and poor farming practices. A visitor to the old Fourth District may still see acres of freshly plowed, pitch-black earth furrowed along gently rolling hills, but often the view is of deep gorges in the land, tracing a path where the topsoil has washed away, leaving the remaining land fit for little else than brush and weeds.

The black land is a thick, clay soil that does not easily absorb water. The slow water absorption coupled with the low, gently rolling hills mean that, without proper soil conservation prac-

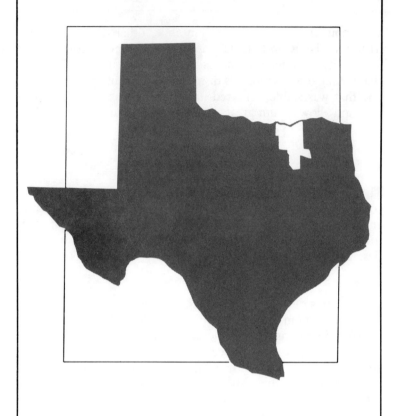

The Fourth Congressional District in Rayburn's
time was a compact, agricultural district. The
finance and insurance fortunes were just outside
the district, to the south in Dallas. The great
cattle ranches were to the west.

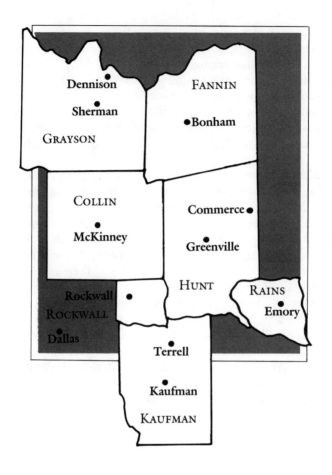

The seven counties that make up the Fourth Congressional District.

tices, the topsoil washes away very quickly. Rainfall in the district averages slightly under forty inches a year, an amount that is usually more than enough for dry-land farming. The figure is misleading in that district summers are frequently hot and dry, with rain infrequent from late spring to fall. Parched land and hot summer days limit the profitability of farming operations. When wet weather does arrive, the black land turns into a thick mud that makes mobility difficult, field work impossible, and the dirt roads bogs.

The small towns scattered throughout the countryside of the Fourth District play supporting roles for the farming enterprises. The largest city in the district was Sherman, in Grayson County, and in 1960, the year before Rayburn's death, its population was only 24,988.[2] Only four towns other than Sherman had 1960 populations greater than 10,000: Denison (Grayson County); Greenville (Hunt County); Terrell (Kaufman County); and McKinney (Collin County). Three of the counties in Rayburn's district, Fannin, Rains, and Rockwall, had no town with a population as large as 10,000. There was little industry in the district, except in Sherman, Denison, and Greenville. Organized labor was never very strong anywhere in the district except Denison, where labor was strong because of the Katy Railroad locomotive repair shops.

The people of the district tended to be poor compared to the state as a whole, probably because of the agricultural economic base and lack of large industry. As is typical of East Texas, there were few people of Spanish origin. The fourteen percent black population was slightly greater than the state's average. Most black men in the Fourth District worked as laborers, and black women worked as household workers. Their poverty and lack of education was far greater than that of the whites. In 1960 the median education for district blacks over 25 was 7.3 years, and the median family income was 1,978 dollars. The educational level for the Fourth District was lower than the median for the state. Family income was far lower than for Texas as a whole.

For Rayburn the center of the district was Fannin County. Though born in Tennessee, he had spent most of his youth in Fannin County and considered the area around Bonham, the county seat, his home. His residence was just outside the Bonham city limits. Fannin County provided strong electoral support for its resident congressman, not surprising when Rayburn's parents and several brothers and sisters lived in the county. Rayburn himself was frequently in Bonham and the small communities throughout the county. It is common for voters to support friends and neighbors, and in Fannin County, that is what Rayburn was. In 1960 Bonham's population was only 7,357, and the whole county had only 23,880 residents. The small size of town and county made it easy for Rayburn to know something about most of the families. If he did not know a Fannin County resident, it was likely that he would know some relation.

Grayson County, with a 1960 population of 73,043, is west of Fannin. It was only a twenty-five-mile drive from Bonham to its county seat and largest town, Sherman. Nearby Denison closely followed Sherman in size. The two towns dominated the county and provided Rayburn with strong support, especially in his later years. He frequently visited Sherman and had many personal friends there. His visits to Denison appear to have been less frequent.[3]

In Rayburn's early years, labor in Denison was quite distrustful of him. He had opposed a federal child labor law and seemed more farmer- than union-oriented. In addition, after World War I he supported the denationalization of railroads, a program opposed by the Denison railroad workers. In 1922 he nearly lost a bid for reelection, largely because of his stand on denationalization. Denison also had a violent railroad strike, and when Rayburn spoke there in 1922, his life was in danger and he had to be protected by the sheriff and by Texas Rangers. Ultimately, martial law was imposed in the railroad town.[4] By the mid to late 1930s, however, he had gained strong support from the railroad unions, especially because of his legislative leadership during the New Deal.[5] Denison's citizens, along with Sherman's and the rest of Grayson County's, became very pro-Rayburn because of his successful efforts to obtain federal funding for the Denison Dam and Lake Texoma, a huge lake project that boosted the area's economy. Grayson County citizens, especially those in the cities, benefited the most, for they were very near the lake. In

the early 1940s Rayburn's efforts again provided a very notice-
able boost to the Grayson County economy when Perrin Field,
a military air base, was located near Sherman.

South of Fannin County was Hunt, the home county for
some of Rayburn's strongest opponents. Hunt had a 1960 population of 39,399, and its county seat of Greenville had a population of 19,087. Greenville is the trading center for the county,
and it dominates trade along the edges of surrounding counties
as well. Commerce, with its 1960 population of 5,789, is the
county's second-largest town. It is the home of East Texas State
University, once known as Mayo Normal College, Sam Rayburn's alma mater. During the 1940s when Rayburn faced some
of his most intense political opposition, the college was headed
by James Gee, one of Rayburn's strongest critics. Gee attempted, with some success, to turn the college and Commerce
into a center of political opposition to Rayburn. It has been
suggested that much of Rayburn's opposition in Hunt County
was cultivated by a local newspaper, the *Greenville Morning Herald,* which was engaged in a long-term circulation battle with a
pro-Rayburn paper, the *Greenville Evening Banner.*[6] It is clear
that the *Herald* was the strongest anti-Rayburn paper published
in the district.

Collin County is now a Dallas suburb, increasingly Republican, and dominated by Plano, a southern Collin County city
with a population of more than 80,000. In Rayburn's day, Collin was an agricultural county dominated by McKinney, the
county seat. McKinney's 1960 population was 13,763, and the
county's was 41,247. Plano was then just a tiny community with
a population of 3,695. Republicans (as noted later in this chapter) simply were not a factor in the county in Rayburn's time.
Throughout Rayburn's district, Republicans were a rarity, generally existing only as "post office Republicans": people who obtained political patronage when Republicans were in national
power but did little or no local-level work for the party. During
the half century that Sam Rayburn was in public life, he never
faced a Republican opponent.

Rockwall County is the smallest county in area in the state. In
1960 much of it was in cotton production. Though Rockwall is
now experiencing suburban growth much like Collin, in 1960 its

county population was 5,878, and its county seat, Rockwall, had 2,166 residents.

Rains County is another tiny county located on the eastern edge of Rayburn's district near the southeastern corner of Hunt. Rayburn spent little time in Rains, probably visiting there no more than twice a year. The lack of personal visits to the county is in part explained by its small population, only 2,993 in 1960. The county seat, Emory, was a town of only 559. Because Rains had no trading center of any size, its residents frequently did business in Greenville. Owing to the practice of voting on the basis of personal ties, friends-and-neighbors voting, and to Rains's ties to Greenville, Rayburn had a minor political problem in that an opponent from Greenville could endanger him in Rains County.[7]

Kaufman County, with a 1960 population of 29,931, was the southernmost county in Rayburn's district. It is dominated by two towns: the county seat, Kaufman, with a 1960 population of 3,087, and Terrell, with a 1960 population of 13,803. A significant source of funds for a Rayburn opponent in the early 1950s came from a group of prosperous Terrell businessmen hostile to Rayburn's perceived liberalism.

Rayburn appears to have spent more time in Fannin and Grayson counties than in the others, where he would visit from time to time, speaking at such events as Lion's Club luncheons, speaking on the courthouse lawn, or walking through little communities introducing himself and shaking hands with shoppers and merchants. In the counties other than Fannin and Grayson, he relied somewhat more heavily upon a network of friends to keep in touch with constituents.[8]

The District over Time

In 1912 when Rayburn was first elected to Congress, his district's five counties had a combined population of 214,721. The district was heavily agricultural, strongly emphasizing crops such as wheat, hay, sorghum, and especially cotton. The little industry that existed was limited to such towns as Denison, Sherman, and Greenville. Farming affected virtually everyone's life. At the time of his death in 1961, the Fourth District remained agricultural, with cotton still a major crop; suburbanization of the counties bordering Dallas had still not taken place. The district had lost many old residents, but that loss was not compensated by in-migration. As a result, the families that lived in the district had long-standing ties to it.

Not only had Sam Rayburn grown up on a farm; he owned a farm and a ranch. He knew agriculture, and he talked farming with the people in his district. To stay up to date for such conversations, he studied U.S. Department of Agriculture crop reports, with special attention to those on cotton.[9] He was among his people in the Fourth District, and he liked the district as it was. His preferred constituency was the black-land farmer, and he was so oriented toward such constituents that friends concluded that Mr. Sam believed everyone should have a family and a piece of land.[10] The experience of poverty formed a bond of hardship between Rayburn and his people. He liked to tell them that it was the Democratic party and Franklin Roosevelt's New Deal that had made farm life a little better and cotton prices higher.

Of course not everyone in the district was a part of this world; there were, for example, the Denison railroad workers. Younger constituents, those too young to remember the Depression, could not understand this world of cheap cotton and burdensome life about which Rayburn so frequently spoke and which, Rayburn claimed, was ended by the Democrats. Vernon Beckham, a Rayburn leader in Denison, remembered during the 1950s telling Rayburn the district was changing, stressing that railroad people and young people did not fit Rayburn's views of the district.[11] Miss Lou and Mrs. Bartley, two of Rayburn's sisters, had been telling him much the same, and he promised to change,[12] though whether he ever did is debatable. Beckham thought Rayburn did broaden his appeal somewhat, but Rayburn continued to give the "four-cent cotton" speech so frequently in the district that it has been burned into the memories of his constituents. Dick Rayburn also suggested that Sam update his appeal to voters. To him Sam explained that he wanted no one to forget those times and that young people needed to be informed about what the Democratic party had done for the country.[13]

It would of course be wrong to say that the district did not change in Rayburn's half century in Congress. In his later years, there were more people employed in the towns and fewer on the farms. Cotton was still the major crop but there was no longer the one-crop dependence of pre-Depression years. People generally lived more comfortable and prosperous lives. Nevertheless, the interests of the district from 1913 to 1961 remained similar. The small farmers and businessmen needed some protection from the great industries of America such as the railroads and the utility holding companies; they needed a cushion against the drops in the economic cycle; and they needed assistance in making life on the farm less difficult.

Populism had had an impact in northeast Texas, and that tradition of rural economic liberalism continued in Rayburn's years.[14] Unlike many parts of the South, the racial issue in northeast Texas did not totally dominate the politics of the region. Nonetheless, though blacks were fourteen percent of the district's population, the Texas Democratic party did not allow them to participate in the Democratic primary until forced to do so by the Supreme Court in 1944.[15] In addition to being a white-primary state, Texas had the poll tax for federal elections until 1964, for state elections until 1966.[16] This tax, required for voting, effectively denied that right to many blacks and poor whites.

Racial demogoguery could appeal to the electorate's baser emotions. From time to time, Rayburn made racial appeals to voters. In 1922, for example, he said, "Some have gone to the negroes and paid their poll taxes to get them to vote for them. I do not make this as a threat, but the negroes of Fannin County are not going to vote in this coming primary. By the Eternal God, my ancestor's blood has been spilled on nearly every hill on this land, that this should be a white man's country."[17] In 1944 Rayburn said, "No one in Congress thinks that Congress has the power to destroy the segregation laws of the state or if it did that it would be silly enough to try. If it should be attempted, I shall do all in my power to prevent it and I believe that I can prevent such an act in my present position."[18] During the 1940s it was necessary for him to reassure the voters that he remained a segregationist. By the time blacks could vote in Democratic primaries, Rayburn had established himself as a national leader close to Franklin Roosevelt, and while he might claim to be a segregationist, he received significant black support.[19] During the Roosevelt and especially the Truman administrations, he was placed in the politically dangerous position of being a leader of a national party that was far more liberal on racial questions than was the majority of his district. This problem caused difficulty for Rayburn for almost all of the remainder of his life, even affecting his behavior during consideration of the 1957 Civil Rights Act (see Chap. 5).

The Fourth Congressional District was opposed to any civil rights legislation. Rayburn shared the racial values of his district and personally believed in segregation. He did not believe in the social equality of blacks and whites. Yet he was less of a white supremicist than many of his constituents. In Washington he had seen how blacks could succeed when given a chance. Unlike many of his Fourth District constituents, therefore, he moderated his white supremicist thinking over the years, did not hate blacks, and was inclined in his last years to support political equality for them.[20] As a leader of the Democratic party, it was inappropriate for him to be a racial demogogue, but in his last years, he would not have appealed to racial hatred. His friends noted that Rayburn shook hands with blacks, a very unusual behavior for a white man in the Fourth District.[21] He spoke about having no racial hatred.[22] Furthermore, while he personally did not endorse the Supreme Court's desegregation decision in *Brown* v. *Board of Education* and wished to delay its implementation, he counseled moderation and compliance with the Court's mandate.[23]

On one occasion Rayburn faced a minor problem that well indicates how he handled racial issues. During the 1950s he received a request for an appointment with a visiting delegation of schoolchildren from the district. A staff member pointed out that the children were black and asked Rayburn if he would see them. Rayburn unhesitatingly agreed. When the day came for the visit, he sent a staff member for a large number of soft drinks, sandwiches, and potato chips; lunched with the children in his office; and behaved in a friendly fashion. The children felt well treated and left in good spirits. Rayburn had won their friendship. No public display was made of his friendliness toward the black children, however. No reporters were told of the visit, and contrary to his frequent practice, he lunched with the children in the privacy of his office rather than taking them to a more visible dining area.[24]

The political stability of the Fourth District was crucial to Rayburn's success. Rayburn himself did change somewhat over the years. He was primarily a prohibitionist in his early years, for example, but he did not advocate that cause for long. A politician with his pragmatic nature could represent similar interests any time during that fifty-year period. A mildly populist appeal was never out of taste during his years in office.[25] No new political interests such as immigrants, unions, urban residents, suburbanites, or Republicans arose during his congressional career.

In addition to the remarkable stability of the district over time, it was a homogeneous district, mostly rural or small-town America. Rayburn was never therefore in the precarious situation of balancing city against farm or white suburbs against the black and brown inner city. District stability and homogeneity gave him political security.

Redistricting

Redistricting can endanger a congressman's political future. A redistricted congressman may be thrown into competition with another incumbent, or he may find his base of support weakened or completely moved to another district. His new district may have interests that oppose him or that conflict with interests he has previously promoted. Rayburn faced none of these problems.

As Speaker of the Texas House, he had worked during the reapportionment based on the 1910 census to carve out a district favorable to his political interests. State Senator B. B. Sturgeon of Lamar County, his strongest potential congressional opponent, was redrawn out of the Fourth Congressional District.[26]

After the 1930 census it was again necessary to make changes in the Fourth Congressional District. It had lost population since Rayburn first went to Congress, even while Texas gained almost 2 million people between the 1910 and 1930 censuses. In 1910 Rayburn's district contained 214,721 people and in 1930 only 209,316. Texas, on the other hand, grew from 3,896,542 in 1910 to 5,824,715 in 1930. The Fifth District, which included Dallas, Rockwall, and Ellis counties, was just to the south of the Fourth District and mushroomed from 197,449 in 1910 to 387,385 in 1930.

Though the addition of two counties to the Fourth District increased its population to 257,879, by Rayburn's death in 1961 the district's seven-county population was only slightly above its 1910 five-county population. People would not be kept on the farm, indeed could not stay, given the weaknesses of farm prices during the Depression years; the "cottoning out" of the land, which meant lower yields brought on by erosion and one-crop agriculture; and the attractions of urban life.

During his only redistricting in nearly one-half a century in Congress, Rayburn kept his old district in its entirety and received two relatively small counties that shared the characteristics of his other counties. He had hoped to get Lamar County because, claimed Rayburn, it had "the same type of people and the same type of land."[27] He had friends in Lamar, one of whom wrote him that Lamar would keep him in Congress for life, or until he went to the Senate.[28] Rayburn also felt certain that he would get Rockwall County. The growth of the Fifth District made it clear that Dallas County alone would constitute a separate district. With the removal of Rockwall from the Fifth District, it was only reasonable that it be placed in the Fourth.

Rayburn's hope for Lamar County, however, went unfulfilled. Instead he got Kaufman, a county similar to those in his district. Rayburn wrote of his pleasure in getting Rockwall and Kaufman counties. Of Rockwall, he noted that "its people, its industries and its land are very similar, if not identical to the other counties of the District."[29] His views about Kaufman County were similar: "I do not know of a county in the State that I would rather have in the district that I represent than Kaufman County, as I feel that the people in that county are fine people and will fit in with the other counties in the district."[30]

Rayburn immediately went to work trying to insure that Kaufman and Rockwall counties would fall in with the district's pattern of voting for Sam Rayburn. His brother Dick Rayburn worked for a cottonseed mill and traveled throughout the northeast Texas area buying cottonseed. Dick was familiar with the people in these counties and did some political scouting there for his brother. Dick reported that Rockwall was "fine."[31] It was a tiny county and would not have been much of a threat even were there any opposition. Dick was pleased with Kaufman's selection, claiming, "I like Kaufman better than Lamar. Lamar is a fine county and fine people but they are a little queer in politics, have been associated with the sandy land too long and will vote too much on that wild idea sometimes." Kaufman County he viewed as a "steadier" county. Perhaps most important, he reported that no one there had congressional aspirations.[32]

One problem was patronage. A Democratic administration was in power, and so the Democratic congressmen were able to select postmasters, rural mail carriers, and others. In Kaufman County Morgan Sanders had been the representative, and Hatton Sumners had been representative in Rockwall County. If Rayburn upset the established patronage structure, he could generate opposition. Brother Dick recommended that Rayburn not become immediately involved in patronage, and Sam agreed. Sam reported that Sanders would handle patronage until 1935 in Kaufman County and that Sumners would do the same in Rockwall.[33] Presumably during that time Rayburn could determine how many of the patronage appointees were acceptable to him.

Rayburn did his best to ease the transition of the new counties from one district to another. He made plans to bring along Rockwall County's former congressman, Sumners, on a trip to the county. Rayburn wrote Rockwall's county judge, Claude Isbell:

> It will be a great pleasure to meet you and the other people.
> I would like to bring Hatton with me when I come. I realize
> that you people have had one of the finest congressmen in the
> United States for twenty years and I also realize that you regret to
> sever relations with him but he and I will work together for
> Rockwall County in the future.[34]

In the meantime, Dick Rayburn was busy contacting his friends and getting them active in behalf of Sam.[35] An attorney in Greenville, in Hunt County, Joseph Nichols, was a Rayburn supporter who had many friends in Kaufman County, whom he contacted in Rayburn's behalf.[36] Judge Isbell, whose position made him an influential figure in Rockwall County, asked Rayburn to recommend his half brother for a job with the Internal Revenue Service in Dallas.[37] Rayburn's brother-in-law W. A. Thomas was a high-ranking Internal Revenue official in Dallas, and Mr. Sam reported that he had written him a strong letter of recommendation, and furthermore, he had done so even before Isbell had made his request.[38] By such gestures, political organizations are built.

Others in Rockwall and Kaufman counties volunteered their support. Walter D. Adams of Forney, in Kaufman County, was, for example, influential in Texas politics owing to his long-time leadership in the Texas Pharmaceutical Association. He offered his support because an old friend of his had also been a friend of Rayburn's and because Adams, like Rayburn, had been a friend and supporter of the orator and Texas senator Joseph Weldon Bailey.[39] Such contacts with friends and neighbors soon provided Rayburn with an organization in Rockwall and Kaufman counties.

The two new counties were relatively minor additions to the district. They posed no great threat to Rayburn in that they were small, did not introduce politicians with congressional ambitions to the district, and reflected the rural interests of Rayburn's other counties. It was not until the 1950s that redistricting, or at least the threat of it, posed a serious problem for Rayburn. In the early 1950s Rayburn opposed Gov. Allan Shivers because Shivers, though a Democrat, strongly supported Eisenhower for president. There was much talk that Shivers and his supporters, known as Shivercrats, would retaliate for Rayburn's stand on party loyalty by redistricting the Fourth District.[40] The logical way to redistrict would be to move the Fourth District south into Dallas County.

Rayburn did not want Dallas County. For years he had been opposed by the leading paper in Dallas, the *Dallas News,* and Dallas appeared to be far more conservative than the Fourth District. In 1954, for example, Dallas elected the ultraconservative Republican Bruce Alger to Congress, and it returned him for a total of ten years. In addition, Dallas was urban and its population was mobile. Programs that bore the Rayburn label, such as rural electrification or Lake Texoma, though important in the Fourth District, would mean little to Dallasites. Parts of Dallas in his district could mean trouble, and Rayburn was worried about these proposals. Shanks has claimed that Rayburn's main fear was redistricting and especially redistricting that would let Dallas overwhelm his district, for Rayburn wanted to keep "a compact district of people similar in occupation and sentiment."[41] Yet, there was a certain logic to moving north Dallas County into the Fourth District. In 1950 Dallas County, the Fifth Congressional District, was much larger than the average Texas congressional district, whereas Rayburn's was much smaller, and as the 1950s drew to a close, that disparity worsened (see App. B, Table 2).

The threat came to nothing. Though Rayburn was hated by many of the Shivercrats, he was, during this period, either the Speaker or the Democratic leader, positions that gave him a great deal of power. He had done, and could do, much for Texas and for individual Texans. If he chose, he could also do much harm. Several of those close to Rayburn believed that he had contacted a number of influential figures in Texas politics and spoken to them about redistricting, making it clear that, were his district not protected, he would no longer support Texas interests such as the oil depletion allowance, tidelands legislation, or federal recognition of community property. Over the years his position had enabled him to build up sufficient contacts and IOUs for favors done all over the state to give him the influence in the state legislature to keep his district just the way he liked it:[42] small enough that it had "no Chamber of Commerce big enough to give me any trouble."[43]

When reapportionment based on the 1950 census was being considered, the small size of Rayburn's district could not be overlooked. Senator A. M. Aikin was named chairman of the subcommittee considering reapportionment. His senior law partner had tried to get Aikin's home county, Lamar, into Rayburn's district in the 1934 redistricting. Aikin himself was a friend of Rayburn's and realized that several of his colleagues were attempting to destroy Rayburn. He told the senators: "If any of you can go up there and beat Sam Rayburn, have at it, but I am not going to sit here and see him legislated out if I can help it."[44]

Shortly afterward Rayburn met with Senator Aikin and Senator Crawford, two of the three men on the redistricting subcommittee. By then, he felt powerful enough to withstand the onslaughts of his opponents, and he told the two senators: "Don't put Cooke County on me and don't put Highland Park [a very wealthy Dallas County town] on me. That silk stocking district doesn't want a Democrat in it."[45] Aikin asked, "Mr. Speaker, you have told us things not to do—what are you telling us really to do?"[46] Rayburn suggested making no changes in current district boundaries and creating instead the position of congressman-at-large for the additional Texas congressional seat resulting from the state population increase.[47]

Rayburn made his wishes clear as well to Att. Gen. John Shepperd, first telling him and then writing him. Rayburn argued that, inasmuch as the population of the Fourth District plus the population of Dallas County merited two congressmen, "Why couldn't it be worked out so that the Dallas District be left like it is and mine like it is?" Though he wanted Lamar County, Rayburn explained that he would not want to take it from his friend Wright Patman. Should he have to take either Denton or Cooke County, he preferred Denton, as he considered Cooke nearly Republican.[48] There was no redistricting, and Texas got a congressman-at-large.

It was an interesting pattern of reciprocal causation. His leadership position in Congress gave Rayburn the political strength to withstand redistricting challenges and maintain a stable, secure district. At the same time, the stability and security of his district enabled him to have the political security and flexibility necessary to play a national leadership role.[49]

National Elections

The people of the Fourth District were overwhelmingly Democrats, though like many southerners they increasingly voted for Democrats in local and state races but for Republicans in presidential elections.[50] Democratic strength was in part the result of Rayburn's influence in the district and his support for Democratic presidential nominees.

Texas remained strongly in the Democratic column in 1944

despite a challenge mounted by conservatives who backed a third-party anti-Roosevelt movement. Roosevelt was even stronger in the Fourth District in 1944 than he was in Texas as a whole (see App. B, Table 3). In 1948 the anti-Truman States' Rights party was even less successful in the state and in the Fourth District than were the Texas Regulars in 1944. Of the States' Rights party, Rayburn said, "Those Dixiecrats are as welcome around here as a bastard at a family reunion."[51] Republicans picked up strength, however, though the Fourth District returned a pro-Truman vote not too much smaller than Roosevelt's in 1944.

It was in 1952 and 1956 that the voting pattern in presidential elections in Texas changed. The strongly Democratic state switched into the Republican column, supporting Eisenhower with fifty-three percent of the votes in 1952 and nearly fifty-six percent of the votes in 1956. In both years, Eisenhower benefited greatly from Gov. Allan Shivers's support. Shivers remained a Democrat and successfully turned the state Democratic party machinery over to Eisenhower. Rayburn, practically alone among state leaders who held elective office, campaigned in Stevenson's behalf in 1952. He supported Stevenson's efforts against Eisenhower again in 1956. In the latter campaign, Rayburn had greater support from state leaders, and most important, Sen. Lyndon Johnson actively supported Stevenson. Rayburn's district also supported Stevenson over Eisenhower in both 1952 and 1956, bucking the Texas trend even though Denison was Eisenhower's birthplace. Even in the Fourth District, however, Democratic voting dropped precipitously from earlier years.

Surprisingly, the Kennedy-Johnson ticket carried Texas by only slightly more than forty-six thousand votes, a tiny margin when one considers that Johnson was a Texan with a well-established statewide political organization. While the Kennedy-Johnson ticket did better in the Fourth District than in Texas as a whole, the ticket's margin of victory there was actually less than the Stevenson-Sparkman margin in 1952. The Rayburn organization did all it could for the ticket, but the Democratic vote was nowhere near the levels of 1944 and 1948. It seems clear that the religious issue explains much of the low level of support for the ticket; many voters just could not bring themselves to vote for a Catholic for president.[52] Nevertheless, the Fourth District cast over fifty-seven percent of its votes for the Democratic ticket compared with only fifty-one percent in Texas as a whole.

The district was willing to stick with Rayburn and support the Democratic ticket and to do so more strongly than the state as a whole. It was even willing to support the ticket in spite of two major third-party challenges, a Republican nominee who was a Denison-born hero, and a Catholic Democratic nominee. Such a record of support for the national Democratic party certainly helped Rayburn in his efforts to function as a national party leader.

2. The Rayburn Style

THIS CHAPTER EXAMINES RAYBURN'S POLITI-cal style, that is, how he attempted to relate to his constituents. Like everyone else, Rayburn attempted to project a particular image,[1] but his was a vastly complex personality. He balanced the roles of Speaker and district representative; he was one of the nation's most able legislators; he was comfortable with the good ole boys in Merit, Texas, as well as with congressmen, senators, and presidents. He could be kind or cold, gruff or friendly, soft or hard. He could defend presidents and criticize them; support them and call them liars to their faces. Richard Bolling may have best understood the complexity of the man and the style:

> [He] was infinitely being presented as this wonderfully simple presence until you got to know him. He was one of the most complex people I ever saw. He presented an image that he made up in his own mind sometime in the late teens of the century or the '20s. That was always the image that he held. But behind that, there was this infinitely complex subtlety.[2]

Rayburn grew up on a small farm and had known poverty in his youth. He had chopped and picked cotton and knew the dif-ficulty of farm life. He stressed his upbringing and his farm ori-gins in many of his speeches within the district. The image he projected was one of a lifelong farmer in government to try to relieve the burdens and drudgery of farm life. He often talked about how his father had given him twenty-five dollars when he went to Commerce to attend Mayo College and how he worked his way through. One of his friends described the impact of his image: "Many times I have heard him tell the story of his little country schooling and his mother and father. I think this is what gave him such great ties to his people. As a country kid myself and going to a three-teacher school, gosh, I could relate to that. So could everybody in his district. We all felt like he was one of us."[3]

"Homecoming in Bonham for newly elected Speaker Rayburn." *When Sam Rayburn returned to Bonham after his first election as Speaker, he was welcomed by a homecoming celebration and parade through Bonham, October 22, 1940. Courtesy of Sam Rayburn Library.*

"Opening the Fannin County Fair." *This fair was a major event in the area and provided Rayburn with the opportunity to meet with thousands of constituents. Here, Rayburn officially opened the fair by cutting the ribbon across the main gate, October 2, 1946. Courtesy of Sam Rayburn Library.*

**"Mr. Sam and Miss Lou on the front steps
of the house."** *This house was the center
of political activity when Rayburn returned
home. It was home for several members
of the Rayburn family including Miss Lou,
the sister closest to Mr. Sam, 1956.
Courtesy of Sam Rayburn Library.*

"Rayburn and Visitors at his Home, 1957."
Rayburn presented the image of a farmer in politics. That image, coupled with his representation of an agricultural district, frequently led visitors to bring him farm produce. Courtesy of Sam Rayburn Library.

"Dedicating the Bonham Domiciliary, 1948." *Rayburn had a major role in locating the domiciliary in Bonham. He spoke at its dedication on July 9, 1948. Courtesy of Sam Rayburn Library.*

"Trades Day in Bonham, early 1920s."
*The square in Bonham bustled with activity
when the farmers came to town to do business.
An Erwin Smith photograph, courtesy
of Mrs. L. M. Pettis.*

He was born Samuel Taliaferro Rayburn, but he found the name too fancy and dropped it in favor of "Sam" at the time he went into politics.[4] He strove to have his constituents identify with him as one with similar origins, for he knew it was important to retain the country-boy identification. A reputation for prosperity or for having a sense of self-importance in East Texas politics was a sign of impending defeat. Rural East Texans wanted as representatives people they could talk to and understand, not aristocrats. So Rayburn was accessible; his house was always open to a constituent, as were his offices in the Capitol.

"Sam," said one of his county leaders, "was as common as an old shoe."[5] If Rayburn ever chewed tobacco in Washington, a long-time aide could not recall it, but in Bonham he always seemed to have a plug in his cheek. He made certain always to spit in the fireplace at his home when constituents were visiting, so that if nothing else, they would take away the idea that Mr. Sam was just a plain fellow. In Washington he wore tailor-made suits, never the khakis, old shirt, and slouchy hat that were his regular Bonham attire. Over twenty years after his death, friends would speak of him dressed in a torn shirt, or in old-fashioned shoes, or in khakis and an old hat, or tying a knot in his shoe-laces because they were too short to tie a bow. Once in Bonham, Rayburn's voice always seemed to change. The East Texas accent became more pronounced, and the drawl thickened. In Bonham he cut his own wood and worked his cattle. He would tease men who smoked "women's cigarettes," by which he meant filter tips. His brand was unfiltered Camels, and he smoked heavily. In Bonham he never rode in the Cadillac limousine given him by members of Congress nor in the Speaker's limousine, but in his well-dented pickup truck or his sister's Plymouth.[6]

Rayburn's projection of a farmer image can also be seen in many aspects of his life in the district. For him, the Fannin County Fair was a major event. He always spent plenty of time around the exhibits.[7] The fair also provided him the opportunity to make political speeches. Once when a storm threatened to rain out both speech and fair, Rayburn stood up on the platform and shouted, "This is a million-dollar rain. It might ruin the fair, but think what it is going to do for the cotton crop and grain crop." Although the storm knocked out all power, fifteen hundred to two thousand people heard Rayburn speak that day—without notes, and as there was no power, without a public address system or lights. Well over an inch of rain fell after three weeks without anything but hard and hot winds.[8] Mr. Sam, those fairgoers must have concluded, knew a good summer rain was well worth the sacrifice of a fair. Another time, President Truman called and requested Rayburn's presence in Washington. Rayburn said that he did not want to go because he would miss the fair.[9]

In the district Rayburn could drink whiskey and laugh with the best of the "good ole boys." While he was not known as a poker player, he was a fair domino player. But in Washington, as one long-time staff member noted, he was the distinguished, reserved, almost worshipped Speaker. Congressman John Brademas described the Washington Rayburn as having "immense moral authority around here. He was Speaker longer than anybody in history. Just his mere physical presence commanded great, great respect. . . . He was a . . . remote figure. You approached him almost as if you were approaching a divinity."[10] The Speaker often scowled in Washington, the severity of his features serving to intimidate congressmen.[11] He insisted on proper decorum in the House. He would even become irritated when congressmen wore sport coats rather than suits. Even after his eyesight weakened, he was able to spot women in the galleries wearing shorts, clothing he considered disrespectful toward the House of Representatives.[12] In Bonham Rayburn seemed relaxed and much more informal.[13] There were two Sam Rayburns, both well suited, if not necessary, for his political well-being.

Character

Rayburn's life style was a simple one that did not change even after he had been Speaker for years. His Washington apartment was pleasant, not elegant, and it was the same one he had lived in for over twenty years. His Bonham home was comfortable, but it was one he built in 1916. Rather than buy a color television, he purchased a piece of multicolored plastic that, placed over the screen of the black-and-white television, gave an approximation of a color-television picture. It was a simplicity of life style that projected an image of honesty.[14]

Rayburn took pride in his reputation for honesty and for keeping his word, and he tried to avoid the appearance of a conflict of interest. Contrary to common practice, after he went to Congress he did not maintain a law office at home so there would be no danger of a conflict between his congressional work and legal business. He also made it a practice not to own stocks or corporate bonds. He explained to a family member that he had once bought stock in a small oil company, and to his surprise, an oil company executive had approached him about special legislative treatment for the company. He angrily dismissed the executive, sold the stock, and resolved never again to own stocks.[15] When he hired his nephew as a staff member in 1948, he insisted the nephew also sell his stocks and corporate bonds.[16] All savings Rayburn kept either in government bonds, in a checking account, or invested in his farm or ranch. He did not accept honorariums for speeches and frequently even paid his own expenses when invited to give one.[17] The person who prepared his income tax recalled that he consistently overpaid his taxes to insure that there would be no criticisms of his deductions.[18]

Perhaps Rayburn's greatest pleasure was the Sam Rayburn Library, which was constructed with private donations. One person made a very large contribution to the library, but the money was returned because Rayburn had suspicions about the donor's character and feared an attempt to buy influence with such a substantial gift.[19] Rayburn did, however, accept donations from oil men and oil companies,[20] some of them in cash and in large amounts. Myron Blalock, for example, provided fifty thousand dollars in cash to the library, saying the money came from several friends, but he died before providing a list of contributors.[21] Several large donors whose money was accepted did seem to expect special treatment in exchange, for example, that their contributions would keep Rayburn from endorsing Ralph Yarborough, a liberal Democrat, for the U.S. Senate. To their dismay, Rayburn did endorse Yarborough.[22]

Little has argued that Rayburn behaved in an ethically questionable manner in this Senate race, adding that, to his knowledge, it was the only time Rayburn behaved in a seemingly improper manner regarding financial matters. In late May of 1958, William Blakely sent the Sam Rayburn Foundation a check for ten thousand dollars coupled with a note saying, "As before—please—no publicity—Just Mr. Sam—you and Me—It is My Plan and hope that you will be hearing from me as time goes on. No Acknowledgement necessary." The arrival of the check so close to the Senate election between Yarborough and Blakely prompted Little to suggest the appearance of a payoff to Rayburn to keep him from endorsing Yarborough. Little noted that, for much of the campaign, it was said that Blakely had Rayburn's support. Actually, Rayburn remained quiet, while his leaders split over Blakely and Yarborough. Buster Cole, for example, invited Blakely to his law office during a visit to Bonham, whereas R. C. Slagle was a leading activist in the Yarborough organization. Rayburn said that his organization was split because he did not dictate to his leaders whom to support, but he did become disgusted with widespread rumors, created in part by several of his leaders' support for Blakely, that Rayburn himself favored Blakely. Little claimed that the seeming conflict of interest was worsened by Rayburn's silence in the campaign. According to Little, Rayburn neither acclaimed the Yarborough victory nor announced that he had voted for Yarborough.[23] Actually, Rayburn did both. In fact, Green considered Rayburn's surprise last-minute endorsement of Yarborough decisive in the Yarborough victory.[24] Blakely was a friend of Rayburn's and a man so wealthy that ten thousand dollars was a pittance. The donation was to the Rayburn Foundation rather than Rayburn himself. The timing of the donation was bad, but there is no evidence it affected Rayburn's political behavior.

Rayburn did not generally accept large gifts. On one occasion, for example, a wealthy oil man transported a very expensive horse to Rayburn's farm. Rayburn was a great admirer of fine horses and there was no one who would know of the gift other than Rayburn, the oil man, and a staff member. Nevertheless, Rayburn returned the horse.[25] There were exceptions to this policy, however. Foreign leaders did give Rayburn expensive gifts. The silver service on display at the Sam Rayburn House, for example, was a gift of the Philippines. One of the few Americans who could give Rayburn expensive gifts was oil man Sid Richardson. He gave Rayburn several valuable paintings and several expense-paid trips to his private island, St. Joseph's, a choice retreat for hunters, fishermen, and luxury lovers.[26] Richardson was a major contributor to congressional Democrats and a trusted friend of Rayburn's, which perhaps explains Rayburn's relaxation of his rule against gifts.

Rayburn exercised more care than most politicians in avoiding conflicts of interest. It was not a national, and certainly not a Texas, political practice to be concerned with ethics. Rayburn's caution may in part be explained by the experience of his mentor, Bailey, who was destroyed politically because of a conflict of interest. Bailey accepted large legal fees from a Standard Oil company while he was a U.S. senator.[27] Yet Rayburn appears to have been sensitive about conflicts even before Bailey's political demise. While still in the state legislature, for example, he engaged in the virtually unheard-of practice of accepting no fees from his law firm for those clients who had legislative interests.[28]

Rayburn's ethical behavior did not go unnoticed. Some of his campaigns for office pointed to it to show that a vote for Rayburn would help elect an honest man. Says a 1932 election flyer, for example: "We submit that Sam Rayburn owns no stocks or bonds, but that his savings are in a farm in Fannin County, Texas; that he was reared on a farm and that, therefore, he has the interests of the farmer at heart."[29] His record of honesty probably benefited him as Speaker as well, for other members of Congress would wish the Speaker to be above reproach.[30]

Rayburn's strong ethical sense gave him a reputation for being rigid on ethical questions. He was known to argue with friends that either a man was honest or he was not; there was no in-between.[31] Rayburn praised the dismissal of students from the military academy, for he maintained that a student who cheated on an examination was a dishonest man who should not be allowed to wear the uniform of a U.S. military officer. He was also critical of Senator Bailey's financial affairs,[32] even though he thought him the most impressive of all the great and important people he had known.[33] These rigid views only reinforced the Rayburn image of integrity.

Rayburn took pride in being a man of his word. Many interviewees emphasized that if he gave his word, he kept it. This was a valuable trait for the Washington Rayburn, because so much negotiation in Congress is based on trust. Politicians considered untrustworthy often find it difficult to work with other politicians. The Bonham Rayburn also stressed and protected the value of his word. He almost never told a constituent that he *would* do something; rather, he would say, "I'll see what I can do" or "I'll look into that."[34] Promises he never gave lightly.

Affirming his humble origins, Rayburn presented the unpretentious, personally honest, accessible image of one concerned about improving lives in the district. Such an image could readily inspire support and trust. Senator Henry Jackson believes a major component of Rayburn's success was his character, which led his constituents to trust and have faith in him:

> Had he been merely a representative, voting as a representative from Bonham, there is no doubt in my mind that a representative . . . from that district would have voted differently than the Speaker. . . . He was a big enough man; he had the stature; he had the respect in his district that they allowed him to do those things. . . . So character, integrity, respect, all those things play a very important role in my judgment in how people vote. That was the genius of Mr. Rayburn. Mr. Rayburn was an institution, and his opponents could get up and say he was a socialist, a radical, he was way out there, but who is going to believe it down there, because he was a respected man.[35]

Jackson was echoed by several Rayburn associates. According to one, his supporters "had the utmost faith in Sam Rayburn. They felt that we couldn't have a better representative in Washington than Sam Rayburn."[36] Another stated: "Rayburn was one of the most honest men in public office that I ever knew. I've known a good many. And I've known quite a few good, honest men like Fred Vinson, the Supreme Court chief justice. But in terms of integrity, I would gauge him, in terms of percentage, damn near 100."[37] Still another noted that Rayburn "was a very uncommon man in that his strengths far outweighed his weaknesses. I believed and I think that everybody that knew him believed he had integrity first of all and in a very basic sense."[38] A fourth interviewee said, "My feeling about Mr. Sam, and I know my father's as well, was that he was going to do the right thing and he was going to do what was right and fair and honest. There would be nothing devious about him, and there would be no sell out. We might wonder why he voted that way, but as far as I was concerned, it might be something that I'd think, well, I'm just not informed enough."[39]

Rayburn believed that votes were often cast on the basis of the character of the candidates. When he campaigned, according to one of his county leaders,

> he would go around and meet people around over the district; he wouldn't promise all sorts of things he knew he probably couldn't deliver on. He tried to tell them something about himself, what kind of man he was. And then, in effect, he said to them, "If you think I am the kind of man you can feel comfortable with having as your representative in Washington, then I would like your vote. Otherwise, then you should vote for somebody else. I can't sit here now and tell you how I am going to vote on all these issues that are going to come up in the next two years, but I will tell you this; I will vote on each one of them only after a study of the pros and cons, and I'll vote to the best of my judgment and conscience."[40]

Large numbers of constituents did indeed view Rayburn as a man of character.

Many took personal pride in Rayburn. One school teacher in Trenton, a small town in Fannin County, used him as a role model to inspire her students. "You think that nobody from Trenton could ever amount to anything," she told them. "Here's a man that came from a black-land farm down here below Windom and from Bonham and lived just like we did and reached the heights and pinnacles he did by being honest and a man of integrity, and yet he was just like we are. That shows you, you can be yourself, you can be honest, and you can still reach the top."[41] Such a personal following allowed Rayburn considerable freedom in Washington because so many of his constituents trusted him.

Character, however important, was not sufficient to explain his success in the district. He also made clear to constituents that he was effective in Washington and brought benefit to the district with such programs as farm-to-market roads and rural electrification.

Interaction with Constituents

When speaking with a constituent, Rayburn would often ask about his family. He was frequently able to name the constituent's parents, children, and other relatives. He was especially good at tracing back a family tree, mentioning something about a forebear.[42] Such displays occurred so often that Rayburn was able to create the impression of a man with a marvelous memory who knew and remembered the people in the district.[43]

It is unclear just how Rayburn accomplished such feats, although both good memory and good staff work were involved. For example, it was customary for a member of the staff to greet visitors and briefly converse with them before going into the inner office to get the Speaker. During these brief conversations, valuable information about the constituents could be obtained. The staff member would learn the constituents' names, where they lived, and if possible some connection with Rayburn. Once when a couple from the district visited the Speaker's office, the woman commented to the staff member that the Speaker had once praised her pecan pie. The staff member asked the couple to wait in the outer office, went into the inner office, and gave the Speaker a two-sentence briefing on the couple's name, their hometown, and his fondness for the woman's pie. Rayburn was then able to greet them by name and talk as though he had done nothing but think of the woman's pecan pie.[44]

Rayburn also kept lists of constituents' names and addresses.[45] In addition, members of his organization functioned as "spotters," people who knew their communities and could discreetly whisper names into his ear or greet those coming toward Rayburn loudly enough for him to hear their names.[46] Around Fannin County, it was said that Rayburn did not need a "spotter," for there he rarely had trouble with names. Even after his eyesight became poor, he could often identify his supporters by the sounds of their voices.[47] Giving speeches in the district, Rayburn also used his skill with names to great effect by frequently mentioning the names of people in the crowd, thus establishing an identification with the audience.[48]

Rayburn put great stress on his accessibility. Often he would invite callers at his house to stay for dinner or supper — a huge

Texas-style meal usually made with vegetables from the large backyard garden and meat fresh-killed from the farm.[49] A telephone call to Rayburn in Bonham would usually be answered by Rayburn himself. Constituents' calls were frequent, leading him to joke that at home he got his exercise by going to the telephone.[50] Aides, when they did answer the phone, were instructed to greet the caller and ask him or her to hold but never to ask who was calling. Rayburn explained that such a question was appropriate in Washington, but a call to his house in Bonham would be from a constituent, and he wanted to talk to any constituent, no matter who it was.[51] Once Rayburn called the Rockwall County judge, Ralph Hall. A secretary made the mistake of asking who was calling. When Hall took the phone, Rayburn roughly reminded him that a "servant of the people" should not care who was calling him; he should take calls from everyone.[52]

Time and again, interviewees commented about Rayburn's lack of pretense. Although proud of his achievements, he consciously strove for a modest appearance. In his view, conceited or arrogant people were not big people. Hardeman recalled Rayburn saying, "We don't put on airs in my family."[53] The modest style won votes. As one handwritten note said, "Friend Sam: I've been with you 100% since our first conversation. Possibly you remember our first acquaintance in your first campaign for Congress. I was hoeing in my garden. We had a long conversation. I think you helped me hoe some too."[54] In Bonham he was indistinguishable in appearance from the other men who walked around the town square. This plainness broadcast the message that power had not gone to his head, that he remembered his origins and who elected him.

Rayburn kept in touch with his constituents when he was in Washington as well. He received all the newspapers from the district and was said to be an avid reader of the *Bonham Daily Favorite*.[55] These newspapers were small enough that they regularly published all births and deaths in the community. Rayburn had a staff member who culled such news. Congratulatory messages went to the parents of new babies, and new mothers would receive a baby care book from Congressman Rayburn. Sympathy letters went to the families of the deceased. Students who received special school honors got letters from the congressman. Farmers in the district received Department of Agriculture bulletins and yearbooks.[56] Often Rayburn's network of friends and supporters would send him names of people who would especially enjoy hearing from him, and he would write them. If his leaders identified an especially pro-Rayburn voting box or particularly effective supporters, it would not be long before those voters or those supporters received a letter of appreciation from Rayburn. He is said to have phoned someone in the district, usually a family member, every day when in Washington just to obtain additional news.[57]

All the letters were designed to convey to constituents that they had a congressman who knew them, cared for them, and was keeping in touch, and they were often effective. Once, for example, Rayburn was on a campaign tour in western Hunt County, riding around in an old car to visit people in the little communities. He had stopped at the two or three stores in Floyd, introduced himself, and visited about an hour. He had done the same thing in Merit and was spending the remainder of his time campaigning in Lane, where campaigning consisted of going to Bill Bruce's store to sit on a keg of nails and talk to constituents. A country woman in an old-fashioned bonnet entered and, after a while, shyly approached Rayburn. "Aren't you Sam Rayburn?" she asked. Rayburn took off his hat (the Bonham Rayburn wore his hat in stores) and said, "Yes, ma'am, I am." Then the woman told him, "I just want you to know how much we really appreciated your sympathy card when we lost our baby." He again expressed sympathy and shortly left Lane. Speaking of the incident, his Hunt County manager noted that the sympathy card obviously meant a lot to that woman, so much so that she probably voted for Rayburn in every subsequent election and probably asked her neighbors to do so as well. In those days, people in the country received little mail, so a letter from a congressman could mean enough to a constituent that the congressman would be repaid with a vote.[58]

A former Rayburn staff member also emphasized the political value of such constituent contacts, noting the many occasions when visitors from the district had come to the Washington office clutching some note Rayburn had once written them.[59] When constituents came to Washington, Rayburn often used their visits to gather information about the district. One county leader reported that when he visited Rayburn, he could never discuss his own mission until he had responded to questions about various district matters ranging from the health of a supporter to progress on a farm-to-market road. Rayburn sometimes devoted thirty minutes to such details before allowing discussion of the constituent's business in Washington.[60] When a staff member once criticized Rayburn for spending 1½ hours talking to a Fourth District visitor, Rayburn, who did not consider the visit a waste of time, responded, "I can learn more about how the campaign is going by talking to a fellow like that than taking time out to talk to the fat cats."[61]

These visits with constituents were also a way of building goodwill in the district. The trappings of the Speaker's office could not fail to awe constituents. In addition, Rayburn would often take a constituent to lunch in the Capitol, perhaps introducing him to such well-known political figures as Lyndon Johnson, Wright Patman, and Robert Kerr. A few constituents he even invited for drinks at the Rayburn Board of Education meetings (regular meetings after a day's congressional session where, at Rayburn's invitation, political figures got together for drinks and political discussions). There they would meet several powerful congressmen and hear politics and politicians discussed and legislative strategy developed. Those who went on the limousine tour of Washington provided by the Speaker's chauffeur could not fail to enjoy the plush vehicle and the curious stares of other Washington tourists.[62]

Rayburn also used constituents' Washington visits to convert opponents. In the 1944 Democratic primary, he had failed to carry Point, in Rains County, a failure primarily due to the hostility of one of Point's most influential citizens. In 1948 Rayburn once more faced the same major opponent. This time, however, before the primary contest, the influential Point citizen, his wife, and daughter went on a tourist visit to Washington, where, at the suggestion of a county leader, they dropped by Rayburn's office for a visit. Rayburn promptly turned his chauffeur and limousine over to the man for a tour of Washington. From then on, that Point citizen was pro-Rayburn, and Rayburn's political difficulties in Point and Rains County were thus reduced.[63]

If constituents needed special help during their visits to the East—theater tickets in New York or restaurant or hotel reservations in Washington—they noticed the special treatment they received from those contacted by Congressman Rayburn. One county leader recalled how, during a visit to Washington, Rayburn went with him to his hotel room for drinks and talk of local politics. Naturally, the Speaker's visit was noticed: "The next morning when I went down, hell, I owned the hotel from then on . . . made all the difference in the world. They opened it up."[64] Constituents who visited Washington with the desire to meet with elected officials or members of the bureaucracy found meetings were, with the Speaker's help, remarkably easy to set up.[65] Such little things meant much to the voters and burnished Rayburn's image of effectiveness.

The House

One-half mile west of Bonham on State Highway 82 is the Rayburn home, on the left. It is a two-story, white frame colonial house with twelve rooms constructed in 1916 and substantially renovated in 1934. Rayburn built it for his parents. His father died soon after the house was built, but his mother lived there until her death in 1927. Miss Lou, his sister, also lived there, as did his brother Tom until he married in 1941. Another brother, William, lived there from time to time until his death in 1943. Meddibel, a sister, moved to the house with her husband in 1941. Her husband did not live long, but she remained in the house after his death. Katherine, another sister, spent much time there, although she lived in Dallas. Minnie Eldridge, a cousin, also lived in the house from 1927 to 1937. Sam, too, lived there when he was not in Washington.[66]

A roomy, rambling farmhouse, pleasant, attractive, but not ostentatious, the Rayburn house was larger than most in the area but often was home to more adults than most. Its furnishings range from beautiful and expensive items, such as the china and silver services, to furnishings that are cheap and tacky, like most of the upstairs furniture. Most of the furnishings are typical of rural middle America. The house is situated on a 120-acre farm, where Rayburn once raised dairy cattle, later changing to beef cattle. Visitors often found him doing farm work. Following the custom in rural East Texas, visitors would go to the back door, enter a small porch, and once inside, usually go to a small day room on the right, directly behind the living room. This day room served Rayburn as an office during adjournments and lengthy recesses,[67] when he always returned to his district. His foreign travels amounted to one trip to Panama made early in his congressional career and paid for with his own funds, and one or two brief trips to Mexico.[68] Rayburn was very critical of congressmen who traveled rather than return to their districts, for he considered such trips politically foolish.[69]

The day room held several chairs, a small bed, and a fireplace, which was the favorite spitting place of the tobacco-chewing Rayburn and his friends. If the group was too large for the day room, Rayburn would take them into the adjoining living room. Generally, however, the living room was used as a waiting area when visitors bunched together. If confidential conversation was in order, Rayburn would take his guest upstairs to his bedroom, which conveniently had a bottle of bourbon tucked away in a closet.[70]

Rayburn's dress, like that of his visitors, was usually informal. Though he would wear a suit when meeting with some visiting delegations, he was usually attired in khaki pants and a white shirt. Known for his rather gruff exterior, he was all business. Interviews with visitors who were not close friends were usually very brief. He would establish some family tie with the visitor, elicit his problem, and give the assurance "I will look into that" or "I will see what I can do."[71] Although long, intelligence-gathering visits like those held in Washington also occurred at home, many of the flood of visitors there were only interested in favors. Rayburn dealt with them politely but quickly. At home there were plenty of opportunities to gather information about people and local issues through observation and consultations with his leaders.

Rayburn's associates recall how, among old friends, he would relax, talk, laugh, and tell stories for hours. His gruffness was a necessary device, they suggest, to protect his time so that he could meet all his visitors during the day. Rayburn was also well aware that persons of great influence attract large numbers of people who wish to profit from the exploitation of that influence. His gruffness may also have been a result, then, of a necessary distrust and of hesitancy with those he did not know well.

Moreover, and perhaps surprisingly, Rayburn was a reticent and almost shy man whose discomfort in social situations was often masked by the rough exterior.[72]

It is difficult to know how many visitors Rayburn would see in a day because no records of his appointments have been kept and because many people came without appointments. At times, a staff member's most difficult job was fitting those without appointments in between those with them. The number of visitors also varied greatly from day to day.[73] In addition to visitors, there were numerous telephone callers requesting his aid. Rayburn's phone system was crude by modern standards—only one line with one phone downstairs and an extension upstairs—but it served its purpose. Callers report brief conversations with Rayburn with no small talk. Long-distance callers were almost certain to complete their business in less than three minutes.[74]

At these home sessions, Rayburn handled quite a variety of problems. One local grocer, for example, butchered his own beef for sale in his store. New federal regulations would have ended that practice, so he phoned Rayburn for an appointment, went to the house, and explained his problem. Rayburn asked him to write a note about the problem and send it to Washington, as he was about to return to the Capitol. The grocer typed his letter and then took it to one of the county leaders to make sure he had satisfactorily explained the problem with the regulation. The Rayburn lieutenant suggested that the grocer redo the letter in pencil on a writing tablet so that it would be sure to get the Speaker's personal attention. The grocer shortly received a handwritten note from Rayburn indicating that the regulation had been changed to meet the objections.[75]

Much of the planning for Lake Lavon occurred in the Rayburn house. Delegations from various communities met frequently with Rayburn to discuss their problems and their need for the huge flood control and water project.[76] Once a delegation even visited Rayburn to ask him to intervene to save a convicted murderer from execution. The murderer had killed one of his relatives, and other members of his family believed him mentally ill. After listening to the story and how the man often thought he was fighting on the front lines in World War II and at other times that he was Jesus Christ, Rayburn called the governor and suggested a stay of execution because of strong evidence of mental instability. The governor agreed, and the man was removed to a mental institution.[77]

Rayburn also held political meetings with his leaders at his house. He made the house the center of the kind of social activity that aids in maintaining political support and a political organization. D. M. Tunnell, his leader in Crandall, in Kaufman County, recalled how, one stormy day, four of Rayburn's Kaufman County leaders found themselves with nothing to do. Without an appointment, they drove to the Rayburn house, where they found Rayburn dressed in his customary khaki, talking with two or three people in the day room. Rayburn invited the four in and entertained them with stories of what was going on in Washington.[78]

Rayburn did not call attention to his personal political successes. He enjoyed talking about the major events and figures with whom he had been associated. Fred Schwengel, an Iowa Republican congressman, became a close friend of Rayburn's because of their mutual interest in history. Rayburn, when he was tired, would call Schwengel to one of his private rooms in the Capitol to relax and talk about the history of the Capitol, or Joseph Cannon, or Nick Longworth, or other major congressional figures.[79]

In the district, as well, Rayburn relaxed among close friends, talking of Joe Bailey, early campaigns, and important political events. To him, one of the most significant events he had been involved in was the secret appropriations for the atomic bomb. He told friends how only a small group of congressmen, including Rayburn, Majority Leader John McCormack, and the Republican leader, Joe Martin, were aware of the bomb project. He explained how he succeeded in going before the House and getting appropriations without telling the members any details of the project. He also told how the secret of the bomb research was nearly published in the pages of a major Eastern newspaper: Following the secret meeting of Rayburn, Martin, and McCormack with Secretary Stimson, General Marshall, and Vannevar Bush, a reporter called him for story confirmation. The reporter's story was a detailed account of the secret meeting. A stunned Rayburn appealed to the reporter's patriotism, begging him to forget the story. The story was never published, but

Rayburn told friends that he knew who was responsible for a leak that could have endangered the nation's security.[80]

All congressmen, of course, are called upon to aid and meet with constituents, but Rayburn stands out for the personal and folksy manner in which he performed this part of his job. Most constituents would never see their congressman if they had a problem but would interact instead with the staff, usually by phone or letter. It is even more unusual for a constituent to see a congressman in his home. Rayburn's intensely personal style, by keeping him in close contact with constituents, was one of his greatest political strengths.[81]

Coupled with personal style, of course, was vast influence and power. Rayburn's success in helping constituents was in large part because government officials recognized that if he presented them with a problem, it would not be wise to be uncooperative. Pete Rodes, his Rains County manager, recalled one instance where Rayburn exerted his influence. Rodes was a banker and approved a large check for a customer who was in Wisconsin buying dairy cattle. The approval was based on an understanding that the sum would be met by a Farmers' Home Administration loan, but the Farmers' Home representative changed his mind and refused to make the loan. This placed the banker in considerable difficulty inasmuch as the amount of the loan exceeded the bank's legal limit. The banker could get no satisfaction from the agency, so he went to Rayburn's house and found him at home. Rayburn told Rodes, "Let me call [Farmers' Home]. I'm not personally acquainted with this man . . . because he's not my man and he's not a Democrat, but let me get him. I think I can have some influence." Rodes reported that the next morning the head of the agency office had driven seventy miles and was at the bank before it opened. "Why," he said, "did you call Mr. Rayburn? Why didn't you call me? Oh, I'll do it. Yes sir, we'll make the loan."[82]

When Rayburn had difficulty satisfactorily resolving a problem, his normal taciturnity gave way. The top of his head turned bright crimson; his voice would rise to a shout; and his language would be filled with obscenities. Wise men would not cross him when he was in such a state.[83] Wise staff members avoided him at such times.[84] Ray Roberts recalled how Rayburn dealt with an uncooperative official. Upon discovering that almost all Work Progress Administration (WPA) officials in the WPA district were from Dallas and that several Fourth Congressional District residents had been turned down for jobs, Rayburn called the WPA administrator for the area and said, "You don't know me, but I am Sam Rayburn and you have got all my district in your organization down there. I would like to have a list of the people you have working in that office." The administrator replied, "Why, Mr. Rayburn, I can't give you that information." The conversation continued briefly before Rayburn said, "I want to tell you something. I want that list by wire on my desk by three o'clock this afternoon. Now if it is not there . . . don't you bother about going to work Monday morning because you don't work there anymore." He then called Harry Hopkins, a top Roosevelt aide who ran the WPA, and said, "Harry, I have just talked to some damn fellow . . . with the WPA. . . . He has all my district, but he has not hired any of my people. I cussed him out and I told him that if I did not get a list of people that he had by three o'clock this afternoon, he was fired. Now are you going to back me up or am I going to Roosevelt?" Hopkins backed Rayburn, and he got the list. As Roberts said, "When he pressed a button, he pressed it hard."[85]

The Rayburn house was not only the center of constituent relations during long recesses and adjournments but where Rayburn met with politicians. Wright Patman, the congressman from the adjoining district to the east, was a frequent visitor. Carl Albert, from the Oklahoma district to the north, visited there, as did Sen. Robert Kerr from Oklahoma, Cong. Jim Wright from Ft. Worth, Sen. Lyndon Johnson, and Missouri Cong. Richard Bolling.[86] Newly elected congressmen, especially Texas congressmen, were often visitors at the house. Rayburn met with them, evaluated them, and discussed committee assignments with them. Such visitors included Cong. John Brademas of Indiana and Texas congressmen Lindley Beckworth, Omar Burleson, and J. T. Rutherford.[87] In addition, reporters frequently visited to interview and do stories on Rayburn.[88] This influx of distinguished visitors could not have gone unnoticed in such a small town and inevitably reinforced the image of Sam Rayburn as the local boy who had made it.

It was certainly clear that Sam Rayburn was a congressional

power when Secretary of the Treasury Fred Vinson and President Harry Truman made visits to Bonham. On both occasions, Rayburn had a reception at the house. Vinson was an old congressional friend of Rayburn's. In 1936 he had been a manager of Rayburn's campaign for majority leader.[89] Later, Vinson became secretary of the Treasury and then chief justice of the United States. His visit provided Rayburn an occasion to hold a reception to meet people and strengthen ties with old friends and supporters.[90]

Truman's visit was quite an event, for Bonham was unused to visits by presidents and presidential candidates. No one doubted that Truman was in Bonham because Sam Rayburn lived there. Thousands of people turned out. Until Rayburn's funeral, the Truman visit must have been Bonham's biggest event. Rayburn wrote, "President Truman isn't just visiting Bonham, he's visiting every nook and corner of Fannin County and his party is as much Honey Grove's, Bailey's, Leonard's, Ladonia's, or Trenton's as it is Bonham's. This is the biggest event in Bonham's history, and I expect 25,000 people or more to be here."[91]

The local paper, full of excitement over the visit, pointed out that Bonham would be in the "national spotlight" because of the visit and would be the "Capitol pro-tem" during Truman's stay. It reported:

> This "once-in-a-blue-moon" distinction, of course, comes
> Bonham's way by reason of Congressman Sam Rayburn, long
> one of the Nation's foremost statesmen and a pillar of the Democratic Party. This will be another of the many recognitions that
> the squire of Fannin County has brought to his neighbors in the
> Fourth Congressional District.[92]

Truman spoke at the Bonham High School field. After the speeches, everyone was invited to the reception at Rayburn's house. Thousands attended, shook hands with the president, were introduced by Sam Rayburn, and milled around the house and yard eating fried chicken, baked ham, and homemade biscuits.[93] The event is still talked of today by citizens of Fannin County, and it further endeared Sam Rayburn to his constituents. The news also reached the constituents that Rayburn had prevailed over the Secret Service's caution and insured that the people of Fannin County would have a chance to meet the president. Rayburn apparently told the Secret Service agents: "These are my friends. I know every man, woman, and child here. I'll vouch for them personally."[94]

A few miles from his home, Rayburn had a 900-acre ranch. He had purchased the land in the late 1930s, improved the property, and stocked it with beef cattle. The ranch, near Ivanhoe, was his hideaway. It had a cabin, no phone, no running water, no lights. When he had had too much of visitors at the house, he would retire to the cabin.[95] In addition to providing a place to relax, the ranch's isolation was beneficial for long, uninterrupted political meetings. Rayburn often met there with his lieutenants from throughout the district to plan campaign strategy.[96] From time to time, visiting congressmen and senators would come there as well to discuss political matters.[97]

On the Stump

Rayburn placed little faith in his oratorical skills. Instead, he used speaking engagements to establish personal relationships. In contrast to the common practice of accepting numerous speaking engagements and rushing from one to another, Rayburn made relatively few speeches except at the end of primary campaigns. He sacrificed a large quantity of speeches for a few speeches at which he tried to interact with as many constituents as possible.

Rayburn never gave the appearance of being rushed; he always took his time at a speaking engagement.[98] Congressman Ed Edmondson of Oklahoma recalled a speech that well-illustrates the personal relationship with voters central to the Rayburn style. Edmondson was visiting Bonham and attended a barbeque where Mr. Sam was the principal speaker:

> We arrived a good forty-five minutes before the program and spent the time visiting with Rayburn constituents as they arrived. [Rayburn gave a rousing speech] and I expected we would head for home after some handshaking. However, we stayed to visit the hundreds of Texans and more than an hour passed before Mr. Rayburn thanked the park caretaker . . . and walked back to his car. "Mr. Speaker," I said, "I could understand when we got here early to greet the folks, but why did you stay until the last

voter had left?" "Ed," said Mister Speaker, "These folks didn't come here to listen to my speech, they came to tell their congressman what was on their mind. As long as one of them had something to say it was my job to listen. And I'll guarantee there'll be a lot more talking about what they told Sam Rayburn than there will be quoting my speech."[99]

Although he lacked the qualities of a great orator, Rayburn did attract large crowds. He was, after all, the Speaker and an important person, so people listened. He had a reputation for speaking matter-of-factly, tending to concentrate on economic matters, especially as they related to the farmer. He was not in the habit of giving lengthy speeches, nor did he tell jokes when he gave a speech. Unlike many well-known politicians of his era, Rayburn believed he was a poor joke teller and avoided humor.[100] Hardeman prepared some of Rayburn's district speeches after he joined Rayburn's staff in 1957.[101] Most of the district speeches, however, were extemporaneous talks with the people. There were times when Rayburn would carry a prepared text and then put it away and speak instead off the cuff.[102]

Rayburn's friends often claimed that he gave only one speech, "the four-cent cotton speech." In it, he would recount the poor economic conditions of farmers during the Hoover administration and then talk about the Democratic administrations and their successful efforts to improve life for the farmers. The implication was clear that Rayburn was a part of those Democratic administrations. It was also clear that Republican electoral victories would bring about a return to a depressed economy.

The speech was not his only one, but it was repeated many times for many years and with few variations—his political mainstay to the end. At the core of the speech was a reminder of Republican hard times and Democratic good ones:

> I can remember four and one half cent cotton. I sold one thousand bushels of oats out here one year for ninety dollars. If I had it now I could get one thousand dollars for it. We sold our cotton at twenty-two and one half a bale. Now we can get a hundred and fifty or more. Cotton seed were burned in those days. They are very valuable now because we do not have too much oil of any kind. Cattle, hogs and oil were selling at a price that it gave nobody a buying power.[103]

When he gave that speech, thousands of small farmers and merchants could not help remembering those hard times. Mr. Sam knew how to reach his audience, and he knew that memories of the New Deal's stress on improving rural life, an effort in which Sam Rayburn was a major figure, would last. He talked also of issues other than rural economic ones, but these speeches were less frequent. Aid to the Greeks, after all, had little to do with the price of cotton. For the small farmers in the district and the small town merchants who depended on those farmers, the price of cotton was life itself.[104]

Rayburn was responsible for some of the most important laws passed by the Congress, including the Securities and Exchange Commission Act, the Utility Holding Company Act, and the Communications Act of 1934, but he rarely spoke of most of his accomplishments. It was not his style to point to his own accomplishments, but he must also have realized that much of this legislation was too complex to be appreciated by his constituents. How does one, for example, make a successful political speech by dwelling on the creation of the Federal Communications Commission when speaking at a ramshackle gas station in Floyd, Texas? The Communications Act was unquestionably important, but Rayburn understood that it was not central to his constituents' lives.

Few congressmen have been as fortunate and as skilled as Rayburn in guiding through Congress several laws—two, in particular—that did rapidly and significantly affect his district. He rarely gave a speech without mentioning rural electrification and farm-to-market roads, both a result of his legislative activities. Electricity revolutionized life on the farm, as Rayburn said it would: "It will take some of the harsh labor off the backs of farm men and women. Can you imagine what it will mean to a farm wife to have a pump in the well and lights in the house?"[105] He might also have asked if one could imagine the reward to a rural congressman who authored rural electrification legislation. That act alone was enough for many of his voters to feel forever indebted to him.[106]

Rayburn was fond of saying, "I want my people out of the mud and I want my people out of the dark."[107] Rural electrification and farm-to-market roads accomplished both. Rayburn stressed his efforts had obtained federal money for farm-to-market roads. In the black lands of the Fourth District, wet weather makes the rural dirt roads impassible. The black earth becomes a bog through which it is difficult to ride horseback and impossible to drive, as one strong supporter who had been a rural mail carrier in the black lands explained:

> I've seen them unhitch mules from wagons and leave the wagons sitting there balled up in mud. There are different stages of that black mud. If it rains just a little bit, it is just slick as glass. If it continues to rain, it will cut ruts and then it will hold water just like a bucket. It doesn't ever dry up in the winter time hardly. Then at a certain stage, it will just roll up and lock the wheels of anything. I walked a many mile carrying that mail and riding horseback. Each foot of a mule gets so big with mud that you can't pick it up hardly.[108]

In speeches Rayburn would recall his own experiences, establishing a bond between himself and the thousands of Fourth District voters who had had similar experiences: "I've been out on a farm and was so lonely that I was just hoping somebody would pass so I could see a horse or a wagon go by. When you are bogged down out there and can't go anywhere, the farmers can't get their children to school, they can't get their produce to market, they can't get to a doctor if they are sick."[109] It was those memories, Rayburn claimed, that caused him to insist that the highway bill provide funds to hard-surface secondary as well as major highways.[110]

Less frequently Rayburn would talk about other legislation. At times he would mention his support for soil conservation, a significant program for a district whose land had been subjected to much erosion.[111] At other times he would mention such acts as the Utility Holding Company Act, not discussing details of this complex legislation that broke up the great utility holding companies but emphasizing how this law had caused Texas Power and Light (TP&L) to fund his opposition. He told of the lobbying tactics that TP&L had used against the act, saying to a district audience, "They not only got everybody that they could write in opposition to that legislation, but we ran across some in Denison where they had actually sat down and listed names of people off of gravestones. I got letters from eight members of one family and one of them was a two year old pickaninny."[112] Listeners may not have learned much about the Holding Company Act from such a speech, but they did get the message that Sam Rayburn was against the trusts.

When Rayburn did go beyond a discussion of four-cent cotton, it is interesting to note his presentation style, well-illustrated in a speech he gave before the Altrusa Club in Greenville. The speech, dealing with some of the dangers America faced in the world, is for the most part a typical "America is great, but we must be vigilant" speech of the type most congressmen probably give scores of times in their careers. During the course of the speech, however, Rayburn stated that modern young people were smarter than he was, for opportunities were greater than when he attended a one-teacher school in Flag Springs with its one teacher certified to teach only second grade. Later in the speech he noted, "I have often said that I had come a long way from Flag Springs, and I have also often said that I feel very close to Flag Springs." He then told the group about his role in obtaining funds for atomic bomb research. Secretary Stimson, General Marshall, and Vannevar Bush, he said, came to see him, told him "the greatest secret of the war," and asked him to get the funding. The initial request was $800 million, and the purpose had to be kept secret. Rayburn said the congressional committee provided every dollar after "I had convinced them that it was a real war effort." Later, when the bomb was completed, he said that he was asked to go see the research effort at Oak Ridge, but he refused, for "I am not much of a traveler except to go to my beloved North Texas," and "I told them I wouldn't go down there because I would not understand any of it. I would just see a lot of buildings, pots and pans, and jars and they could not have explained it to me, anyway."[113]

Such a speech delivers a combination of messages: Here is a man who had few opportunities in life, but he made the best of them. In spite of that, he is a man who remembers his origins. No place attracts him as does home, in spite of numerous opportunities for travel. Yet, here is a home boy who did so well that he played a major role in ending the war by funding the atomic bomb. In spite of that vast power, he is still just like the audience; he thinks the research for the bomb occurred in some peculiar kitchen where things are so mysterious that they cannot be understood. In sum, "I am one of you. I came from your world, love that world, and always will be part of it. I also happen to be one of the most powerful people in America."

Also of interest is what Rayburn did not say in his speeches. He supported legislation, especially the 1957 Civil Rights Act and some labor legislation, that would not be popular in his district. Without his support, it is unlikely that the 1957 act would have been passed. With the exception of Denison, organized labor was very weak in the district; yet, Rayburn opposed such antilabor legislation as the Taft-Hartley Act and the Landrum-Griffin Act.[114]

One might think that a politician would feel compelled to explain his position on an issue if that position did not appear popular with constituents. Rayburn simply avoided those issues, speaking of them rarely if ever. Instead of trying to justify an unpopular position to an audience, he would stress his personal skills, visit with as many members of the audience as possible, establish some identification with them, and talk of four-cent cotton, the Rural Electrification Administration (REA), and farm-to-market roads. On those few occasions when he did offer an explanation for an unpopular decision, he would explain that there might be things he did not agree with personally but had to support because of his leadership position. A leader in the House, he would suggest, had to compromise and be a team player. That meant it was sometimes necessary to go along with disagreeable things. As one of his county leaders said, "Every once in awhile, I'd raise hell about some position he took on something and he'd say, 'Look Bob, those damn guys in the East, those big city guys have got us outvoted. I'm making some compromises to keep them from running plumb over us.'"[115] After Rayburn became a part of the Democratic leadership and was meeting with President Roosevelt in regular weekly conferences, he explained to the McKinney Rotary Club, "Now, I had to make a choice. Some of those policies I didn't want, but I was asked to be on that team and I was determined that, whether I stayed in Congress or not, I was going to play as a team member." He explained that he felt honor bound to carry out the policies agreed to by the majority at the weekly leadership conferences, though he might not be in that majority.[116]

Contribution to the District

Rayburn was fond of telling an old political story made famous by Vice President Barkley.[117] In the Rayburn version of the story, he was out campaigning and stopped at a little country store. The storekeeper was an old friend of his but remained strangely quiet as Rayburn greeted him and recited the favors he had done him. Very perplexed, Rayburn asked the storekeeper, "Surely you are not for my opponent? How can you be for my opponent after all I've done for you?" The storekeeper replied, "But what have you done for me lately?"[118] Rayburn knew the ultimate test of a politician's worth was his ability to satisfy constituents, and he knew that they had insatiable appetites.

Sam Rayburn had a reputation for being a congressman who delivered.[119] After the two best-known contributions to the district, farm-to-market roads and rural electrification, a close third was Lake Texoma, a gigantic lake, the tenth largest man-made lake in the United States, covering eighty-nine thousand surface acres and able to hold 2,722,000 acre-feet of water. It is located in both Texas and Oklahoma and is formed by the Red and Ouachita rivers. The water, impounded by the Denison Dam, is salty because the Red River flows through areas that contain much salt. As a result the dam and reservoir allow little water use, but they protect thousands of acres from floods, have great recreational value, and supply hydroelectric power. Rayburn worked for years to obtain this project for the district. Once Franklin Roosevelt promised five hundred thousand dollars for it, but then it turned out that funds were not available to carry out that commitment. Rayburn's expressions of displeasure over this turn of events were sufficient to lead to a cabinet discussion of the problem, an indication of his influence and tenacity.[120] Mr. Sam was also faced with strong opposition from Oklahoma, especially from Gov. Leon C. Phillips, who opposed the project on the grounds that it would flood valuable Oklahoma farmland. That opposition led the Oklahoma legislature to instruct its congressional delegation to oppose the project. Puett claims that Rayburn, who was majority leader, suggested to the Oklahoma delegation that, in respect for the state's desire to protect its farmland, the state would get no federal funds for any water project. The result was the Oklahoma legislature's prompt withdrawal of its negative instructions.[121]

Another major water project was Lake Lavon, located in Collin County on the east fork of the Trinity River. Lake Lavon cost $12 million and stores 425,000 acre-feet of water. Unlike the water carried by the Red River, the water of the Trinity River is fit for consumption. Lavon provides almost one-fourth of its capacity to water-starved communities within the district. The lake is not a power source, but like Texoma it has recreational value and has a major soil conservation and flood control purpose.[122]

Along with the Lavon project Rayburn was instrumental in obtaining an experimental soil conservation program that involved construction of numerous small water-retention reservoirs along the streams flowing into Lake Lavon. The reservoirs were constructed at government expense on private property donated by the landowner. Such reservoirs reduced silt accumulation in Lake Lavon and provided a valuable water resource to the landowner.[123]

These projects were visible, tangible symbols of Rayburn's influence in Washington. He and his leaders could point to them as proof of Mr. Sam's value to the district. For farmers who had suffered from the periodic flooding of the Red and Trinity rivers, town dwellers dependent on rapidly depleting wells for their water, concessionaires at Lake Texoma, and sportsmen who used the lakes, Rayburn was clearly a valuable resource.

A potentially anti-Rayburn force could have been created out of the lakes' development, especially huge Lake Texoma. Many landowners had to sell their land to the government so that the lakes could be built. Rayburn could not completely blunt the opposition; many landowners did become angry over being forced to sell. Their number, however, was few compared with the number who benefited. Rayburn tried to insure that landowners were satisfied with the price paid them by the government. He made sure that Lee Simmons, his old friend and Grayson County leader, was appointed to assess the property of the landowners. Simmons was a well-known, well-respected person in whom Rayburn had great trust. Simmons was probably appointed specifically to insure that landowners got a price for their land that would reduce their hostility over its forced sale.

Simmons was also in a position from which he could inform Rayburn of political problems developing with specific land-owners.[124] Fenner Leslie, another longtime Rayburn friend and supporter, was appointed special assistant to the U.S. attorney in the Land Division of the Attorney General's office. Leslie worked closely with Lucius Clay in handling land acquisition for Denison Dam and Lake Texoma. As Leslie described his job:

> Sam Rayburn was solely responsible for my being appointed assistant United States attorney. I was in his district, and there was talk that he would lose votes if he took land away from the people and I tried to treat them all right. He carried Grayson as well as he did Fannin County and he didn't lose any votes in Grayson County for that purpose.[125]

Much of the land taken by Lake Texoma and Lake Lavon was overflow land, land subject to frequent flooding, so many land-owners felt no special affection for it. As long as they got a fair price, they held no grudge against Rayburn. Another factor that reduced landowner opposition was that, during Rayburn's life-time, most land in the district was inexpensive and much of it available for sale. With good farmland in the 1950s available for sixty dollars an acre, land taken for the projects could easily be replaced.[126]

Rayburn also aided in locating four military air bases in the district, one near Sherman, another near Bonham, one near Greenville, and the fourth near Terrell. All the bases were flight-training facilities opened during World War II. Perrin Field, near Sherman, was by far the largest. During the war about fifty-five hundred pilots graduated from its basic flying school. It was closed in July 1945 but reactivated in 1948 for several years. Majors Field, near Greenville, was far smaller than Per-rin.[127] After the base closed, it served to attract aircraft-oriented industry to the town. Even today the base is used as an aircraft maintenance and repair facility by E-Systems, a large employer in Hunt County.

Along with all the other projects, Rayburn was influential in obtaining a veterans' domiciliary in Bonham and a veterans' hos-pital in McKinney. The domiciliary, which provided a home for veterans unable to care for themselves and without a home, had three hundred domiciliary beds and fifty hospital beds. It opened in 1950 and provided 262 jobs, mostly to Fourth District residents.[128] The McKinney Hospital, which received War Department approval in September 1942, had 1,500 beds and was designed to serve the North Texas area as a center for the care of World War II wounded.[129] In 1946 the hospital was transferred to the Veterans' Administration; though it was reduced to 620 beds, it was not closed until after Rayburn's death.[130]

The Rayburn effort in helping to get a new National Guard armory for Bonham illustrates his style in obtaining projects for the district. While the Bonham Chamber of Commerce was engaged in a downtown beautification effort, several members of the beautification committee were at Rayburn's house and talked to Mr. Sam about the project. He was just back from a trip to South Carolina, where he had talked to five hundred people in an armory. That speech, still on his mind, prompted him to suggest that what Bonham needed was an armory, for it had no place big enough for five hundred people to gather. The committee members pointed out that Bonham did not have a full National Guard unit and therefore was not eligible for a new armory. Chamber of Commerce members had already checked into the possibility and been told they were not even on the list of eligible places. Rayburn suggested, however, that they work with Robert West on the armory and see what could be done. West, a close friend of the Speaker's and a leader in the Honey Grove community, had just worked on a project that brought a new armory to Honey Grove and so knew procedures and appropriate officials. The Chamber of Commerce committee members expressed an interest in pursuing the project.

That night, after the committee left, West drove to Rayburn's house and met with him about the armory. About one month after that meeting, West arranged a trip to Dallas to meet Gen. Carl Phinney, head of the National Guard in Texas. Aubrey McAlester, publisher of the *Bonham Daily Favorite* and a man active in civic affairs, accompanied West. The two had only visited briefly with Phinney when the general mentioned that Bonham was scheduled to get a new armory. It was clear to McAlester that Rayburn had put the word out that he wanted a new armory for Bonham even if it meant changing the regulations.

The new armory not only provided Bonham with a meeting place but cleared up an eyesore for Rayburn. The armory was located next to the Sam Rayburn Library on land that had been occupied by weeds and poor, unattractive housing. Rayburn, concerned that the housing detracted from the library, had planted an evergreen shield on the property line. A suggestion to Gen. Ernest Thompson, who was in charge of building armories, that Rayburn would be pleased to have the new armory on the neighboring property resulted in the choice of site.[131]

In Fannin County alone, Rayburn could point to numerous projects and programs of his that directly benefited the county: (1) rural electrification; (2) farm-to-market roads; (3) soil conservation; (4) Jones Field, the pilot-training base near Bonham; (5) the Bonham Domiciliary; (6) Lake Fannin; (7) Bonham State Park Lake; (8) Coffee Mill Lake; (9) Lake Davy Crockett; (10) the Bonham National Guard Armory; and (11) the Sam Rayburn Library.[132]

Over the years, Rayburn was also instrumental in bringing numerous temporary projects to the district. For example, during the Depression he was influential in obtaining several Civilian Conservation Corps camps for the district.[133] During World War II his efforts led to the location of a prisoner of war camp in Kaufman County. Because POWs worked on neighboring farms, the camp functioned to relieve the labor shortage on the farms.[134] He capitalized on these very visible projects, which were such obvious reminders of his effectiveness in Washington. These projects were coupled with effective work at more routine levels such as obtaining an upward adjustment in the federal payment toward construction programs and aiding localities and businesses in cutting through red tape. He was also known as a congressman who was interested in constituents' individual problems. He could be a great help to those having problems with government agencies or wanting jobs with either the government or the private sector.[135] Such effectiveness built up a vast storehouse of personal and community level debts which were owed Rayburn by constituents. Payments on these debts, of course, were made by supporting and voting for Mr. Sam.

Personal Life

Marriage and divorce. It was widely believed, even among his friends, that Sam Rayburn was a bachelor. Few knew that he had been divorced.[136] Until very recently, a divorce was extremely damaging to a Texas politician. Rayburn's friend (and brother-in-law for a short time) Cong. Marvin Jones was also married briefly. Records of Jones's marriage and divorce conveniently disappeared. His biographer suggested that divorce was a political liability and that erasure of the records made Jones an "official bachelor."[137] It was the expectation at the time that marriage, no matter how unhappy, was for life; political retaliation against divorced politicians was likely. Perhaps this explains why Rayburn sought to project himself as a confirmed bachelor.

His marriage on October 15, 1927, was to Metze Jones. Sam was forty-five when he married, and Metze was twenty-seven. The marriage took place only months after the death of Rayburn's mother, whom he worshipped, and lasted only two months and three weeks.[138] Several stories have circulated about the reasons for the divorce. Shanks has stated that Metze publically criticized Rayburn's drinking during a cocktail party in Washington and that Rayburn felt such criticism was improper because it endangered his political career. Sam and Metze thus quarreled, and the marriage came to an end.[139] Steinberg noted that Metze "ate him out" when Rayburn drank at a Christmas party given by Cong. James Parker. He also wrote that "Metze was rabid against alcohol" and that Sam had said the Christmas of 1927 "was the driest Christmas I ever spent."[140] Dorough simply suggested that there were differences between the two related to Rayburn's love of Congress and the strenuous nature of Washington's social life.[141] It is unlikely that the full story of the divorce will ever be known. Metze apparently never spoke of it, nor did Rayburn, except to his friend Fenner Leslie and, apparently, to D. B. Hardeman. Leslie never spoke of the divorce, and Hardeman provided only limited information to Shanks. Rayburn conveyed the impression that he had never been married. Knowledge of the marriage was not widespread in the district inasmuch as it had been so brief, the couple had not spent much time in Bonham, and the wedding had been outside the district, in Cooke County. Never was there a hint of scandal associated with the divorce; Rayburn remained on excellent terms with Marvin Jones, Metze's brother; and no newspaper chose to highlight the divorce.[142] The result was that it was so forgotten that, when a political opponent attempted to use the divorce against Rayburn, the charges were not believed.[143] By then people "knew" that Mr. Sam was, and always would be, a confirmed bachelor.

When Rayburn was in Washington, he enjoyed the company of several women. At least one was a well-known Washington socialite. He was especially fond of one woman, the widow of a cabinet officer, and regularly dined with her.[144] These relationships were always discreet. Once, for example, Rayburn started taking Vice President Alben Barkley's widow to parties. When the press began writing about his interest in Mrs. Barkley, Rayburn stopped seeing her, and Mrs. Barkley issued a public denial of the rumors of romance: "Oh, for goodness sake. He's a wonderful friend and he was my husband's friend. I enjoy his company immensely and that's that."[145] The Speaker was by no means a regular on the Washington social circuit, but he did enjoy socializing and female companionship as long as it was unpublicized. One longtime aide suggested that his insistence on an unpublicized social life was based on his concern that social life not detract from his image in the district. He wanted the people back home to believe that Washington had not changed him and that he was the same person he had always been.[146]

Religion. In a rural, strongly Protestant district like the Fourth, a congressman might well use a church affiliation to build a strong political base, but Rayburn did not. He did not join a church until he was seventy-four, and then he attempted to do so without publicity, which proved impossible for such a well-known figure. He chose the tiny Primitive Baptist Church in Tioga, Texas, apparently because his father had been a Primitive Baptist and Tioga was the site of the nearest church.[147] The many other Baptist churches in the district were almost all Southern Baptist.

Before joining the church, Rayburn had been under some pressure by friends to become a member. One, Judge Grover Sellers, told Rayburn that his image was harmed by his failure to become a church member. Rayburn explained to Sellers that he had waited until too late in life to join, for now the Methodists would be upset if he became a Baptist, and the Baptists would be upset if he became a Methodist.[148]

Then events in 1956 profoundly affected Rayburn's thinking about religion. Miss Lou, Rayburn's sister, died of cancer. With the possible exception of his mother, Miss Lou was closer to Sam than any other person; her loss was a major blow. Soon after, he lost his nephew Charles Rayburn and his sister-in-law, the wife of his late brother Jim. According to Steinberg, "Rayburn's attendance at three family funerals left him in a state of shock."[149] It was only a few months after these deaths that Rayburn joined the church. One aide noticed that after Miss Lou's death, Rayburn's correspondence first began to contain references to God.[150]

Rayburn was distressed over the publicity his church membership received. He pleaded with a district paper, the *Sherman Democrat,* to write nothing about it.[151] In 1960, however, his membership did become a useful political tool. John Kennedy's Catholicism was very disturbing to the Bible Belt Protestants of Texas. Anti-Catholicism was fanned by ministers throughout the state. Religion was an issue in the presidential campaign as it had not been since 1928, when Al Smith, also a Catholic, had been the Democratic nominee.[152] Sorenson even believed that Rayburn was anti-Catholic and that he believed a Catholic could not and should not be elected president.[153] If that was Rayburn's attitude, even Sorenson believed it changed with Kennedy's speech to Protestant ministers in Houston in which he discussed the religious issue. Rayburn was very impressed with Kennedy's performance, saying, "As we say in my part of Texas, he ate'em blood raw."[154]

Rayburn's religion, which had been a very personal matter, suddenly became a tactical ploy in a Rayburn-style offensive against religious bigotry. Responding to charges that John Kennedy owed "allegiance to the Pope of Rome," Rayburn argued:

> I am glad being a Baptist of the hard-shell type, that I have no religious prejudices. I have served in Congress with hundreds of Catholics. By no speech they ever made, no vote they ever cast, did they indicate they were Catholic, Protestant or Jew. I know

this statement to be true. Please think again and vote for the man, regardless of religion, whom you think can best serve our beloved country.[155]

Rayburn stayed in the forefront of efforts to carry Texas for the Kennedy-Johnson ticket. There is a folksy eloquence to his arguments, for example, "I am a hard-shell Baptist. But if no one gets to Heaven but us Baptists, it'll be a mighty lonely place. And, they'll have to expand the other place,"[156] and "I cannot agree with you that Kennedy should ever say, under any circumstances that he would give up his church any more than I think a Baptist should say it. If a Protestant should say that he would give up his church before he would give up an office, I think he would certainly be condemned universally."[157]

Old age. By the mid 1950s Rayburn, though still healthy and active, was beyond his seventieth birthday. He had told one staff member and one close associate that he had planned to retire in the early 1950s, but he later concluded that he would stay in Congress until he died or until he was unable to function effectively.[158] Then in 1956, at seventy-four, he suffered a rapid and dramatic loss of vision caused by hemorrhaging of the blood vessels in his eyes. He was left with very blurred vision, and he saw black spots. Vision in the left eye was 8/200 and in his right, 20/200. The vision in the left eye could not be corrected, though right-eye vision was correctable to 20/40.[159] He could not see to read nor distinguish facial features until a person was within a few feet. He could walk only because he could distinguish light from shadows. Rayburn very quietly sought the assistance of eye specialists. Their conclusions reached him through the mail when he returned to Bonham. His aide read him the news that nothing could be done and that further deterioration could be expected. Rayburn showed no reaction. Grief-stricken, the aide continued to read Rayburn his mail.[160]

Rayburn never discussed the problem, nor did others. His staff noticed that he was asking them to read more to him than he had in the past, and after a while they read him everything, but the reason was never mentioned.[161] There was a point beyond which one did not go with Rayburn; personal aspects of his life were beyond it.[162] His staff was absolutely loyal and dedicated; he was loved as very few employers are. They asked and said nothing about his sight, even to one another. This avoidance of personal matters is also evident in regard to the divorce. Even a few years afterward, a staff member noted that he would never have thought it appropriate to mention the marriage.[163] Two of his closest friends did not even feel it appropriate to mention the marriage decades after the divorce.[164]

So Rayburn's vision was never mentioned. The parliamentarian made sure that someone was always on hand at the Speaker's chair to provide names of those approaching the chair or seeking recognition. The staff was always on hand in the offices to help identify visitors. A staff member began to accompany the Speaker to social functions and was instructed: "When people come up, tell me who they are."[165] Close friends such as Dale and Scooter Miller noticed the problem. Scooter would discreetly stand within hearing distance of the Speaker and greet by name those approaching the Speaker to greet him.[166] The same sorts of devices were used in the district. An aide or a friend familiar with the names of Rayburn's friends and supporters was always nearby to whisper a name in the Speaker's ear or loudly greet a constitutent.[167] These techniques worked so well that many of the Speaker's friends either noticed nothing or thought the Speaker only a little nearsighted.[168]

Such ruses were important. By 1956 the age issue had already been used against the Speaker for more than a decade. It had always been deflected by assertions of Rayburn's effectiveness and by his self-presentation as a strong, energetic person. Any overt admission of blindness would project a conflicting image of a dependent old man suffering the ravages of age, an image politically damaging not only in the district but in Washington, where the Speaker maintained control partly by the appearance of power and strength.

The secret was well kept;[169] congressional friends noticed it only because there were occasions when it could not be. Omar Burleson, for example, frequently ate in restaurants with Rayburn. When it came time to pay the bill, Burleson noticed that Rayburn could no longer count change and correctly concluded that he could not see to distinguish the coins.[170] Such secrets can also do political damage, however. Try as they might, aides could not recognize every supporter and, though his memory for voices was remarkable, Rayburn could not distinguish every voice. Once, for example, a suppporter was insulted when he was near Rayburn but was not greeted by him. Angered, he began going around his community telling friends he had been shunned by the Speaker and that Mr. Sam must be getting highbrow. Eventually, news of the insult and the supporter's angry comments reached Rayburn. Despite a necessarily tough political skin, Sam Rayburn cried.[171]

In 1961 another and far more serious ailment befell Sam Rayburn. He began to suffer severe back pain. Initially he thought it was lumbago, but the pain continued and grew more severe. In his last months there were times when he became disoriented. Before his pain became too severe, he continued his habit of taking walks in the area around the Capitol, but his sense of direction failed him so that he twice needed assistance in finding his way back to the Capitol.[172] He saw several physicians, but it was not until shortly before his death that his problem was diagnosed as cancer of the pancreas, incurable, and already widespread.

Between when he was first stricken and this diagnosis in Baylor Hospital, Rayburn bravely concealed his pain, which was so bad that he could barely move. No one except those closest to him realized how ill he was. Carl Albert, for one, noticed that he began to have great difficulty moving from one position to another and became alarmed, but Rayburn insisted that he was fine.[173] His staff noticed that Rayburn, who always liked a short nap in the early afternoon, began to take longer ones. After a while he began to add a morning nap. Later he had to be aided off his couch. Often when moved from his couch, he suffered such pain that tears streamed down his face. Though his chauffeur, George Donovan, told no one until after the Speaker's death, Donovan became so alarmed he began walking Rayburn into his apartment and sitting with him until Rayburn fell asleep.[174] Toward the end, Rayburn twice had to be assisted from the Speaker's chair.[175] At home in the district he maintained the front of good health, claiming his only problem was lumbago. But he was rapidly losing weight and had no appetite. His pain became so severe that he became irritable and irascible.

Through the last year of his life Rayburn struggled to maintain an appearance of strength and energy. A sign of weakness in a politician could tempt challenges from younger aspirants to his job. In both the House and the district, once the extent of his problems became known, maneuvering began that foreshadowed the post-Rayburn era.

There is some indication that advancing age and his vision problems changed Rayburn's political style. In Washington he circulated less among the members than he did in his younger days.[176] To many members he appeared distant, and he did not talk directly to them. In the district there are also those who thought him more distant in his later years. Some believe the eyesight problems slowed him down;[177] others, that he could not tolerate the hot Texas summers as well as he once could.[178] Still others have suggested that he found himself well established in his later years, his opposition destroyed, and thus found it less necessary to be constantly engaged in political activities.[179] Richard Bolling has suggested that he had fought so many political battles that he had, in his later years, a sense of déjà vu, a sense that there was no value in jumping into a political battle.[180] Perhaps all these points have some value in explaining his activity in his later years.

Any decline in activity in Washington or the district was, of course, only a matter of degree; the substance of Rayburn's political style remained the same. Near blindness did not slow him down enough to cause him to remove himself from party politics either at the national or the state level. His state party maneuvering in 1956 is discussed in Chapter 5; here it is enough to say that his eye problems did not keep him from forming an alliance with Lyndon Johnson and Price Daniel and taking control of the state Democratic party. At the national level, he chaired the 1956 Democratic convention. He also offered himself for the vice presidency in that year.[181] He probably was motivated by the belief that an open convention fight over the vice presidency was a foolish idea that would both create unpredictable results and split the party.[182] Hale Boggs, a Rayburn protégé who was close to Adlai Stevenson, carried the proposal to Stevenson, who rejected the offer on the grounds that it came too late. The vice presidential choice was already open to the convention, and

Stevenson believed he could not change his mind at that point.[183] The fight over the nomination therefore took place against the Speaker's wishes.

Conclusion

There are two outstanding characteristics of the Rayburn style. First, his personal behavior seemed oriented toward building constituents' trust. It has been suggested that there are three ingredients of trust: qualification, identification, and empathy. *Qualification* requires that the legislator be viewed as capable of handling the job. Rayburn's behavior clearly stressed this aspect of trust. In emphasizing the legislation he had been involved in, especially that which benefited the district, he projected the image of a master legislator. *Identification* requires that a legislator project an image resembling the constituency. Rayburn tried to convey the image of a farmer in Washington, even to the point of riding in a dented pickup truck rather than his chauffeur-driven limousine. Finally, *empathy* requires that a legislator try to understand and care about constituents' problems. Rayburn's extraordinary accessibility stressed his concern for and interest in his constituency.[184]

Second, Rayburn efforts to promote projects for the district and his interest in individual constituent problems seemed to be an effort to create a reservoir of goodwill in the district. A voter has a difficult time voting against a legislator who has been of help to the community or to himself even if that voter disagrees with the political behavior of the legislator.[185] Trust and constituent work in the district worked to make Rayburn a revered and unbeatable political force. They also helped give him the political freedom to be a national leader.

3. The Rayburn Organization

VEN WITH A STABLE, HOMOGENEOUS DISTRICT and a strong constituency orientation, a congressman needs a political organization to build and maintain a power base. This chapter explores the Rayburn political organization, a strong and very successful grass-roots organization of friends and neighbors. Rayburn did not depend on his staff for campaign aid, nor did he ever use professional campaign assistance. His reliance on the media was minimal, and he did not place great emphasis on frequent political appearances. Yet his organization was so strong that members of it still wield political power in the old Fourth District counties.

Rayburn relied on volunteers for his campaigns. Each county had at least one, often several, campaign managers, who would activate Rayburn supporters in each community. The degree of organization varied from county to county, but the pattern was to have key persons in every community and, in some cases, in every voting box. Their responsibility was to visit friends and neighbors and get out the Rayburn vote. The county campaign managers would work with these key people, contact friends and neighbors, obtain campaign contributions, and schedule campaign appearances. In Rayburn's absence some would also make campaign speeches. What Rayburn had was a long-term and politically sophisticated organization of men who would, for the most part, describe themselves as "country boys."

The organization was in its most active state during those election years when Rayburn had opposition, but he kept in touch with his county leaders even in nonelection years or when he had no opposition. He tried to visit each community in his district at least once a year. The county manager and the key people in the communities would be called upon in off years to assist in these visits by escorting Rayburn through the community or setting up a luncheon for him.

Rayburn's lieutenants tended to be local people with long-

standing ties to the community, leaders who knew almost everyone in their towns, an easy task in communities that tended
to be small with little in-migration. These people served as
"spotters" on Rayburn visits and informed him of what was
important to the community, whose ego needed cultivation,
who was opposed to him, and why. He encouraged them to
write him regularly when he was in Washington, and a large
number of them did. The result was an intelligence network that
provided detailed reports on everything important and much
that was unimportant that was occurring in each little town in
the district.

The organization was not rigidly structured, and lines of authority were often unclear. Rayburn exercised loose control. The
first among equals in the organization was the Fannin County
manager, who was the leader in Rayburn's home county. From
1948 until Rayburn's death, this was Bonham attorney Buster
Cole, who functioned as overall campaign coordinator and in
Rayburn's absence would call strategy meetings of the other
county managers.

The informal style of many of Rayburn's campaign efforts
would astound the modern congressional candidate. Much
would depend on whether Rayburn had the time and the incli-
nation to campaign, and many, though certainly not all, of these
efforts were on the spur of the moment. His Hunt County manager, for example, recalled that Rayburn would make campaign
visits that were sometimes unannounced, the visits for the most
part consisting of going to country stores, renewing acquaintances, and talking to the people who happened to be there.[1]
His Rains County manager noted that on one occasion Rayburn
called him and told him of a forthcoming campaign visit in
two hours. Rayburn asked him to try to get together a group
on the courthouse lawn in Emory, where he intended to give a
speech. The manager was able to gather a large crowd, but only
because of a peculiar coincidence. A murder had occurred in
Lone Oak, and the victim was unidentified. To discover the
victim's identity, the body was placed on display in a hardware
store located near the courthouse in Emory. Such an unusual
occurrence in tiny Rains County had attracted people to view
the body and talk about the murder, resulting in a huge audience ready made for Rayburn's speech. In fact, Mr. Sam was

so elated over the huge turnout on such short notice that the Rains County manager never told him that a cadaver had been the main attraction.[2]

Characteristics of the Activists

The activists in Rayburn campaigns came from a variety of occupations. Among his key people were insurance salesmen, farmers, ranchers, lawyers, postmasters, a gasoline distributor, a furniture store owner, newspaper publishers, bankers, a car dealer, a railroad worker, local politicians, grocers, and the owner of an ice cream company. Many were civic minded, and if they did not hold full-time elected offices, they often held part-time positions in low or nonpaying jobs such as the school board or city council. Frequently they were active in the Chamber of Commerce, civic clubs, church groups, and veterans organizations. Their motives for dedicating their time, money, and energy to Sam Rayburn's political interests were varied and complex.

One cannot discuss the Rayburn activists' reasons for strongly backing him without emphasizing the role of friendship. Rayburn was careful to cultivate personal friendships. He went out of his way to perform little acts of kindness, which can of course build intense personal loyalties. These little things, trivial when considered in the abstract, were frequently mentioned by respondents as reasons for their work in Mr. Sam's behalf. One of his leaders, for example, had a son crippled by polio. Rayburn saw to it that the boy received help from the Warm Springs Foundation. Another told of a long telegram of condolence to his widowed mother sent by Rayburn within hours of her husband's death. One leader mentioned Rayburn's help in obtaining care at a veterans' hospital for a seriously ill foster father. One spoke of visiting Rayburn's house when his son was just a small boy. Rayburn took the boy on a tractor and spent more than an hour driving the excited youngster over the farm. In Rayburn's earlier years in politics when his patronage powers were limited, before he had the seniority and power to bring projects to the district and before he was a national leader, it was Rayburn's skill at cultivating friendships that put together an organization.[3] Friendship was to remain a basis for Rayburn's organization throughout his career.

Other leaders mentioned long-term family loyalties that virtually compelled them to be friendly toward Rayburn. He had the ability to maintain friendships over decades. He kept them in part by being intensely loyal. According to Rayburn's Fannin County leader, Buster Cole,

> he made new friends continuously. At the same time, he never forgot his old ones. On one occasion, he learned that one of his old friends and early political supporters was very much down on his luck with an elderly wife dying with a serious malady. Out of his pocket he took one hundred dollars in bills and instructed one of his helpers present at the time to take it over to this old friend. In his early days he had a supporter over in the Bells area. That one died long ago, but his widow lived on and on, well past the one hundred year mark. Each year, as long as she lived, Mr. Rayburn made a special effort to go visit with the lady.[4]

Cole said that "in Mr. Rayburn's later life, locally if somebody wanted something—let's say that he was twenty-five years old—if his folks or his grandparents had supported Mr. Rayburn forty years before, hell, that was all Mr. Rayburn wanted to know."[5]

As death and illness claimed his earliest supporters, Rayburn showed remarkable openness to the younger generation. He could be the friend of a twenty-year-old as well as an eighty-year-old. Fenno has suggested that one serious problem for older politicians is that at some point they will find that death or disability has claimed most of their generation of supporters, leaving them open to attack by the next generation.[6] Rayburn, however, cultivated the younger generation and asked them to become part of his organization. In a district as stable as the Fourth, fathers introduced their sons to Rayburn and the organization. Those sons, in turn, introduced their sons to Rayburn and the organization. By the end of Rayburn's life, it was not unusual for three generations of a family to have been his supporters.[7]

Though his most intimate friends, Lee Simmons, Fenner Leslie, H. A. Cunningham, and Judge McMahon, were of Rayburn's generation, he was always around young people.[8] Even in Washington, rather than socializing with his age cohort, he enjoyed parties with Cong. and Mrs. Gene Worley, Mr. and Mrs. Dale Miller, and Sen. and Mrs. Lyndon Johnson, couples a generation younger than he.[9] Rayburn also tried to convey within the district the image of being an energetic personality. Actually, he slept long hours at night and often took afternoon naps, but in the public eye he was always active. Once when Rayburn had put in a hard campaign day driven around the district by a young staff member, the latter told Rayburn that he was tired. Rayburn responded, "I never was tired in my life."[10]

Rayburn appealed to young people and could readily win their friendship because of his power and importance. The ambitious among the young wanted his friendship if only because it was a door to opportunities that come to the protégés of the powerful. In his later years, Rayburn appears to have become a kind of father figure to many in the organization. They looked upon him as a role model of a successful politician who had made it in America, from the cotton farm to the Speaker's chair in Washington. He was for some, perhaps, what their fathers had never been.

There were still more reasons that Rayburn's organization held together so well and functioned so effectively. All the members, of course, held an interest in politics. Some saw involvement in the Rayburn campaigns as a means of furthering their own political ambitions. Rayburn obtained several political appointments for key persons in the organization, and it was well known that he had great influence in traditionally senatorial appointments such as U.S. attorney, U.S. marshall, and federal district judge. His friends were also rewarded with postmaster positions, and at times Rayburn would intervene in the civil service selection of rural mail carriers in order to appoint key supporters, their friends, or their relatives. There were part-time positions as well where Rayburn's influence could be felt, such as attorney and appraiser for government agencies. Rayburn's great power also made him influential with private businessmen and state officials. A strong recommendation from Rayburn could virtually guarantee a good job to the recommendee. Lawyers close to Rayburn found that association with him brought them clients from both the private and public sectors.[11]

Although Rayburn had a general policy of noninterference in

other political races, a local politician or political aspirant could benefit by taking an active role in the Rayburn campaign. The local candidate could thus develop valuable associations within the Rayburn organization. A local political figure who was identified as a friend of Mr. Sam would garner much support from the organization in his own campaign. This was an informal mechanism. Grover Sellers, for example, was a state judge. Judges are elected in Texas, and his judicial district partly overlapped with Rayburn's congressional district. Sellers would let his friends and supporters know of his admiration for Rayburn, and Rayburn would return the compliment by letting his friendship for Sellers be known to Rayburn's friends and supporters. It was a relationship of mutual advantage.[12]

Rayburn was generally unwilling and perhaps unable to endorse candidates for office openly, for such endorsements might split his organization. For example, if one faction of the organization supported one candidate for county judge and the other faction another candidate, an open endorsement by Rayburn could only alienate some of his own supporters. Sometimes two Rayburn supporters would seek the same office, and Rayburn's policy of not making endorsements protected him from certain loss of support.[13]

Rayburn's political organization was not designed to dominate all elections within the district but to elect Sam Rayburn. He was upset at signs that his organization was to be used for any other purpose. Jake Pickle, for example, was at one time on Sen. Lyndon Johnson's staff. One of his tasks was to build a statewide political organization for Johnson, and as part of that effort he was in Grayson County, where he met and was impressed with E. B. Chapman. Chapman was, Pickle suggested, an ideal person to handle Johnson's campaigns in Grayson County. He was well known, a prominent businessman, and active in civic affairs.[14] The problem was that Chapman already was one of Rayburn's county leaders. Booth Mooney, a Johnson aide who was quite friendly with Rayburn, warned Johnson that Rayburn was unhappy about his leaders being approached. Rayburn had told Mooney that he wanted his leaders to devote their full attention to Rayburn's campaigns.[15] As things developed, members of Rayburn's organization did strongly support other major candidates. Roland Boyd was a very close political and personal friend of Lyndon Johnson as well as Sam Rayburn. R. C. Slagle, Jr., was a leader for Beauford Jester, Price Daniel, Lyndon Johnson, and later Ralph Yarborough, as well as Sam Rayburn. D. M. Tunnell and Vernon Beckham were also strong Ralph Yarborough supporters. Buster Cole was close to Price Daniel. Nevertheless, the organization was Rayburn's. His endorsements were generally limited to the Democratic presidential nominees, especially the Kennedy-Johnson ticket, and to both Lyndon Johnson and Ralph Yarborough in their Senate races.

Another political motive for some supporters was that several seemed to have believed they could succeed Rayburn. They apparently expected Rayburn to retire and to be able to determine his replacement. Mr. Sam was clearly aware of these congressional ambitions. In a speech in 1959 he said that a lot of young hopefuls in his district "were waiting for this old fellow to fall by the wayside. And there are a fine lot of them too."[16] Little believes that as early as 1948 many district politicians were waiting for Rayburn to die or retire so that they could replace him. Given Rayburn's strength in the district, most of these politicians maneuvered for Rayburn's actual or inferred blessing.[17]

At least one Rayburn leader with congressional ambitions spoke to Rayburn about his possible retirement and obtained a tentative retirement date and promise of support from Rayburn. That plan, however, was based on Rayburn's private belief that Dewey would win in 1948 and that the House would be Republican. Rayburn explained to his county leader, "Well, I'd quit now, Bob. I wanted to be Speaker longer than anybody and I had a chance, but I still lack a term to go and it looks like the Republicans have got it. I ain't gonna quit a sinking ship. I'm going through with it." Rayburn did specify, however, that he would quit in 1950 but was released from that commitment when those assumptions of Republican victory proved erroneous.[18] Again in 1951 Rayburn thought of retiring. When James McDade left the staff in 1951, Rayburn surprised him by saying he would only serve one more term in the House and then retire.[19] Such thoughts of retirement seem to have been only passing fancies, but they did accomplish a useful political purpose of keeping ambitious members of the organization behind Rayburn. Why challenge an extremely powerful and popular congressman who may retire soon and bestow his blessing upon a hard working and loyal organizational leader?

In the event of Rayburn's death, membership in the organization was considered likely to be crucial to a victory for the successor; in fact, it was a key to victory in the first post-Rayburn congressional race. Ray Roberts and R. C. Slagle, Jr., were two leading members of the Rayburn organization and also the two leading candidates in the race. Though their candidacies split the Rayburn organization, they still dominated the field trying to succeed Rayburn. Roberts took the greater number of votes largely because of his service in the Texas Senate. His senate district overlapped the congressional district to a significant degree, and he had produced an impressive record in the office. Thus, Roberts had close identification with Rayburn along with excellent name recognition throughout most of the district.

Rayburn's leaders could also benefit from the status obtained from associating with Sam Rayburn. Their known association caused people to go to them for favors and assistance. Because of Rayburn's national status, the local people who had his ear were even more influential in their communities. It was well known, for example, that Rayburn often asked his leaders' advice when political appointments were to be made, and job seekers thus frequently sought endorsements from the leaders.

Several of the leaders implied that one reason they were so active in Rayburn's behalf was the feeling that, by aiding Rayburn, they were participating in something important. It was a way they could have a role in history. It was not easy for a small town lawyer, banker, businessman, cotton farmer, or railroad worker to have an impact on the national political scene, but by working for Mr. Sam's political interests, they could. The Speakership created the aura around Rayburn that inspired such support.

There were other rewards as well. Leaders who visited Rayburn in Washington received special consideration and were introduced to senators and congressmen. If they had government business, they were provided with introductions from Mr. Sam. Some of Rayburn's leaders received his assistance in becoming delegates to national conventions and were provided with Rayburn-sponsored backroom educations on convention politics. Rayburn chaired the 1948, 1952, and 1956 conventions and played a key role in Johnson's presidential efforts in 1960. A delegate role was therefore an invaluable experience for any lucky Rayburn friend. A tiny number of Rayburn's leaders were also assisted in being named presidential electors.

There is no booster like the booster of a small town. Many of Rayburn's leaders were dedicated supporters because they believed key civic projects could benefit from his influence in Washington. One small-town school board member, for example, was impressed that Rayburn could obtain a funding formula adjustment from the federal government, an adjustment that increased the federal funds available for rebuilding a burned school building. Another leader was very interested in soil conservation and saw Rayburn as the force behind efforts to control flooding and erosion along the Trinity River and its tributaries. Several leaders were impressed with Rayburn's efforts on behalf of Grayson County including construction of Lake Texoma and the Perrin air base. Some of the boosters recognized that development could not come to the Fourth District without an adequate water supply, and Rayburn, they knew, was an essential force behind the huge Lake Lavon water project. Other leaders were rural electrification enthusiasts and saw Mr. Sam as the legislative father of the REA.[20]

Through the efforts of Sam Rayburn and his civic-minded supporters in the Sherman area, Sherman was in the finalist category for the location of the Air Force Academy, which was ultimately located in Colorado Springs. An event occurred during the effort to secure it for Sherman, however, that would have indicated to any civic-minded, or status-minded, constituent that Sam Rayburn was a valuable man to have in Washington. Sherman citizens lobbying for the academy were in Rayburn's office when he called the White House and said he had some friends from Sherman who would like to see the president for about ten minutes and that they were coming over. Eisenhower was of course available for the Speaker's friends and did visit with them. The number of congressmen who could get their constituents in to see the president, especially without notice, must have been few.[21]

Selection of Leaders

As might have been expected, there was no procedure or set pattern for the selection of Rayburn leaders. The main criteria were that the leaders have some influence in their communities and that they be willing to work in Rayburn's behalf. County managers were Rayburn's intimates, men closer to him than any except perhaps his family, two or three staff members, and a very small number of congressmen. It is interesting to note how these intimates were selected and recruited and how a new generation of leaders was developed as the older generation diminished. A few case studies of the selection process reveal much about the reasons for Rayburn's political longevity.

One of Rayburn's first leaders in Grayson County was Carl R. Nall, a druggist. It is unclear how Nall became associated with Rayburn, but he must have been an ideal choice for leader in Sherman and Grayson County, for he ran Sherman's most popular drug store and was a friendly, outgoing, back-slapping type. In later years Rayburn appointed him postmaster in Sherman. One of Nall's closest friends was Bob Slagle, an officer of a cotton-gin manufacturing company and a bookkeeper for Carl Nall's drug store. It was natural, then, given the friendship between Slagle and Nall, that Bob Slagle, Jr., would know and admire Sam Rayburn. Young Slagle attended law school, returned to Grayson County, where he became involved in local politics, and ran unsuccessfully for state representative and county attorney but was appointed assistant prosecutor and later criminal district attorney at the age of twenty-six. All the while, he retained his close friendship with Carl Nall and because of that association, worked in Rayburn's behalf. As Nall grew older, the youthful Slagle naturally picked up additional responsibilities for Rayburn in Grayson County, at the same time advancing politically himself. He became the youngest district judge in Texas, for example, and later was chairman of the Democratic party in Grayson County. It was a natural progression from child in Nall's drug store to leadership in the Rayburn organization in Grayson County.[22]

E. B. Chapman was a gasoline wholesaler and one of Rayburn's leaders in Grayson County. He began working in Rayburn's behalf in the late 1930s. His entry into the Rayburn organization came through Lee Simmons, who was Chapman's father-in-law and one of Rayburn's oldest and most influential supporters. Chapman also shared Rayburn's pleasure in fishing, and their relationship grew stronger over the years. Simmons was one of the most colorful of Rayburn's leaders. As a youth he killed a man in a gunfight and narrowly escaped lynching. Later he became sheriff of Grayson County. In 1912 when he was running for sheriff, he met Rayburn, who was running for Congress. The association grew, and Simmons, after serving as warden at the state prison in Huntsville for six years, increasingly devoted his energies to promoting Rayburn's interests. For many years Simmons worked as manager of the local Chamber of Commerce. He appears to have viewed Sam Rayburn as a man who would greatly benefit the economy of the area. He also served as superintendent of Denison Dam, a position obtained through Rayburn's influence. Simmons had an enormous number of contacts in the county and was invaluable to the organization.[23] In his later years, Simmons and young R. C. Slagle worked together in Rayburn's behalf in Grayson County, Simmons handling the older generation and Slagle the younger.[24]

Samuel Fenner Leslie first met Mr. Sam about 1900. He recalled when Rayburn, still living on the family farm near Windom, visited the Leslie home. When Rayburn became a school teacher, Leslie got to know him better, but it was in 1910 that their friendship developed into a close one. Rayburn was running for the state legislature, and Leslie was running for Fannin County attorney. The two frequently traveled together, riding horseback over Fannin County and meeting voters. Those campaign rides clinched a friendship that would last until Rayburn's death. From the time of Rayburn's service in the Texas House of Representatives, Leslie was known as one of Rayburn's leaders. He recalled one of his primary responsibilities as a campaign manager:

> One responsibility of mine was for Fannin County and I would make appointments—about ten or twelve in the county—for certain days, advertise them and would start in the north, go east to a little town or two and to Honey Grove. We would take two days at this, come on in, start at another voting box, Dodge

City—go on down to Gober, Hail, and to Bailey, which is ten miles south of Bonham, the county seat. This was where I was raised, and where my brother lived at that time. Then we would go on to Trenton and Leonard. Leonard was quite a voting box and a pretty good little town. We would appear there usually at night. My business was to stop his speaking so we could make the next box in time. He'd raise and say he wasn't through talking. I remember an occasion at Ladonia. He said, "I want to talk to these, my friends" and I said, "Well, you'll lose a lot of friends if we don't get to Gober." That was just made up between him and I.[25]

Leslie along with another Bonham attorney, H. A. Cunningham, were Rayburn's most influential Fannin County leaders until the 1948 campaign, when a younger man, Buster Cole, assumed major campaign responsibilities.

Buster Cole was born outside of the district in Hopkins County and moved to the district as a young boy. His ambition was to become a lawyer, and he spent a great deal of time working around the law offices of Cunningham and Lipscomb. After attending college, Cole returned to Bonham and went to work for the firm. Both of the firm's partners, Henry Cunningham and R. T. Lipscomb, were strong Rayburn supporters and leaders in the Rayburn organization in Fannin County. Cunningham was especially close to Rayburn, whom he first came to know in 1906 when Mr. Sam was running for the Texas legislature and Cunningham was running for Fannin County attorney. The two young office seekers became fast friends. Over the years Cunningham handled many legal matters for Rayburn. By 1948, however, Lipscomb had died, and Cunningham was seventy-seven years of age and less active, so Cole, who had been assuming more and more duties within the Rayburn organization, became Rayburn's Fannin County campaign manager and the coordinator of the seven-county campaign, a position he held until Rayburn's death.[26]

Vernon Beckhan was the foster son of Bob Dunn, who had been one of the Rayburn leaders in Denison. Dunn was a crane operator for the Katy Railroad and was stricken with a crippling muscular disease. Dr. M. M. Morrison, an opponent of Rayburn's in 1912 and 1924, took a strong interest in the case and, after much effort, diagnosed the disease. Unfortunately, the disease was progressive and incurable. Still, Dunn was grateful for the physician's diligent efforts and worked in Morrison's behalf against Rayburn in 1924. Morrison ran a disappointing race, winning only 15,032 votes to Rayburn's 24,105. Interestingly, the defeated Morrison became a strong Rayburn supporter in later years, apparently because he admired Rayburn's refusal to attack him personally during their races. This alliance between Morrison and Rayburn made Dunn pro-Rayburn. In addition, Rayburn aided Dunn by getting him medical care at a veterans' hospital. Dunn became a strong and tireless Rayburn supporter until forced by the pain of his illness to become less active. Meanwhile his foster son was growing up and inherited Dunn's many friends and acquaintances in the Denison area. Upon the suggestion of a Denison newspaper publisher who was also a Rayburn leader in Denison, Beckham began to be invited to leadership meetings and soon assumed his foster father's role.[27]

This selected list of the Rayburn leaders well-illustrates how Rayburn, unlike many older politicians, did not rely exclusively on leaders of his own generation but let younger people into the organization. Indeed, he encouraged it. As a result, his organization never went stale or died away. Younger members gradually obtained more power as the aging process slowly released the grip of the older generation.

This kind of recruitment process clearly requires a stable district like Rayburn's, which was a five- (and later seven-) county network of family ties, friendships, and associations. Sons grew up among the friends of their fathers and inherited those ties as well as forming their own among their peers. There was no massive in-migration to disrupt this long-standing network, nor was there the anomie of urbanized society. People knew their neighbors and almost everything about them. Within such a stable system as the Fourth District, a self-perpetuating organization of community influentials functioned as a foundation for Rayburn's political longevity.

Role of the Organization

The organization leaders had as their primary role winning elections for Sam Rayburn. The leaders were well known and established in their communities and could call upon friends and neighbors to vote for Rayburn and to, in turn, ask their friends and neighbors to vote for Rayburn. One leader thus described the range of his friends and neighbors network:

> In 1948 when I got elected district judge, there were sixty thousand people in Grayson County. I called twenty-one thousand of them by name. I mean that's how hard I'd worked. There wasn't a road I didn't know, there wasn't a family I didn't know. . . . Hell, I was born here, raised here, went to grammar school, high school, college, district attorney, district judge, county chairman, active law practitioner. . . , Shriner Mason 32nd degree, Knights of Pythias, Elk . . . past commander of VFW.[28]

The friendship network of his leaders could corral a substantial number of votes.

The leaders would also arrange rallies and luncheons for Rayburn, print flyers, and obtain other publicity to announce his visits. They would also call friends, who would contact friends, so that there would be good attendance at rallies. At other times, they would make arrangements for Rayburn to speak at high school graduations, at the end-of-school picnics traditional at the country schools, and at family reunions. Mr. Sam, like most congressmen, was in considerable demand as a speaker, so often the task was one of coordination of dates rather than making arrangements for a speech. At times there would be "speakings" where candidates for all offices would give a short speech or their supporters would give speeches in their behalf. The leaders would arrange for Rayburn's attendance or for one of them to speak in his behalf.[29]

When campaigning in his behalf, the leaders would stress a number of points. One trait that was frequently stressed was Rayburn's accessibility. One of the leaders would argue:

> [Rayburn] looks after us. When we want a congressman to do something, we can talk to our congressman. He ain't off in Europe on a trip. He's down here at Bonham where you can talk to him. If I phone him in Washington or you write him a letter, you get an answer. . . . If you want to talk to him, he is available. When he is home on these recesses, you can phone or drive over to Bonham and you can talk to the Speaker.[30]

The leaders would also stress Rayburn's enormous power. To refute the argument that Rayburn was a national leader and not representing his district, they would argue:

He appoints people to all these committees. What do you mean he ain't representing us? If he appointed you chairman of a committee and he came over and said Grayson County needed something, don't you know Grayson County would get it? How'd we get this dam [the Denison Dam]? They talk about he was Roosevelt's ass-kisser, but when Roosevelt was passing out all this money for soil conservation and rivers and harbors, how'd he get $48 million to build the Denison Dam if he hadn't been a good friend of Franklin D. Roosevelt and gone along and helped him? Nobody's the big boss up there. Everybody helps everybody. That's the way you get along. The *Dallas News* hollered, "Rayburn says you go along to get along." You damned sure do.[31]

Other campaign responsibilities included walking around town with Rayburn and introducing him to people on the street and in the stores. Elections are won in the Fourth District by getting out and meeting people, renewing acquaintances, and pressing the flesh.[32]

The leaders donated some money for Rayburn's campaigns, and they collected campaign money as well.[33] Rayburn also contributed his own money to his campaigns.[34] Campaign expenditures were laughably small compared to today.[35] In an uncontested campaign, expenditures would be only a few hundred dollars, mostly for newspaper announcements that Sam Rayburn was running for reelection. Most of his contested campaigns apparently did not cost more than a few thousand dollars, though one leader did estimate that the 1944 campaign, one of Rayburn's toughest, cost forty to fifty thousand dollars.[36] It appears that little if any campaign money came from outside of the district, although some of Rayburn's friends in the oil industry may have made donations. A one-hundred-dollar donation was considered by the Rayburn leaders to be a large one; most were far less.[37]

Expenses were minimized by the highly personal nature of the campaigns and the complete reliance on volunteers. Emphasis on personal contact was possible, of course, because of the small population and compact size of the Fourth District. Rayburn was able to travel around the district with ease and keep in touch with his political leaders. The stability of the population made it easy to know voters, their family ties, and their political values. Thus, a friends-and-neighbors campaign style was possible.

Little or no television was used by Rayburn or his leaders. Radio spot ads and radio speeches were used, but not heavily. The leaders frequently placed election announcements in the local papers and also paid the costs of these announcements. There were a large number of papers in the district, mostly low-circulation weeklies. Rayburn liked election announcements published in every paper except those few that showed strong hostility toward his candidacy. Rather than prepare the announcement, the general practice was to pay the fee and ask the paper to prepare the announcement.[38]

The *Dallas News,* the ultraconservative Establishment paper in Dallas, had a wide circulation in Rayburn's district, and he was a frequent target of its editorials. On one occasion, some of his leaders were so outraged at the negative coverage given Rayburn that they purchased an advertisement in the *News* that said, in part:

> The Democratic Primary is over . . . and Sam Rayburn received about the biggest majority ever obtained in being re-elected for his 21st term as Fourth District Congressman. We in the Fourth District, while not so rich are still a prideful people. Now . . . Mr. Dallas News, we know you send a lot of papers up in our district, and we read them; but . . . your editorial page runs a little askew. . . . In that last minute editorial you said: Mr. Rayburn represents Washington. He represents Truman. He represents New York and Michigan and Massachusetts. But he no longer represents Texas. . . . Now it seems that on July 8, 1951, sixteen days before the election, you carried a story. . . . Congress voted $1,000,000 Monday to begin construction of the Dallas Floodway this year. . . . Although the Senate originally had recommended $2,000,000 the House had omitted Dallas funds entirely . . . but when things looked blackest for Dallas, Speaker Sam Rayburn . . . went to bat.[39]

In the view of some of Rayburn's associates, the opposition of the *News* did Rayburn little harm. It was the city paper, and it was seen as interfering in matters of no concern to Dallas. Its opposition also made it easy for Rayburn's friends to campaign in his behalf by running against the rich city people in Dallas. As one of his supporters explained:

> I'd walk these streets and say . . . "They're spending this money like water and they're getting it out of Dallas. I don't want a Dallas Congressman; I want a Bonham Congressman. I want a Fourth District Congressman. I don't want to sell my Congressman to Dallas. . . . I want to be able to go talk to him and if he don't vote the way I want, I want him to tell me why, and not have to ask Mr. Carpenter of TP&L."[40]

When newcomers moved to town, members of the organization would often try to contact them and convince them of the merits of retaining Sam Rayburn in Congress. As most of the towns were quite small, it was easy to meet new people and discover their political beliefs.[41] Organization members would also keep Rayburn informed about the up-and-coming young politicians in the community and their ambitions. Working on the assumption that it is harder to oppose a friend than a stranger, the leaders would try to bring Rayburn and these new politicians together.[42] Rayburn would also have the leaders check on government programs about which there had been constituent complaints. One Kaufman County leader, for example, recalled a gentleman who frequently conducted unofficial inspections of the levee construction designed to prevent flooding along the Trinity River. This constituent and unofficial levee inspector would write Rayburn about problems with the levees, and the Speaker would call upon his leader to verify the problems. If he got verification, Rayburn would then get immediate corrective action.[43]

Organization leaders frequently provided Mr. Sam with information on the reputations of job applicants or favor seekers. Job supplicants would often talk to organization leaders in the hope of support for their applications. Rayburn did often ask the advice of his leaders on patronage appointments, especially if none of the applicants was a close friend of his. If, for example, there was a vacancy in a rural mail carrier position in Rains County, he would usually contact his county leader to request a recommendation.[44]

Often more than one Rayburn supporter would be an appli-
cant for a position, which could offend those not appointed.
Rayburn temporarily lost the support of the *Rains County
Leader* because he appointed one friend as postmaster instead of
the one the paper backed.[45] With rural mail carrier positions,
the rule was that an appointment would be made on the basis of
the highest test score unless the congressman intervened to support one of the next two highest scorers. Rayburn had a long-
standing policy of not intervening if the highest scorer and one
or both of the next highest were his friends. As he wrote, "In a
place like Bonham, where probably all of the three will be my
close friends, I am sure that I will feel like allowing the one who
received the highest grade to have the office as in a case like that
I would not be accused of showing favoritism between two
good friends."[46] The policy did not always satisfy the disappointed applicants, and Rayburn might have to call upon his organization leaders to persuade the disgruntled applicants that it
would be best to remain Rayburn supporters.

A leader in Rains County recalled just such a situation involving a rural mail carrier's position with two Rayburn friends as
applicants. One was about forty, had only a small family, had
worked in the post office, was a veteran, and was high scorer on
the exam. The other was in his twenties, had a huge family, was
a veteran, and had the second-highest score on the exam. Both
had supported Rayburn, but the latter had a huge extended family, which meant about fifty votes; the former accounted for
only a handful. Rayburn had been Speaker for years when this
patronage problem arose. He took such disputes seriously and
drove to Emory in Rains County, where he combined business
with pleasure by doing some fishing with his country leader:

> RAYBURN: I have put off talking to you about this thing. You
> have been strangely silent about who you want for this and I
> think now is the time for us to talk.
> THE LEADER: Mr. Rayburn, I am still silent. Clearly the older
> man earned it . . . by being first and he earned it by his years of
> work, and if they don't go for anything, why it's kind of a bad
> system. On the other hand, it would clearly be to your advantage
> to appoint this younger boy because you would get a lot
> of support.
> RAYBURN: The [older] boy gets it that's number one.

THE LEADER: I think that's a good decision and I think we can keep these people.
RAYBURN: Will you go talk to them? I don't want to go talk to them.

The leader found both the young man and his father bitterly disappointed over the decision. He explained, "You're young and there's lots of other things that are going to come up. Bear in mind this boy earned this thing. It would have been bad to slap somebody in the face that earned something." The young man and his family continued to support Rayburn, and in four or five years another rural mail carrier position became vacant and the young man was appointed to it.[47]

A final activity of the organization, one greatly encouraged by Rayburn, was keeping him informed of events in the district. Leaders wrote him about births, deaths, illnesses, opposition, progress on government projects, possible opponents, and the political pulse of the community. Rayburn also encouraged such reports from all constituents, and the result was an intelligence network that was central to his political style, for it gave Rayburn important information about the district during the long periods he was in Washington while giving the information providers a sense of being a part of the political process. One who is in regular correspondence with a congressman on district matters will probably be his regular supporter.

Tensions Within

The organization was not always a smoothly running political machine. At times, personal rivalries threatened its effectiveness. In 1944, for example, there was hostility between Lee Simmons and Sherman attorney James Buster. Simmons, Buster thought, was trying to ostracize him from the organization. Rayburn wrote Simmons and others in the organization to ask them to try to be nice to Buster, which they apparently were, for Rayburn received a report from Carl Nall that Simmons was "now going out of his way to be congenial with him [Buster]." The problem, explained Nall, was jealousy over friendship with Rayburn. For the election, Rayburn's friends were trying, however, to unite.[48] But the truce did not last long; it was soon necessary to try to patch things up again. Buster had delivered two pro-Rayburn speeches over the radio and had paid for them with his own funds. He had planned three more but canceled them because Simmons had told him to stop. Buster was hurt and brought the affront to the Speaker's attention.[49]

A similar spat broke out among Rayburn supporters in Greenville. The Horton brothers and Miss Ollie Coon became angry with Gus Hodges, whom they accused of disloyalty to Rayburn because he was friendly with one of the Poole family and with G. C. Morris. One of the Hortons was publisher of the pro-Rayburn paper; Miss Coon was its society editor. Hodges was the Rayburn-appointed postmaster, and he did make the mistake of being friendly with a Poole, of the family that published the rival paper, and with Morris, a major Rayburn opponent. The tensions were serious enough that Rayburn's brother-in-law in Dallas, W. A. Thomas, spoke with Hodges, as did Charles Tune, a Rayburn leader from Terrell. Both determined that he was completely loyal to Rayburn even though he sometimes made a poor choice of friends. Thomas then worked with Hunt County leader G. C. Harris to unify the warring pro-Rayburn factions, "at least until the campaign is over."[50]

In 1948 problems broke out in Sherman between James Buster and R. C. Slagle, Jr. Slagle was one of the strongest personalities in the Rayburn organization and one of its politically most influential figures. He was sometimes spoken of as a successor to Rayburn and at other times as a potential political rival. There were times when it appeared that Slagle was the dominant figure in Grayson County politics. Buster resented Slagle's efforts to dominate the county's politics, suspected that it was a first step in a Slagle effort to succeed Rayburn, and threatened to work against Slagle's efforts. He also suggested that Slagle's friends were encouraging Judge David Brown to run against Rayburn in 1948. The alleged strategy was that Brown would be demolished by Rayburn and would be defeated so badly that he would no longer be a rival to Slagle's congressional ambitions.[51] As was Rayburn's practice when such problems erupted, he did nothing to exacerbate the conflict. While he thanked Buster for his friendship, he made no mention of Slagle in his reply and offered no encouragement to Buster's anti-

Slagle views. Instead, he shared grief with Buster over the recent death of Carl Nall. Rayburn also tried to focus Buster's energies on Judge Brown and urged efforts to convince Brown not to make a congressional race.[52]

Rayburn also had problems with organizational leaders who aroused hostility among voters in their communities. In 1944, for example, Rayburn was contacted by some constituents who were hostile to some of Rayburn's Grayson County leaders. Essentially, the dispute was over county politics. The unhappy constituents asked Rayburn to intervene and get his "henchmen" to change their county policies.[53] Rayburn politely refused, claiming:

> I have certainly never taken any stock in any Grayson County races and I never expect to. Of course, I assume that my close friends, like yourself, line up on different sides in different county races, but that certainly does not mean that they go against anybody at my suggestion. So anything that happens in Grayson County politics cannot be charged to me.[54]

Rayburn's practice of praising his correspondent, playing down conflicts, and trying to focus the correspondent's attention on Rayburn's primary campaign is seen in his response to post office problems in Blue Ridge. One of his Blue Ridge (in Collin County) leaders wrote Rayburn that personnel problems in the post office involving a Rayburn-appointed postmaster were hurting Rayburn. The leader suggested that the postmaster and one of his assistants were disliked in the community and that the postmaster was making life difficult for a well-liked postal employee.[55] Rayburn's reply was to request further information on the post office difficulties, to praise his correspondent, and to ask for unity among his supporters: "I am hoping that all my friends at Blue Ridge can work together as I feel that taking all elements there are supporting me, including such men as yourself, can get that box in good shape."[56]

The Family

Rayburn came from a very large family, and some of its members played significant roles in the Rayburn organization. In his earliest years in politics, several family members apparently campaigned long hours in his behalf, for example, his brother Frank Rayburn, a physician in Bonham.[57] His death in 1928 was a personal as well as a political blow to Rayburn. Three other brothers, Tom, Jim, and Dick, and a brother-in-law, W. A. Thomas, also had roles in the organization.

Tom was four years younger than Sam and a farmer. He managed Rayburn's agricultural interests and was well known and liked among farmers in the Bonham area. For years Tom was superintendent of the livestock barn at the Fannin County Fair, a position that brought him into contact with numerous Fannin County farmers. Tom frequently attended political rallies with Sam and would visit with his friends and neighbors, campaigning in his brother's behalf. In the earliest days of Sam's career, Tom was well known throughout the district as a baseball player. It was said that Tom's baseball playing gave him better name recognition than Sam. Baseball took Tom into several counties and made him a political asset.[58]

Brother Jim was a rural mail carrier for many years. He often informally polled mail customers on his route so that Sam would know what people in the area were thinking.[59] Somewhat more politically active was brother Dick, who was two years younger than Sam. Dick was in the cottonseed oil business, which required him to work with farmers and travel all over northeast Texas and southeastern Oklahoma. Dick used these trips to visit with his friends in his brother's behalf and gather useful political information. In the earlier years of Rayburn's tenure, Dick was also frequently seen at political rallies. He was the most outgoing and friendliest member of the family. His wide circle of friends made him one of the most politically important members of the family. His political judgment was considered excellent by other members of the organization.[60]

W. A. Thomas was the husband of Katherine Rayburn, Sam's oldest sister. W. A. was originally from Hunt County and, with Rayburn's support, he obtained the position of director of the Internal Revenue Service in Dallas. Thomas was involved in some of Rayburn's earliest campaigns and remained active even after moving to Dallas. Before his move, he held county office in Fannin. Probably the most politically oriented of Sam's relatives, one close friend described him as a man who "loved politics." After moving to Dallas, W. A. played a major role in the 1928 Smith-Robinson presidential campaign. He was also an early supporter of Texas Sen. Tom Connally. Until his illness and death in 1946, W. A. worked in Rayburn's behalf by contacting friends in the district and coordinating Rayburn's appearances throughout the district.[61]

When Sam came home to Bonham, it was said that these family members would gather at the house to spend a night or two. During that time they would provide Sam with an enormous amount of political intelligence on the district.[62] By the late 1940s, however, the political activities of family members appear to have been minor compared to those of his unrelated political volunteers, for age, illness, and death had taken their toll of family members. Such a large family, many of whom lived within or near the district, did serve, however, as a major political asset for years.

The Staff

Lyndon Johnson was fond of saying that "Sam Rayburn ran his office from his ass back pocket."[63] There is considerable validity to that statement. Rayburn ran his offices in a highly personal manner, he kept few notes, received few staff briefings, and handled much House and district business from the back of an envelope.[64] He had no professional speech writer on his staff. He wrote most of his speeches, sometimes with the assistance of political reporters and personal friends such as Cecil Dickson and Bascom Timmons. After 1957 D. B. Hardeman, a lawyer-politician-intellectual, joined the Rayburn staff with the formal title of research assistant, but he functioned in a variety of roles ranging from friend to speech writer. Within the district, Rayburn's speeches were hardly ever prepared and were given without any notes.[65]

There was no press officer to handle district coverage. Rayburn once tried to hire Booth Mooney for such a job, but Mooney was working at the time on Lyndon Johnson's staff. Though he accepted Rayburn's offer, neither he nor Rayburn felt comfortable telling Johnson that Mooney had been hired away, so Mooney continued on Johnson's staff.[66] Rayburn received district press coverage from stories local papers picked up from the wire services, articles from Washingon news services with Texas subscribers such as the Bascom Timmons' agency, and most importantly Rayburn's personal contacts and friendships with local publishers and reporters. He had an especially good relationship with the *Greenville Banner,* the *Denison Herald,* the *Sherman Democrat,* the *Bonham Daily Favorite,* and the *Terrell Tribune.* He provided the papers, which were among the largest circulation papers in the district, with numerous on and off-the-record interviews. He would even arrange interviews with other notable figures for these papers. He was news and was most generous with his time when it came to these papers. Their response, of course, was appreciation, support, and even special issues honoring him. In several cases, publishers and editors of local papers had major roles in the Rayburn organization.[67]

There was only one office in the district, on the square in Bonham, and for most of Rayburn's career it was only staffed when he was in town. One or two staff people would work in the office during those periods to make appointments, meet visitors, and handle correspondence. For four years Rayburn did have one staff member in the district office who was full time. This person's work, however, was very limited, the position being primarily a sinecure.[68]

Over nearly one-half a century in politics, Rayburn employed only thirty-eight staff members, never more than seven at any one time. At this writing, the House Speaker employs twenty-seven staff members.[69] Rayburn's thirty-eight staff members included both those who served on his regular congressional staff and those who managed the Speaker's office. Two were chauffeurs, George Donovan when he was Speaker and Nick Nicastro when he was Democratic leader. Numerous other patronage positions were available to Rayburn in his leadership positions, and he made use of these patronage powers to appoint people from the Fourth District to jobs in such places as the legislative clerk's office and the Capitol police. In Rayburn's day it was common to expect such patronage appointees to work part time in the congressman's office and even campaign for him. Except for a few brief periods when Rayburn was shorthanded in his congressional office, he did not call upon these appointees to perform any work for him in campaigns, the Speaker's office, or the congressional office.[70]

With the exception of his chauffeurs, all members of the staff had strong ties to the Fourth District, and most were born there. Rayburn was unwilling to hire those without ties to the district because the jobs paid well in comparison to wages in the district and he viewed these jobs as valuable plums for those who were responsible for putting him in office. He also wanted people in his offices who knew the people in the district and who could understand their problems.[71]

Some staff jobs were apparently used as rewards for his organization's leaders. His earliest staff member, for example, was Hal Horton, the brother of Fred Horton, publisher of the *Greenville Banner* and one of his Hunt County leaders. Alla Clary, who worked for Rayburn from 1919 until his death, was the sister of U. M. Clary, a very early Rayburn supporter who had worked hard in Mr. Sam's behalf in the Prosper area of Collin County. Dan Inglish was the son of a close friend of Rayburn's. The senior Inglish was with the strongly pro-Rayburn *Bonham Daily Favorite,* was one of Rayburn's earliest supporters, and had been a Rayburn appointee to a state position when young Sam was in the Texas House. Bill Wilcox was the son of G. I. Wilcox who owned the pro-Rayburn *Sherman Democrat.* Ted Wright's family was also strongly pro-Rayburn.[72]

Staff members were often quite young, and several attended law school part time while working on the staff. In this way, Rayburn provided them with an excellent job while they attended school. Unlike some congressmen who employ only staff members from the district, Rayburn never terminated a staff member and so never suffered any political repercussions from firing a local person.

Because of the prodigious correspondence maintained with constituents, most of the congressional staff functioned as stenographers and secretaries. Alla Clary was first secretary for Rayburn for over forty years. Thus she knew the members of the Rayburn organization and could determine which mail needed his personal attention and which could be handled by staff. She also functioned as the office receptionist and set up appointments for Rayburn. If his time needed protection, she would protect it. Indeed, Rayburn said that her value was that she could say no when necessary. She could also be rude when it was unnecessary, from time to time creating embarrassing situations. For example, when Carl Albert first went to Congress, he went to Clary and asked to see Speaker Rayburn. Albert's appearance was then very youthful. Clary told him that Rayburn did not have time to see pages.[73] At times Rayburn would become very frustrated with Clary, and she recalled that he had threatened to fire her many times.[74] More than any trait in a staff member, however, Rayburn valued loyalty, and Clary was loyal. When Lyndon Johnson told Rayburn that Clary should be fired, Rayburn reacted with anger. Other staff members also came to know the organization well, for many remained with Rayburn for several years.[75]

The Speaker's office had a small staff designed to greet visitors and prepare briefs on legislation. Staff members would also be assigned to the floor of the House when Rayburn could not be present and when matters under consideration were of special interest to the Speaker. They would watch the progress of legislation, attend some committee hearings, and report problems with legislation.[76] Lines of authority and staff duties within and between the two offices were sometimes unclear, with staff members doing whatever Rayburn assigned, often without knowledge of what other staff members were doing.[77] It was said that Lyndon Johnson and his staff made fun of Rayburn's for its small size, informal style, and northeast Texas country ways.[78] For Rayburn, however, the office was just as he wanted it. It provided jobs for the people in the district, and more important, it could communicate, East Texas accent included, with his constituents.

Rayburn had at least six unwritten rules that were soon clear to staff members: (1) Loyalty was a prized trait. (2) Confidentiality of office operations was essential. (3) Appointments to see Rayburn would be made but were not required. Anyone who walked into the office could generally see the Speaker if that person was willing to wait his turn. (4) Constituents were to receive rapid responses to letters and requests. Rayburn's name, rather than the staff member's name, was to be affixed to correspondence. Rayburn did not sign all his mail, but he made certain that staff members could sign his name with a signature that looked authentic so constituents would believe their problems got the Speaker's personal attention. (5) Visitors from the Fourth District were, if at all possible, to see Rayburn and to have priority over others wanting to see the Speaker. (6) Rayburn was to see all handwritten letters from people in the district. This last rule was based on Rayburn's belief that those who wrote handwritten letters, especially with a pencil on lined paper, rarely wrote their congressman, had probably made an effort to write, and did so out of the conviction that they had something to say. After Rayburn's eyesight became too poor for him to read, staff members read these letters to him. Rayburn believed a satisfactory personal reply from the congressman was likely to guarantee a vote.[79]

Rayburn's offices were designed with the district in mind. One employee in the Speaker's office recalled how, in the first days of his employment in 1955, he learned how strongly Rayburn felt about running a constituent-oriented office. Rayburn was then as politically secure in the district as it was possible for a congressman to be. The new staff member was handling the office by himself one day because the other two employees were otherwise occupied. The employee was seated near the entrance to the Speaker's office, and Rayburn was presiding in the House.

> Anyway, these people showed up. . . . The guy had on khaki pants and a brown coat. The lady was well dressed, but very country dressed. You could tell they were not from Washington, D.C. They had a couple of kids with them. They were standing out in the hall just staring in at the ceiling and the offices, which were very lavishly appointed. So I walked over to them and asked them if I could help them. They had been on a tour and had asked a guard where Sam Rayburn's office was. They were from the congressional district. . . . They just wanted to look in and see his offices. I said, "Well, sure." I said, "I know he would love to see you, but he's tied up today and all these people are here to see him." And they said, "Oh well, we understand that. . . ." They were up here for two or three days on a trip. They were farmers in Fannin County and just wanted their kids to see Washington. So they looked there for a minute and I went on with my business.

A light and buzzer on the side of the staff member's desk then summoned him to the Speaker's chair in the House.

> [Rayburn] asked me two or three questions. I had a list of people there to see him. He was sitting there listening to me with one ear and also watching and listening to the action on the floor. I said, "There was a family from Fannin County that came up here and got lost off the tour and looked in." He said, "Well, who were they?" I said, "I don't know. . . ." He said, "You didn't get their names?" . . . And he just came unglued and he said, "I'm going to tell you something, you go find those people and bring them back to my office. And don't come back until you do." I said, "They've gone on. I don't know if I can find them." He said, "You find them. And you need to get with it right now. And get to finding them." Well, I took off like a scalded dog and I found them over on the Senate side. . . . Anyway, I got them back over there. . . . He left the chair . . . sat them down and had known their parents and grandparents. . . . And he made them feel so comfortable and so relaxed. He said, "Bob is going to make arrangements for us to have lunch in the Speaker's room. . . ." They would be driven back to their hotel by George Donovan, the chauffeur. . . . That afternoon he explained to me very clearly, "These are the people I represent. These are the people that pay my salary. These are the most important people, more important than the guy who is out there with the appointment wanting something. These people are not wanting something other than good representation."[80]

Throughout his career Rayburn was remarkably sensitive to the feelings of his constituents. In 1957, for example, he was trying to hire a janitor for the Sam Rayburn Library. The job was not a high paying one, but the salary was good for the Bonham area and the work steady. Rayburn asked Karl Trever, an archivist on loan from the federal government to help set up the library, for his recommendation. Trever recommended a black man who had done construction on the library and made an impression with his energy and his skills. Rayburn hesitated because there were many white men who wanted the work and would be upset at the appointment of a black. Trever persisted, and Rayburn did give the job to the black man. At that time Rayburn had been in Congress for forty-four years and had had no serious opposition for nine. He was an institution in his district. Yet still he worried about the political repercussions of a mere janitorial appointment.[81]

Another indication of this sensitivity is his technique for responding to gifts. Rayburn liked to drink whiskey and often received bottles as Christmas presents. Out of respect for the pro-temperance feelings of many of his constituents, however, his thank you notes would not mention liquor; instead he would thank the donor for the "fruit." Should such a note somehow fall into unfriendly hands, his signature would thus not be associated with the word *whiskey*.[82]

Rayburn's chauffeurs also played an important constituent-relations role. They were frequently called upon to provide tours of the Capitol and surrounding areas for Fourth District visitors. George Donovan, in particular, was a master tour guide and was devoted to Rayburn. He was a friendly man who knew every tourist attraction in the area and who would describe buildings with appropriate reference to Sam Rayburn. He would, for example, point out the White House and tell the visitors how he sped through the streets to get Rayburn there, ignoring police and traffic signals, so that Rayburn and Roosevelt could talk about the attack on Pearl Harbor.[83]

After Rayburn became Speaker, he was concerned that the Speakership would distract him from district affairs. He decided to hire someone to concentrate on protecting his district interests. Acting upon the recommendation of Lyndon Johnson, Rayburn hired Ray Roberts, who was from the Fourth District and had worked for Johnson in the National Youth Administration, to concentrate on district matters, especially trying to win government projects. Roberts was one of a small group known as the "Little Cabinet" who developed contacts with the middle-level bureaucracy that enabled them to obtain advance information on agency plans and projects. World War II limited Roberts' service on the Speaker's staff to one year.[84] With his departure, no one was placed on the staff with a specific district-oriented function. With the departure of Roberts and the unsuccessful effort to hire Booth Mooney to handle his press relations, Rayburn concentrated control over district matters in his own hands.

When Congress adjourned, Rayburn would return to Bonham, taking one or two staff members with him. At least one of the staff members would be male because Rayburn often used staff as drivers for trips within the district. His chauffeur stayed in Washington. Rayburn used men as drivers because he felt it was unseemly for an unmarried man to be driving around the district with a woman.[85] The staff that went with him to the district also handled correspondence and managed phone calls, appointments, and unannounced visitors at Rayburn's home. With the exception of one staff member who was an able public speaker, no Rayburn employee gave speeches on his behalf. In 1957 the Sam Rayburn Library, privately funded by donations, was dedicated in Bonham. A Rayburn staff member left the Speaker's office to assume the directorship. Rayburn assigned the library director to gather politically relevant information for him, and the library was used from 1957 until after Rayburn's death as a place where constituents could go and receive assistance.[86]

The staff was structured toward maintaining Rayburn's personal relationship with constituents. Thus it made its contribution to Rayburn's remarkable hold on the district.

4. The Campaigns

THIS CHAPTER EXPLORES THE DISTRICT POLI-tics, the Rayburn style, and the behavior of the organization in the context of five Democratic primary elections. Rayburn faced numerous challenges in Democratic primaries during his half century in Congress. In those days the win-ner of the Democratic primary won the election, for there was no Republican opposition. It was thus the primary that was the focus of his campaign energies. Though Rayburn had no opposition after the 1954 election, this was unusual; he did face opposition in seventy-two percent of his primary elec-tions (see App. B, Table 4). His first election to Congress, in 1912, was a very close race. He did receive the greatest number of votes, and in those days only a plurality, rather than a majority, was necessary for victory. After 1917 a runoff election was re-quired if no candidate received a majority, but Rayburn never had to participate in one.[1]

Several of Rayburn's primary elections were close, especially those in 1916, 1922, 1930, 1932, and 1944.[2] The 1916 primary was a close one because he faced very strong opposition from Andrew Randell, the son of Choice Randell, who had been only recently the district's congressman. Andrew was on good terms with Woodrow Wilson, who was very popular in Texas. In addition, some of Rayburn's votes, especially one against child labor leg-islation, had angered his labor constituency in Denison.[3] In 1922 Rayburn faced a strong challenge from a state senator, Ed Westbrook. Westbrook had run a much weaker race against Rayburn in 1920, but in 1922 he benefited from being better known in the district, the continued decline in farm prices that had begun after World War I, and a violent strike of the railway union in Denison, which resulted from a government wage reduction. Rayburn was opposed by the unions because of his support for returning the railroads to private hands af-ter they had been under government control owing to the war and because of the general unhappiness resulting from the wage reduction.[4]

In 1930 and 1932, Rayburn's victory was only by fifty-one per-cent of the vote, his political weakness then being due to the

Depression and to constituency feeling that some sort of change was needed to improve economic conditions.[5] Both in 1930 and 1932, Rayburn's challenger was Choice Randell, whose son had run so strongly against him in 1916. Randell finished about forty-five hundred votes behind Rayburn in 1930. A minor candidate, however, B. L. Sheley, received over thirty-seven hundred votes, so Rayburn barely had a majority and was almost forced into a runoff. In 1932 Randell ran a much weaker race, finishing third in a field of three; but a Greenville printer named Jess Morris ran a strong second place to Rayburn in this, the first of his three races. With Roosevelt's 1932 victory, Rayburn became a leading congressional force on the Roosevelt team. His primary victories showed him much stronger in the district in 1934, 1936, 1938, 1940, and 1942.

In 1944, however, Rayburn faced a strong challenge from state senator G. C. Morris, who was one of the state's most respected legislators. Morris attempted to capitalize on wartime dissatisfaction. He was clearly Rayburn's most serious political threat from the time Rayburn assumed the majority leadership in 1936 until his death in 1961. An all-out effort by Rayburn forces in 1948 destroyed Morris as a challenger and virtually wiped out the opposition's hopes of ever eliminating Rayburn. He was only faced with two more primary challenges after the 1948 campaign, and in both he overwhelmed the opposition.

The five Rayburn primary challenges examined in this chapter are his last four, including the especially significant 1944 and 1948 campaigns, and one of his earliest campaigns, in 1916. These five show how Rayburn as a congressional leader dealt with his opposition. In addition, a comparison of the later four with the 1916 race reveals the differences between the beginning politician and the established party and congressional leader.

Before the election-by-election examination of the five campaigns, it is useful to note two points about them (see App. B, Table 5). One is the importance of friends-and-neighbors voting in Fourth District Congressional races.[6] Rayburn's greatest strength was in his home county of Fannin. Andrew Randell's strongest county was Grayson, his home county. G. C. Morris's strong county was Hunt, his home county, and Reagan Brown's was Kaufman, his home county. McRea, whose home county was Fannin, was weak there because it was also Rayburn's home county. Rayburn's support tended to be strong in adjoining Collin and Grayson counties, weaker in adjoining Hunt and the other more distant counties. Inasmuch as seventy-four percent of the votes cast in 1916, and over sixty percent of the votes cast in 1944, 1948, 1952, and 1954 were from Collin, Fannin, and Grayson counties, Rayburn's strength in those counties was especially important to his political success.

The second noteworthy point is that the only candidates who ran well against Rayburn in those five elections were those who could build upon some political base. Randell, for example, built upon his father's political base, and G. C. Morris was a state senator whose counties included Collin, Hunt, Rains, and Rockwall. Other candidates held no offices or had only narrowly based positions. In fact, with the exception of Jess Morris in the Depression year of 1932, Rayburn's strongest opponents in all his close reelection campaigns had significant political bases such as the old Choice Randell organization or a position as state senator.

The Early Days: 1916

Did Rayburn's political style, organization, or campaign techniques change over his nearly one-half century in politics? A definitive answer cannot be given because interview respondents could only provide limited information on the early years and because much on his early career is missing from Rayburn's files. It is only from 1932 and especially from 1940 that considerable quantities of private papers are available. One exception, however, is 1916. For inexplicable reasons, there are extensive correspondence files for that year. In 1916 Rayburn had served only two terms, and the files allow much insight into his style during that year.

The young Rayburn was faced with two primary opponents in 1916: Dr. T. W. Wiley and Andrew Randell. Of these, Andrew Randell was a serious opponent and very strong. He was the son of Choice Boswell Randell, a lawyer in Sherman and congressman from the district for twelve years immediately before Rayburn. He had attained the second-ranking Democratic position on the Ways and Means Committee, even then one of the most important committees in the House. When Joseph Weldon Bailey, Rayburn's political mentor, resigned from his U.S. Senate seat in January 1913, Choice Randell ran for that office instead of for reelection, leaving the Fourth District seat without an incumbent when Rayburn won it in a narrow victory in his first race. Randell, however, was unsuccessful in his bid for the Senate; he was defeated by Morris Sheppard.

Randell, left without an office, returned to his legal practice in Sherman. A six-term ex-congressman who had held a major position in the House and who had not been defeated by the incumbent is a serious threat to any congressional incumbent. Rayburn wrote, "I think it had just as well come now as any time, for the reason that I have known ever since I was elected to Congress that I was going to have to fight the Randells sooner or later."[7] Apparently, Choice and his son Andrew agreed that Andrew should make the race. Andrew was closer to Rayburn's age and was a lawyer. He had been educated at Princeton, where he had studied under Woodrow Wilson. Wilson, now president, was extremely popular in northeast Texas, and the contest quickly boiled down to the issue of whether Rayburn or Randell was more pro-Wilson.[8]

Rayburn claimed that Wilson wanted him retained in Congress and cited a letter from Wilson praising his legislative work. Randell, on the other hand, emphasized his Princeton ties to Wilson and was able to obtain a letter from Wilson stating:

> I learn that certain things I have from time to time said in praise of the work of Mr. Rayburn in the House have been interpreted to mean that I was opposed to your nomination. It is hardly necessary to assure you that this was an unjustifiable construction. I do not feel at liberty to express a preference in any congressional fight and would certainly take no such position when a friend like yourself was involved.[9]

Rayburn's strategy for the campaign was one that he continued to use in every campaign afterward. It was, in fact, a strategy that he had claimed to use even in his first reelection bid in 1914. He wrote a friend that he planned to let the opposition campaign against him while he was in Washington. Then about one month before the primary he would make a whirlwind campaign in the district. Rayburn considered that it would be politically advantageous for him to remain in Washington, above the fray, attending to the public business. His friends could then point to the mean-spirited nature of the opposition, who were sniping at the hard-working Washington official, who was away and could not defend himself. The important work while Rayburn was in Washington would be done by his friends in the district.[10]

The fact that Rayburn was from Fannin County, had family there, and had served in the state legislature gave him a strong personal political base. Frank Rayburn, Sam's brother and a general practitioner in Fannin County, apparently worked especially hard in Sam's behalf.[11] In addition, it appears likely that Rayburn also built upon former Senator Bailey's political base.

Rayburn had been a Bailey man at a time when Texas was split between pro- and anti-Bailey Democrats. Bailey combined an amazing collection of political beliefs. He was at one time a prohibitionist, but later he strongly opposed statewide prohibition. He adamantly opposed the imperialism of the U.S. government at the turn of the century, and it was said that he introduced William Jennings Bryan to the free-silver issue. It was Bailey's personality and not his policies, however, that made him one of the most loved and one of the most hated men in Texas. He had a massive ego, and while he was loyal to his friends, he was brutally cruel to his opponents. His ego and his vicious nature evoked extreme hostility in his opponents. He persisted in adding to the criticism by representing firms while serving in the Senate and obtaining large legal fees from them. His enemies considered those fees, loans, and business deals unethical and thought some of his financial arrangements were bribes. Ultimately, criticism of Bailey's finances helped to bring about his resignation from the Senate.[12]

In 1916, however, Joe Bailey would still have had many friends in Rayburn's district, and they probably knew that Rayburn was pro-Bailey. It was a Bailey speech that inspired Rayburn to go into politics, and he obtained the Texas House Speakership with Bailey's help.[13] In the 1890s Bailey had represented the Fifth District in the U.S. House, a district that had included Collin, Fannin, and Grayson counties. He had done well enough as its representative to serve on both the Ways and Means and the Rules committees. He had also been Democratic leader in the

House. The Bailey supporters in the district would also have been pro-Rayburn because Choice Randell was well known as an anti-Bailey politician.[14]

Rayburn also had support from Silas Hare, Jr., whose father had served in Congress from 1887 to 1891, when he had been defeated for renomination by Joe Bailey. The senior Hare had been overwhelmed by Bailey's oratory. It was said that Bailey, for the only time in his life, cultivated an opponent's friendship; Bailey and Hare became friends.[15]

Also in Rayburn's favor was his practice of spending all of his time in the district when Congress was adjourned. He met people, made friends, and put together his organization. In those early years, he only made one trip outside the country, to Panama. All the rest of his time he spent in the district. In those days the time between sessions was quite lengthy. With no time-consuming business such as a legal practice, he could devote all the time that he wished to his political efforts.[16]

Numerous letters in the 1916 files illustrate how hard Rayburn worked to cultivate the friendship of key persons in the district. In these letters Rayburn asked for support and for information that might benefit his reelection. It is clear that by 1916 Rayburn already relied on personal contacts to campaign in his absence and to supply him with information about his strengths and weaknesses in communities in the district. The beginnings of his intelligence network can be seen: "I want you to write me frequently what your impressions are. Do not just write to make me feel good, but tell me what you think of the situation and write me often and keep ginger in our friends all the time."[17] The result was that in 1916 and throughout the remainder of his career, he received regular reports from his supporters on sentiment in every community in the district.

Rayburn wrote that he had written friends of his in almost every voting box in the district, sometimes just two or three and sometimes many. He asked these friends to look after his interests while he was in Washington. Many responded that they would help and also provided advice. If their letters were flattering or optimistic, Rayburn would write them that overconfidence defeats candidates and that they should not assume victory. As he assessed the situation, Andrew Randell's strength would come from his father's old political organization, but

Rayburn was "two campaigns ahead of Randell."[18] That is, the senior Randell had not run a district-level campaign since 1910, whereas Rayburn had run in 1912 and 1914. Randell's organization, compared with incumbent Rayburn's, was thus likely to be rusty. Rayburn predicted that his weakest county would be Grayson, Randell's home county. He expected to be very strong in Fannin County, his own home county. Collin County, Rayburn thought, was in his corner, and Rains would go for him two to one. Rayburn thought he would carry Hunt County by more than twenty-eight hundred votes.[19]

As the campaign progressed, both Randell and Rayburn stressed their support of Wilson. Rayburn pointed out his effectiveness in Congress. He had successfully sponsored a bill that would make railroads responsible for the full value of goods damaged in transit. Such a bill would be of considerable benefit to farmers, who in those days relied heavily on the railroads for shipment of their crops and livestock. He also pointed to his efforts to secure the passage of the Rayburn stock and bond bill, which would regulate the issuance of stocks and bonds by railway corporations. The bill was important, argued Rayburn, because it would require railroads to have lower capitalization than their present inflated sum. The lower capitalization would result in lower freight rates, a benefit to both farmers and merchants.[20]

Rayburn ran into trouble in Denison because of his vote against the federal child labor bill. He suggested to his supporters that, though labor would be hostile to him because of that vote, it was a vote that could be explained to their satisfaction. He suggested that, if his supporters ran into problems on that issue, they should say he voted against it because it was a question the states should deal with rather than the national government. They should also point out, Rayburn suggested, that Texas already had a child labor law that was better than the federal one. Furthermore, that state child labor law had been strengthened with Rayburn's support when he was a member of the Texas legislature. He also suggested they assure laboring people that he was a friend of labor and was on the committee that was about to report favorably on an eight-hour day for telegraphers.[21] To clinch his argument, he demanded, "I wonder if these same people wanted me to vote for a National prohibition or National woman suffrage, as they are primarily on all fours."[22]

The Randells attempted to portray young Sam as a "wet," whereas Andrew Randell was a prohibitionist. They argued that "wets" had elected Rayburn Speaker of the Texas House, which proved he was antiprohibition.[23] In fact, many antiprohibitionists probably voted for Rayburn because he favored a local option rather than the statewide prohibition supported by an opposing candidate for the Speakership.[24] Moreover, Senator Bailey was probably able to swing some of the antiprohibitionist votes to Rayburn, for he had support among both prohibitionists and antiprohibitionists.[25] Prohibitionists were very strong in northeast Texas, so such a charge could have been damaging, but Rayburn was so well known as a prohibitionist that it is doubtful the charge had much impact. He was a featured speaker at prohibitionist rallies, and he also wrote constituents that he favored prohibition and had consistently done so since 1906, when he first was old enough to vote.[26] Another reason the charge was apparently ineffective might have been that Choice Randell was himself believed to be antiprohibition.[27]

Later in his political career Rayburn would abandon the prohibitionist cause, although prohibition remains a serious issue within the Fourth District to the present time. One reason for abandoning prohibition may have been that he began to drink once he went to Congress. Rayburn regularly drank after he began to be invited to John Nance Garner's Board of Education meetings held after the day's congressional session. When Rayburn became Speaker, he followed Garner's practice of mixing alcohol and politics during regular evening sessions. Rayburn occasionally drank heavily, although in the district he never drank in public or with people other than close friends.

One of the most interesting aspects of the 1916 campaign is how Rayburn was presented to the voters by his friends and himself. They projected the image that was to persist with little modification through more than four decades of congressional service: the good farm boy who worked hard and was doing well. Rayburn was described as "working all the time" and as having the "ability to represent his district in an intelligent manner and labor[ing] faithfully to perform all duties" and as "our personal friend."[28] The image was of a man of the people, "born on a tenant farm in Fannin County" [sic—born in Tennessee, not a tenant], a "plow boy at sixteen," who worked his way through Mayo College and now held an "important and influential position in Congress." Still more:

> His father and mother were without a home. With the first salary he received as Congressman, after paying his own obligations, he bought them a little farm and established them on it, and made provision for them to pass their last days in peace and without cares. And last summer and the summer before, while Congress was not in session, instead of being away at some fashionable resort, Sam with overalls and jumper was out there at home, helping harvest the hay and gather the corn for the old people before he went back to Washington to the discharge of his duties.[29]

It was claimed that Sam had worked in a cotton field until he was more than sixteen, so he knew what it was to work fourteen to sixteen hours a day in the hot sun. Andrew Randell, on the other hand, was a city boy. He had lived in Sherman, Texas; Washington, D.C.; and Princeton, New Jersey. His father had supported and educated him without Andrew having to work. Andrew, it was claimed, "had silken palms that had never been soiled."[30]

Rayburn responded to the continuing criticism of his vote on child labor. He told voters that the legislation banned interstate shipment of cotton produced by the labor of children under fifteen. Surely, persuaded Rayburn, farm families needed the help of their children in the cotton fields. For his part, claimed Rayburn, he knew what daylight-to-dark work was, and it had not hurt him. He went on to mock the American Federation of Labor's plan to reduce the length of the federal workday: "I worked fourteen to sixteen hours a day in the hot sun on a Fannin County farm, and I voted to make these white-handed, bay windowed gentry work at least eight hours a day under an electric fan, and sitting on easy cushioned seats."[31] Rayburn's image of a hard-working farmer in Washington stood in contrast to Randell's as an educated city slicker, and the pair of images destroyed Randell's chances of upsetting Rayburn. Randell garnered only 9,572 votes to Rayburn's 13,116.

The 1944 Campaign

In 1944 Sam Rayburn was faced with one of the most serious political challenges of his career and his first major electoral threat since achieving the Speakership. He faced two opponents: George Balch, a minor candidate, who was a conservative anti–New Deal minister from Hunt County, and Grover Cleveland Morris, a serious contender, who was a state senator from Greenville. Morris had been a state representative and had had a brilliant career in the Texas legislature, where he had established a statewide reputation as an opponent of Gov. "Pappy" O'Daniel's transactions tax. He was the author of a successful substitute tax measure that financed old age pensions from a tax on natural resources.[32] He was a respected and effective legislator even though he was only in his thirties. Morris was clearly one of the up-and-coming political figures in his senatorial district, which significantly overlapped with Rayburn's district.

The war had occupied much of Rayburn's time and made it difficult to return to the district; the emergency made it necessary for the Speaker to stay near Washington.[33] As one of his Grayson County leaders pointed out in a letter to Rayburn, the war had created a conflict between his leadership role and his district role, for by being Speaker he was unable to get to the district and mend political fences.[34]

Nor were things going well for Rayburn in Texas politics. He was not on good terms with the former governor and now senator "Pappy" O'Daniel, a one-time flour salesman who stunned the nation by skyrocketing into major offices with showmanship, a hillbilly band, and superb radio oratory. Governor O'Daniel had defeated New Deal– and Rayburn-backed Cong. Lyndon Johnson in a special Senate election after the death of Sen. Morris Sheppard. O'Daniel moved increasingly to the right and became an outspoken critic of Franklin Roosevelt, the New Deal, and Washington politicians in general.[35]

Concurrent with O'Daniel's rightward drift was the growth of an anti–New Deal faction in the Democratic party in Texas. Anti-Roosevelt sentiment had never been far below the surface. It had risen earlier in 1940 when John Nance Garner made his ill-fated try for the presidency and when party infighting occurred over Roosevelt's try for a third term. By 1944 the antis were stronger and well funded, some of the heaviest contributors being wealthy oil men. Independent oil men who were leaders in the movement included Hugh Roy Cullen, Arch Rowan, E. B. Germany, and Al Buchanan. Other leaders were Hiram King, who was the lobbyist for Sinclair Oil; Clint Small, the lobbyist for Humble Oil; E. E. Townes, the former chief counsel of Humble Oil; R. A. Weinert, attorney for Socony-Vacuum; Crude Oil Company President George Heyes; and possibly Joseph Pew, the president of Sun Oil and the Republican boss of Pennsylvania. George Butler, the attorney for Jesse Jones, who was a wealthy Texan and Roosevelt appointee, was also a contributor. Other leaders included theater lobbyist D. F. Strickland; the *Houston Post* owner Oveta Culp Hobby; and Lone Star Gas attorney Neth Leachman.[36]

The split in the Texas party between the pro- and anti-Roosevelt factions ultimately resulted in a split delegation to the 1944 convention. The anti-Roosevelt faction later formed the third-party movement known as the Texas Regulars.[37] The Regulars' platform called for, among other things, a return of states' rights destroyed by a communist-controlled New Deal, restoration of the supremacy of the white race, government of laws rather than bureaucracy, a return of the Bill of Rights instead of rule by regimentation, and a return to Democratic party integrity destroyed by communists.[38]

Rayburn was weakened by the loss of several of his best young leaders to the war. The 1944 campaign effort was of necessity led by older men, especially seventy-three-year-old Henry Cunningham, a close Rayburn friend and political lieutenant from Sam's earliest days in politics. The war had also caused dissatisfaction with national leaders. In fact, the anti-Roosevelt faction in Texas had hoped to capitalize on feelings brought about by the war as well as on hostility to the rise of organized labor; anger with the Agricultural Adjustment Act for causing over-acreage cotton to be plowed under; hostility to Vice President Henry Wallace; anger over *Smith* v. *Allwright,* which banned the white primary; dissatisfaction with the third term; and concern over the use of the army to settle the Montgomery War dispute.[39] Farmers had been badly hurt by a virtually nonexistent labor supply. The problem was slightly alleviated in Kaufman

County, where Rayburn was successful in locating a German prisoner of war camp. The POWs worked on neighboring farms in the county. There was no way, however, that sufficient labor could be supplied to all the farmers whose laborers and sons were in the military or working in defense plants. Farmers were also upset by a scarcity of materials and an increase in government regulation, both brought on by the war effort. At the same time, Rayburn was more and more frequently identified as a national leader and was often being discussed as a vice-presidential contender.

The situation was not a comfortable one for Sam Rayburn as he faced the 1944 Democratic primary campaign. Opponent G. C. Morris was a former state representative and a two-term state senator with two years remaining in his second term. George Balch was not a real threat, but his speeches proved irritating. Balch claimed that Rayburn was "too big for his breeches," let people from Dallas wine and dine him, and went to parties where he drank. On one occasion, said Balch, Rayburn had a drinking party at his apartment in Washington, where he told the guests: "Listen, fellows, did you know that I represent the driest district in Texas, and here I am drunk as a fiddler's wench,—I wonder what those old boys back home would think if they could see me?" Not only was Rayburn a drinking man, Balch said, but he was "rich and opulent, fat, corpulent, proud and arrogant." If that was not enough, the Speaker was also opposed to Pappy O'Daniel.[40]

By early January 1944 Rayburn began to get his organization into gear. The toughest county in the campaign was expected to be Hunt, Morris's home county. Rayburn was fortunate that G. C. Harris volunteered to undertake the management of the Hunt County campaign.[41] Over the next few months, Harris was to find life difficult; there were times when it seemed to him that, save a handful of citizens, the entire county was composed of Morris supporters.[42] Harris was an excellent Hunt County leader, however. He was reputed to be one of the best courtroom lawyers in the area, and he managed to combine that reputation with a friendly and outgoing personality. Rayburn knew that Harris had "the respect and confidence of literally thousands of people," and both Rayburn and one of his leaders, Greenville publisher Fred Horton, strongly favored Harris for the job.[43] Harris so enthusiastically plunged into his work in behalf of Rayburn that he went to Austin for three weeks to research Morris's legislative record.[44]

Morris was well funded.[45] He was making inroads. He visited Collin County and was campaigning among rural school teachers. Rural teachers' opinions were respected, and Morris knew they were often leaders in their communities. The times were ripe for Morris's anti–New Deal appeal, for the war had increased living costs with no corresponding increase in the teachers' salaries.[46] It was not long before the Teachers for G. C. Morris for Congress Club was formed in Hunt and Rains counties. A leaflet distributed by the club opposed "the further entrenchment of any system of planned economy." It supported freedom of speech and religion, saying that our government was a "Christian Democracy." Most important, the leaflet criticized the burden that the government had placed on farmers. It emphasized the high cost of farm labor, the scarcity of materials and equipment, and bureaucratic governmental reporting requirements. After noting that the United States was going to win the war no matter who was in Congress, the leaflet endorsed Morris and praised his qualifications for the job.[47]

Morris supporters also spread the story that Rayburn did not want to serve in Congress but was instead interested in the vice presidency. Such a story was risky because it showed Rayburn was an important figure, but its purpose seems to have been to cause voters to vote against him inasmuch as he would soon be vice president anyway.[48] It was also said that he had been in Congress too long and that it was time for a change. Seniority, it was argued, was not really that necessary for a good legislator. Rayburn, the Morris faction argued, was not even a good legislator. Morris argued that Rayburn had lost touch with the district. During several radio speeches, Morris asked his audience, "How many times has Mr. Rayburn whittled with you across the fence?" Morris also made reference to Rayburn's "haughty voice and personal appearance."[49] The lack of time the Speaker had been in the district during the war was clearly being turned against him.

Though Rayburn may have brought temporary prosperity to Greenville with the opening of Majors Field, a military air base, Morris's supporters claimed it would be closed immediately af-

ter the war.[50] They also accused Rayburn of making a deal with
TP&L, the utility that had opposed him in previous years because of his sponsorship of rural electrification and the Utility
Holding Company Act.[51] Rayburn, they claimed, had turned
over the power to TP&L that was generated by Denison Dam
in exchange for the company's support.[52]

The racial issue was not as strongly addressed as it would be
in 1948, but Rayburn was soundly criticized by the *Greenville
Morning Herald* for failing to vote when an appropriation for
the Fair Employment Practices Commission (FEPC) was considered by the House. The editorial, clearly aimed at racial prej-
udices, noted that the FEPC is "SIXTY PER CENT Negro controlled"; further, "You probably do not know that in many cases
through this Nation Negro executives are working white girls as
their secretaries; or that in other cases white executives get less
money than Negroes with the same ratings."[53] As far as the paper was concerned, Rayburn's excuse that he opposed the appropriation but did not vote was a lame one. He could have
voted, asserted the editorial.[54]

Race was a part of the campaign, but Morris also attempted
to capitalize on the dissatisfaction brought upon by the wartime restrictions, the growing opposition to the New Deal, and
opposition to a fourth term for Roosevelt. Rayburn was a symbol of the New Deal, especially because of his Speakership, and
to strike him down would be to strike down a symbol of
twelve years of Democratically caused social change. Rayburn
was, claimed Morris, a yes man for Roosevelt, a man who
thought like a northerner, and one who appealed to Negroes
and the CIO.[55]

Rayburn used a variety of approaches to handle the Morris
challenge. One was to work to build and repair old ties with
constituents, an aspect of Rayburn's campaign effort that apparently never stopped. An example of this approach can be found
in correspondence between Rayburn and W. A. Hawkins, "the
Careful Druggist" in tiny Savoy, and a Rayburn supporter.
Hawkins reported matters of political and social consequence in
Savoy as part of the Rayburn network. During this campaign he
reported that Lewis Brown was sick; that Miss Lou Arterberry,
a respected lady in the little community, was aging and could no
longer leave her home; that John Large was an old timer who

would appreciate hearing from Rayburn; and that Rayburn should touch bases with Wiley Hodges because he probably controlled eight votes. Mr. Sam promptly wrote short, friendly notes to all these people, wishing them his best in 1944.[56]

Rayburn's interest in getting every possible vote is legendary in the district and evident in a letter he wrote to his Fannin County manager, Judge H. A. Cunningham:

> Out at Ivanhoe [a small community in Fannin County] there are about forty Eubanks. One year they voted for me but as usual about 95% voted against me. As I remember it, I lost about 44 votes at Ivanhoe in 1942. I was informed about this by a friend of mine there who helped poll the election who said that a great majority of these came from that family. Albert Huff tells me that Sherman Eubanks is the "bell ringer" of the crowd. I think it is a matter that will bear looking into because they go together.[57]

To counter the unhappy feeling about the war, Rayburn told the *Bonham Daily Favorite* that the chief executive and all the people wished the war would come to an early end. He was straightforward in pointing out, however, that the war could last much longer. In addition, he appealed to the patriotism of his constituents and warned that peace would also bring problems. He stressed, "I want to see the United States shoulder its responsibility in the post-war world and do as good a job as our boys on the front lines are doing."[58]

Rayburn and his leaders pointed out to teachers that their unhappiness rested not with him but with G. C. Morris. It was Morris who was a member of the Texas legislature, and the state bore the ultimate responsibility for education in Texas.[59] Morris's age was also used against him. Organization members kept asking why a man his age was not in the army. As indicated by this report from Carl Nall, a leader in Grayson County, the question was an extremely damaging one for Morris. Nall reported that one of the organization leaders, Jim Buster, had been visiting with people in the community and campaigning in Rayburn's behalf, and:

> Old Judge Steed had a chat with him a day or two ago and wanted to discuss your race. He asked him, "Is it a fact that you are the only Grayson County lawyer that ever spoke out for Mr.

Rayburn?" Jim said, "Judge, you can answer that. Did you ever know of anyone?" He said, "No." He also said that Morris might make a better showing than some others in the past. Jim asked the old man how his boys were, knowing they were in the army. He has four in the army. Jim said, "Judge you are not interested in Morris are you?" "Well," he said, "I am sorter neutral." Jim said, "I wonder why Morris isn't in the army. Every boy you have are four to 18 years older than he." The tears begun to drop from his cheek. The old man is 78 years old and looks mighty bad.[60]

In Rayburn's behalf it was argued, "We need some gray hair and some gray matter in Washington to represent us"[61] (Rayburn, of course, had little hair, gray or otherwise).

The reports that Rayburn was being considered for the vice presidency were used to good effect by Rayburn and his supporters. They argued that the best way Fourth District voters could help him and the Democratic party would be to give Mr. Sam the biggest majority ever. Then he would be in a very strong position to receive the vice-presidential nomination.[62] Sometimes opponents of Rayburn's were even whipped into supporting him with the vice-presidential issue. For example, District Judge Jake Loy was a prominent judge in Grayson County. He had congressional ambitions and was bitter because he believed Rayburn's supporters had opposed him in a local election. Lee Simmons reported that "he has told me several times that while he would like to succeed Rayburn in Congress that he was glad to support him and do what he could for him in order that he might become Vice President." Simmons told Loy that support for Rayburn would put Loy in a better position for Congress later than would opposition to the Speaker.[63]

Rayburn may well have desired the 1944 vice-presidential nomination. John McCormack had often visited Roosevelt with Rayburn and had noted ominous changes in Roosevelt's physical appearance.[64] Rayburn had in confidence told one of his Grayson County leaders that he did not think Roosevelt would live long.[65] It was likely that the person chosen to be vice president in 1944 would finish the term as president. Rayburn was faced with a crucial decision: He could go to the Democractic National Convention and work for the vice-presidential nomination, but if he did he might lose the congressional nomination to G. C. Morris. The Democratic primary election was July 22, and the convention was July 19. The timing of the two events could not have been worse for Rayburn. He chose to stay in the district and campaign against Morris, and he continued to do so even after McCormack called to persuade him to go to the convention on the grounds that his presence could mean a chance for the vice presidency.[66]

One consideration Rayburn must have had in mind was that the Texas delegation to the convention was split between both pro- and anti-Roosevelt factions, a very embarrassing division for any Texan trying for the vice presidency. Rayburn later told one of his Collin County leaders that he had spoken with Roosevelt about the vice presidency but had concluded that it would be impossible to get the nomination because the Texas Democratic party split could not be healed by the prospect of it.[67] There had been a boomlet for Rayburn for vice president in 1940.[68] In 1944 word leaked from the White House that Roosevelt favored Rayburn for the vice presidency; word also leaked that the president favored several others, however.[69] Rayburn had been the choice of party leaders in early 1944. He had lunched with Edward Flynn, the political boss of the Bronx and former national Democratic chairman, and with Edwin Pauley, a well-known oil man and former party treasurer. Together the three agreed to work against the renomination of Vice President Henry Wallace. Rayburn indicated his willingness to be considered as a candidate, and Pauley set up speaking engagements for him to enhance his visibility. Later in 1944, however, Flynn met with Roosevelt and by then the field was narrowed to Truman. Flynn still thought Rayburn a good choice for the office but thought him at a disadvantage because he was a southerner and because of the split in the Texas delegation.[70]

Little believes that Rayburn knew he had no chance for the vice presidency. He had planned to go to the convention as late as July 15 but used the campaign against Morris as an excuse not to attend. By then Rayburn may have known that Roosevelt had not been mentioning his name to party leaders.[71] Green has suggested that Roosevelt thought Rayburn was needed in the Congress and that party leaders had concluded Rayburn was too independent minded.[72] By staying in Texas, Rayburn avoided the embarrassment of going to a convention in search of a nomination that he could not have.[73]

The talk of Rayburn as vice president, however, was causing others to consider their candidacy for the congressional seat. Even Mr. Sam's state representative was tempted to file for the office. He wrote Rayburn that a few had urged him to get into the race, but he had told them, "I don't think I could beat Sam."[74] The state representative was having second thoughts given the possibility that Rayburn might be nominated for vice president only three days before the primary, timing he thought would greatly benefit Rayburn's opponents. They could say that Rayburn should not be elected because he was going to be vice president, and the state representative wanted the opportunity to make the same assertion if it were in fact true. He asked Rayburn for some indication of what was going to happen.[75] Rayburn responded that he doubted that he would be nominated, but if he were, he expected that the district would want to provide an overwhelming majority. His concern was that a popular opponent from Fannin County would weaken his majority in one of his strongest counties.[76] He was sufficiently alarmed by this potential threat that he also wrote Judge Cunningham and asked his assistance in "get[ting] some sense in his [the state representative's] head."[77] Cunningham, ever faithful to Rayburn, did as asked and made it clear to the state representative that, not only would a race against Rayburn be unsuccessful, but it would greatly damage any future political aspirations that state official might have. Cunningham reported that the representative got the message.[78]

Cunningham was not merely making an idle threat. The Rayburn organization contained dedicated souls who did not take kindly to public officials who made their opposition to Rayburn public. Gus Hodges, for example, was a Rayburn-selected postmaster in Greenville. Hodges and other Rayburn supporters in Hunt County became alarmed that Hunt County's very popular county judge was going to campaign for Morris. Hodges felt it would be wise to keep the judge occupied with his own reelection because a coalition with Morris would be very strong in the county. An opponent would force the judge to campaign on his own behalf. The Rayburn supporters, therefore, promptly encouraged the Greenville chief of police to run. He was a World War I veteran and had been wounded in the war. Hodges even provided fifty dollars to aid with his expenses. Whether the judge would have campaigned for Morris if he had no opponent is unknown. What is known is that the judge ran a hard campaign for himself and did not campaign for Morris.[79]

In another case a judge in Grayson County was opposed by some pro-Rayburn voters including Rayburn leader Carl Nall. The opposition developed because Nall had learned of the judge's plans to run against Rayburn and because of statements made to six people to the effect that the judge and his wife would not support Rayburn. The judge realized he had made a mistake and apologized after his defeat for an office. He also pledged support for Rayburn and contemplated his own political future as excluding Congress.[80]

Rayburn's supporters kept an eye on the opposition as well as on local politicians and supporters who might go astray. When Morris gave a radio speech, Rayburn's friends were listening, to transcribe it for Rayburn and report to him on its effectiveness.[81] Some would attend Morris rallies, count those in attendance, and report the names of those who introduced Morris or who were most vocal in his favor. It was a formidable intelligence network.[82]

Rayburn's supporters also had his impressive record upon which to base his campaign. The Majors Field training base for World War II was located in Hunt County through Mr. Sam's influence. A leaflet was circulated to point out that this base had brought great prosperity to Greenville, prosperity that benefited almost everyone in the district.[83] The location through Rayburn's efforts of a German prisoner of war camp in Kaufman County was said to have saved two thousand acres of cotton that would otherwise have been lost because of the labor shortage. When there was an effort to move 100 to 150 POWs out of the camp, Rayburn prevented the transfer. Farmers were so pleased with the camp that efforts were being made to enlarge it.[84] Rayburn also sent letters to REA members informing them that he was the author of the Rural Electrification Act and that he had gotten the bill passed because he thought it would be a work saver for the farmer and his family. He noted as well that he had tried to be cooperative and helpful in dealing with farmers' problems through the years.[85] Rayburn also sent out letters that emphasized his role in the war effort:

> Ever since Hitler and his gang broke loose in 1939 Congress had been in almost continuous session. I have been doing my best in Washington as your Congressman and as Speaker of the House to make our Army and Navy the best trained, the best equipped and the best cared for and the most effective military force in history. Under the leadership of our Commander-in-Chief, with the cooperation of our military and naval leaders and with the cooperation of you and millions of other patriotic Americans that job has been done. I am proud to have been your representative on the team that brought about this wonderful achievement.[86]

His friends spoke on the radio in his behalf, as did he after he returned to Texas for a whirlwind tour of the district before the primary. Sherman lawyer Jim Buster spoke over the radio emphasizing legislation in which Rayburn played a major role, including that which promoted the interests of World War I veterans; the Securities Exchange Commission Act; the Utility Holding Company Act; the REA, which had brought electricity to 9,032 farms in the district; and farm price support laws. He also stressed the recognition and honor to the Fourth District in having the Speaker as its congressman.[87]

Another Rayburn supporter, Greenville lawyer Benton Morgan, made a radio speech in which he equated a vote for Rayburn with a vote for patriotism and for the soldiers overseas. He challenged Morris's patriotism saying:

> If he is going to walk shoulder to shoulder, side by side and eye to eye with these young men after the war is over, I want to know and the mothers, fathers, wives, brothers and sisters of a million and a half young men who are as old or older than Mr. Morris, who are in the armed forces fighting for victory around the world, want to know why he is not fighting side by side and shoulder to shoulder and eye to eye with these young men today.[88]

The speech was so effective that one strong Morris supporter, who had worked with Morris's leaders and supplied a 250-dollar campaign contribution, went to those leaders and said that the Morgan speech had "settled Morris for all time." He then went to Rayburn leader Gus Hodges to say that this had been his first and last venture into politics.[89]

G. C. Harris also gave a radio speech that proved the effectiveness of the medium. He criticized Morris over the Sherman radio. There was a large picnic in the Greenville park, and those in attendance heard the speech over a loudspeaker and broke out in applause. When Harris returned to Greenville, people came out of stores to shake his hand and praise him for the speech.[90] Another of Harris's speeches turned Morris's voting record in the state legislature against him. He pointed out that Morris had coauthored a bill to abolish the Texas Department of Agriculture and the office of agriculture commissioner and had voted against appropriations for inspections incident to the eradication of the Mexican fruit fly, citrus canker, and pink bollworm, whereas Rayburn had been a friend of farmers. Harris also noted that Morris,

> as recently as 1941, as a member of the Texas House of Representatives, went on record in referring to Sam Rayburn as a great American statesman, experienced in the affairs of government in so many ways surpassed by none, as one who had served well and efficiently, and as one who had served his state and nation unselfishly, constructively and patriotically.

Harris also pointed to the leadership Rayburn had shown in the war and criticized a comment Morris had made about Guam sounding "like a mess." Harris claimed that Morris showed "disrespect to the boys who fought, died and were captured on that island."[91]

Rayburn returned from Washington with only a few weeks to campaign and set about it vigorously. On July 7 he spoke in Greenville, introduced by two local ministers who had both lost sons in the war. The high school band played patriotic songs, then Rayburn read a message from General Marshall praising the valor of Texas units in the war. His speech that followed urged support for the war and stressed his support for segregation.[92] The praise for segregation may well have been designed to counter a whisper campaign criticizing Rayburn's failure to block the FEPC appropriations.[93] For the next day, July 8,

Rayburn's campaign schedule lists appearances in Farmersville, Blue Ridge, Westminster, Anna, Melissa, Weston, Celina, Prosper, and Frisco, all small communities in Collin County.[94] On July 12 he visited Josephine, Nevada, Lavon, Wylie, Murphy, Plano, Renner, Lebanon, Allen, Parker, Lucas, Culleoka, Princeton, and Farmersville, more small communities in Collin.[95]

One of the most disturbing charges of the campaign was the one that Rayburn had sold out to TP&L by providing them the power from the Denison Dam. It was causing Rayburn problems, and he released a reply to the press.[96] He explained that he had wanted power at the Denison Dam to be under the control of a federal agency but that materials needed for power transmission, such as copper and wood, were strategic materials in short supply. For the duration of the war and six months thereafter, therefore, the government had entered into a contract with TP&L to buy and distribute the power, for it was the only organization with the necessary distribution lines in North Texas. It was to pay 1,205,000 dollars each year for the power, and a price reduction of 400,000 dollars for consumers would be required, of which three-fourths would go for business and residential customers including REA. Rayburn argued that this was a fine trade, whereby the people in North Texas were saving more money in one year than he had drawn from the Treasury in his thirty-one years in Congress. He promised, however, that when the war ended, "authority will be set up, if I am here, that will distribute the power and operate the whole thing."[97]

Rayburn's point about distribution was valid, but there is no question that the power company and Rayburn were on friendly terms in later elections even though TP&L had been very opposed to Rayburn in earlier years. Perhaps it is simply that the management of the power company realized that they could not beat Rayburn and so called a truce. Perhaps more enlightened management felt Rayburn was too powerful to continue to challenge. Or it may be that the Denison Dam contract lessened the threat of public power and was an important step in the truce between Sam Rayburn and TP&L.

In 1946 Rayburn anticipated, but did not receive, major opposition from utilities again. He had angered them by keeping the Southwestern Power Authority budget from being trimmed from $23 million to $3,328,000. Rayburn had supported a successful compromise budget of $7,500,000, but the utility industry had opposed the compromise because that was enough to build public power lines in Texas, Oklahoma, and Arkansas so that power from government dams could be carried to REA cooperatives and municipal utilities.[98] During Rayburn's next campaign in 1948, his old political enemy the conservative and wealthy TP&L executive John W. Carpenter even offered a hand of friendship. He wrote Rayburn a letter expressing admiration for him. It said that Rayburn was considered a great citizen and that Carpenter wished to inform him "that while a public utility cannot be in politics, I personally have my own rights and liberties and am strong for you and I hope, trust, and pray that everything will come out well for you in your campaign for re-election." Carpenter also wrote, "If I, John W. Carpenter, can do anything for you in any way, do not hesitate to have the same brought to my attention because it is my desire to honor you and be helpful to you."[99] Although there were to be tensions between Rayburn and the utility industry over appropriations for REA and the Southwestern Power Authority, TP&L chairman Carpenter and TP&L president Bill Lynch developed a close enough relationship to Rayburn that they were among his invited guests at the dedication of the Rayburn Library.[100]

The friendliness with TP&L may be because the holding companies no longer were in control of it by the 1940s. Robert Bartley, Rayburn's nephew, was closely associated with his uncle in the 1930s and 1940s, working with Dr. W. W. Splawn, Rayburn's brilliant staff member, on the Interstate and Foreign Commerce Committee. Splawn and Bartley worked closely with Roosevelt's aides, Tommy Corcoran and Ben Cohen, on the Holding Company Act, the legislation that broke up the giant utility holding companies and one of the most controversial of New Deal laws. As chairman of the legislative committee, Rayburn sponsored the act and pushed it through the House. More than any other action, Bartley believes this one turned monied interests against Rayburn.

In the Fourth District, the Holding Company Act broke the control of New York's Electric Bond and Share. Before the breakup, John Carpenter represented Electric Bond and Share's interests, and it was during this period that enmity existed between Carpenter and Rayburn. Rayburn once told the powerful Carpenter, "The trouble is, you are just an office boy for those fellows [Electric Bond and Share]." Such remarks were not endearing. After the breakup Carpenter no longer had to represent Electric Bond, and he did become friendly with Rayburn.[101]

Rayburn also noted in the last months of his life that his troubles with the power companies were primarily in 1936 and that by 1940 the operating companies were pleased with the holding company legislation:

> After I had my big fight with the Power Companies in 1935, when I sponsored the Public Utility Holding Companies Act, they gave me a terrific fight in my district in 1936. John W. Carpenter told me four years after the law was enacted it was the best thing that had ever happened for the operating utility companies because they could control their companies at home and not have to get on the telephone or telegraph every night to ask Electric Bond and Share or other big holding companies what they could do.[102]

Rayburn and his friends thought defeat in 1944 was a distinct possibility. His old pal R. B. Ridgway even reminded him that about 1911, before Rayburn's decision to run for Congress, Rayburn and he had planned to open a law office in Ft. Worth. Ridgway offered to take Rayburn as a partner in his Austin law office, asserting, "We could do very well in an office here."[103] But the organization and Rayburn were successful. Rayburn won with 24,306 votes to Morris's 18,672. Balch received only 933. It was not the last of G. C. Morris.

The 1948 Campaign

In 1946 Rayburn had no opposition, but in 1948 he was again faced by two challengers. His rival G. C. Morris had chosen to wait for 1948 to challenge Rayburn again. In 1946 Morris was up for reelection to the state senate and chose to run for that office. David Brown, a Grayson County judge, the other opponent, was considered a less serious challenger, but he was still more of a threat than Balch had been in 1944. Balch and Morris

were both from Hunt County, and friends-and-neighbors voting thus meant the main base of support for both was in the
same county. Brown, however, was from Grayson County. That
left Rayburn with the possibility that Morris and Brown could
each carry his home county. The result might be a runoff
between Morris and Rayburn, for if Brown siphoned off votes
in usually dependable Grayson County, he might deny Rayburn
a majority.

In 1948 Rayburn had the misfortune of having an unpopular
man as president and the good fortune of having Harry Truman
as that man. Initially, Rayburn was privately convinced that
Truman would lose the election. People were even unhappy
with him in the Fourth District, the home of brass-collar Democrats. Worse, Thomas Dewey had distant relatives in Grayson
County, making the Republican candidate attractive even to
Rayburn's home folks. It was Harry Truman, however, who
changed Rayburn's mind about his prospects for the presidency.
Rayburn rode with the president on his whistlestop campaign
through Texas, a campaign that included an address and reception in Bonham. After observing Truman campaigning and observing the crowds, Rayburn changed his private assessment of
Truman from "loser" to "winner."[104]

The whistlestop tour of Texas was not, however, until March
of 1948. At the start of Rayburn's campaign, Truman looked
very weak. His stand on civil rights hurt him greatly throughout
the South, including the Fourth District.[105] Morris's strategy
was to tie Rayburn with Truman and his civil rights program.
Essentially, the argument would be that all those in the Democratic leadership including Rayburn must be removed from office because they were too New Dealish, pro–civil rights, and
soft on communism.

One oil millionaire from Ft. Worth, George Armstrong, was
especially adamant in his criticism of Sam Rayburn. He bought
numerous newspaper advertisements calling for Rayburn's defeat, did so for Lyndon Johnson as well, and argued that all New
Dealers should be defeated because they were planning defla-
tion and depression to promote communism. Despite the considerable sums spent on this media effort, he was not very successful, for his views were too extreme for most people. For
example, Armstrong thought Hitler was "a sober, deliberate,

determined man," that Franklin Roosevelt was a war criminal, and that Harry Truman and Dwight Eisenhower were probably communists.[106]

By far the most serious charge against Rayburn during the campaign was that he was pro–civil rights. He had been very quiet in opposing Truman's proposals, and he had even persuaded the Texas congressional delegation to refrain from joining in the southern condemnation of Truman. He began receiving early warnings from home that race might prove to be a damaging issue. His Hunt County leader, G. C. Harris, reported on a well-received Rotary Club speech in Greenville where the president's civil rights proposals were attacked by a speaker who claimed to be a "Southerner first and a Democrat next." Harris warned that the issue was a dangerous one, for people in the district were generally opposed to Truman's proposals.[107] Harris also wrote that Morris was sending up trial balloons and seeking encouragement to run. The Texas Regulars, Harris reminded Rayburn, dwelt at length upon racial matters in 1944, but with little effect then because of Roosevelt's popularity and the war in progress. Harris warned that, with Roosevelt dead and the war over, the racial issue "could reach great proportions."[108]

Rayburn was quick to recognize the significance of Harris's reports and agreed that the people were agitated over the civil rights program. He wrote Harris that little, if any, of the program would be passed by Congress, adding that he opposed the program except for repeal of the poll tax laws. Though he noted that he had voted against repeal of the tax, he had done so only because he believed the federal government should not interfere with what he regarded as a local matter. Were he in the state legislature, however, he would vote for a constitutional amendment to repeal the tax.[109] He also enclosed a copy of a letter he had written only a week before to a Greenville couple, the Norris Heads, who had inquired about his position on civil rights:

> I will say that I have voted in this Congress against Federal repeal of the poll tax law. I have voted several times against the so-called Federal Anti-lynching Law and will do so again. I have been opposed to the Fair Employment Practice Commission and

still am and shall vote against it and against any bill that has any tendency towards crippling our segregation laws or any other part of the program that has to do with, in what I consider, interference of our local rights.[110]

This letter was to play a central part in the campaign and was to be widely distributed throughout the district. It provided evidence that Rayburn was genuinely opposed to the Truman program and was not pushed into opposing it by Morris inasmuch as the letter was dated before Morris's entry into the campaign.

Nevertheless, Rayburn was in a difficult position. As Speaker it would be most embarrassing for him to attack a Democratic president openly, yet the people in the district were up in arms over the proposals. Harris was concerned about how he could protect Rayburn's interests in the district without damaging his position as Speaker. He wrote Rayburn that he had considered releasing a statement to the press that would flatly oppose Truman's program but had reconsidered out of concern that such a statement would be improper for a Speaker. Harris warned, "I have heard people, well along in years, life-long Democrats, express bitter opposition and disappointment over the matter."[111]

In early March it was clear that Morris was going to run and that the civil rights issue was going to be difficult, just as Harris had predicted. Lee Simmons, one of Rayburn's oldest and most trusted leaders, insisted that Rayburn would be defeated on civil rights if he did not speak out immediately against Truman's proposals, for people took Rayburn's silence on civil rights and his successful effort to prevent the Texas delegation from attacking Truman to mean that Rayburn was pro–civil rights. Resentment against the program was strong, and Simmons noted that Morris was saying, "Not only has he [Rayburn] failed to step out against this attempt to destroy the segregation laws of our state, but it is apparent that he favors the Civil Rights Program. I am opposed to any program which would tear down the segregation laws of the South." Simmons pointed out that many old friends and contributors were saying that they had "voted for Sam Rayburn for the last time." It had reached the point, he argued, where "it is strictly a question of whether you and Mr. Truman are both going down." Simmons added that this was his opinion before conferring with other leaders but that a conference with three others showed they were even more disturbed than he.[112]

Within days Rayburn released to local newspapers copies of his letter to Mr. and Mrs. Head. He wrote Simmons that the letter was the strongest statement he could make. He noted that the *Greenville Banner* had published the letter on the same day that Morris was to speak over local radio. Morris failed to appear for the speech, and Rayburn wrote, "I think that [the publication of the letter] upset him until he didn't desire to speak."[113] When Rayburn returned to the district for his usual last-minute campaign dash, he again stated his opposition to civil rights. In Commerce in Hunt County, for example, he spoke on the city square to a crowd of about six hundred, stating his opposition to the civil rights program and citing his record of voting against such proposals.[114] Morris was checkmated.

With the civil rights issue out of the way, Rayburn was far stronger in 1948 than in 1944. For one thing, his younger lieutenants were home from the war, men such as R. C. Slagle and Buster Cole who would and could work hard in his behalf.[115] For another, Morris did not have a war record, and it was unlikely that returned veterans would support such a young nonveteran. (Rayburn was not a veteran either, but here his age worked in his favor.) Rayburn and his organization decided this was the time to put a stop to strong campaign challenges. As his campaign coordinator said, "In 1948 we decided we would break their backs once and for all. . . . We organized from top to bottom."[116]

In May Rayburn wrote his assessment of the race and his strengths: Morris had been unable to generate the funding he did in 1944, but even then he had been beaten fifty-five percent to forty-five percent. Campaign donors do not bet often on losers. Rayburn's intelligence reports were good, and he had "not received any alarming reports from anybody in the District and in most places they say, even Grayson County, that I am in good or better shape than I was four years ago." He had just spoken to a visitor from McKinney, Ray Roberts, who thought "Collin . . . in better shape, by quite a good deal, than it was four years ago." Rayburn had gotten a huge veterans' hospital constructed in McKinney in 1942. Given the construction of the hospital, the organization in McKinney had probably not worked as hard as it should have but simply assumed "everybody would be for [Rayburn]." He had carried McKinney by only a small majority in 1944, and that misjudgment would not happen again. The huge soil conservation, flood control, and water project known as the Lavon Dam Project, now in its early stages, was brought to the district through Rayburn's influence. Located on the East Fork of the Trinity River, "the Lavon Dam Project should help me out in all the Trinity bottom on the East Fork and that includes quite a lot of Rains, Kaufman and Collin Counties. My friends in Kaufman County have set up a strong county-wide organization and are really going to work."[117]

Good news had also come in from Grayson County. Though Judge David Brown had insisted on running, in spite of much advice to the contrary, he was not at all strong.[118] Brown was only twenty-eight and had little political experience other than being a county court-at-law judge. His platform was a conservative one that opposed the civil rights program and the "coddling of any minority group." He favored governmental economy, preparedness, reduction of the public debt, a return to Jeffersonian principles and good roads. His main claim as a politician appears to be that he was a World War II veteran.[119] Rayburn's Denison leader concluded that Brown would not have the feared effect of pulling away his Grayson County support: "I cannot see where it [Brown's race] will make much difference."[120]

The organization was in gear, and the network working well. Rayburn received reports that President Gee of East Texas Normal College, formerly Mayo, Rayburn's alma mater, was speaking in Morris's behalf and strongly favored him.[121] He learned of a meeting of the Hunt County Bar Association where an effort was made to pass an antiadministration resolution. The resolution was successfully stopped on procedural grounds by Rayburn's ally Harris.[122] In Celina, Rayburn learned that several men in the American Legion opposed him.[123] That alarmed him enough to ask Ray Roberts to check into the situation and see what could be done to gain support.[124]

Morris sent a campaign letter to Will Murphy of Crandall. A postscript on the undated letter stated, "I am writing you this

letter at the request of a mutual friend, Dr. W. F. Alexander of
Terrell, Texas. Please write me if you feel free to pass out some
literature among your friends."[125] But Murphy was a Rayburn
supporter and sent the letter to Dick Rayburn, who notified his
brother that he had checked on Alexander and discovered that
he was related to two Rayburn supporters, Judge Crisp and Pat
Coon. Dick planned to contact them to convert the physician to
the Rayburn cause.[126]

Morris used a vehicle equipped with a public address system
in the 1948 campaign. Contrary to expectations that such a vehicle would be effective gathering crowds and amplifying street
corner speeches in the numerous tiny communities that a
Fourth District congressional candidate had to visit, the use of
the automobile actually hurt Morris because Rayburn and his
supporters had nothing like it. They began to charge that Morris had obtained the vehicle from rich contributors and that
Rayburn did not have the money for one. On one occasion, for
example, Philip Willis, a Rayburn supporter, infiltrated a crowd
of about sixty to whom Morris was speaking. Willis was displaying a Texas *Senate Journal* in his hand. After State Senator
Morris had spoken, Willis said he would like to ask Mr. Morris
some questions. Morris had his driver turn up the music on the
sound truck and drive away, leaving Willis the perfect opportunity. He told the crowd that there were "not any Trusts or Corporations furnishing me with a public address equipped automobile"; he would, he said, speak in his "old-fashioned way" in
behalf of Rayburn. After his old-fashioned, no-sound-truck,
pro-Rayburn speech, eleven of the sixteen people who had
shaken hands with Morris came up to Willis, congratulated him,
and patted him on the back.[127]

It was no accident that Philip Willis went to the Morris
speech. Rayburn and his leaders liked to have their supporters
mingle with the crowds at anti-Rayburn speeches so they could
obtain reports on crowd size, enthusiasm, and the viability of
the issues being raised. Mr. Sam also liked his trusted friends to
mingle with the crowds at his own speeches and report on what
the crowd was saying.[128] Once when two of his secretaries
were circulating through a crowd at a Rayburn speech, they
heard a group of men talking about strategy for beating Sam
Rayburn. In the group they discovered a politician until then

considered a Rayburn supporter. Because he prized loyalty, Rayburn initially refused to believe the report; but after further investigation, he tearfully confirmed to the secretaries that they had been correct. Soon the politician publically endorsed Morris, an endorsement that ended the politician's political future.[129]

Morris also obtained the services of a professional campaign manager, C. Garland Smith. The Rayburn supporters managed to turn this against him as well. Smith was a political professional, a man with no counterpart in the unpaid, volunteer Rayburn organization. Two Rayburn supporters, Harris and Allen Clark, told a radio audience about this paid outsider who had been such a successful campaign professional. When Smith arrived in the district, he used a newly painted automobile. As Roland Boyd, a Collin County Rayburn leader recalled:

> We all started on our radio talks and our other talks by saying, "I wonder who was paying for all this. This fellow [Smith] takes an awful lot of money to hire him. He's a pro; you can't hire him for chicken feed because he's the best. We're not about to spend our money painting any fancy automobiles because this [campaign funding] is ours on Sam Rayburn's side. I just wish you'd get Morris to say where that other money is coming from."[130]

The effect of such speeches was devastating.

Even by 1948 Rayburn had been in office for thirty-five years, so one charge (made as early as the 1930s) was that he had been in office too long. That charge was handled by questioning the value of such an attack, as Boyd did, for example, speaking in Rayburn's behalf:

> "Mr. Rayburn's opposition is trying to convince you that Sam Rayburn has been there too long," I said, and pointed in the direction of the First Baptist Church. . . . "Now that church has been there a pretty long time. I don't believe we ought to burn it down just because it has been there a long time. I think we ought to decide if it is doing good or bad and if it is doing good, let's keep it."[131]

Just as things were not going well at all for Morris, even nature hurt him. On May 3, 1948, a tornado struck McKinney in

Collin County, killed three people, injured forty-three, and did
$2 million in property damage.[132] The Rayburn forces claimed
that Morris, while in the Texas Senate, had supported deductible clauses on insurance. It was a charge Morris adamantly denied.[133] Many in McKinney had to pay a deductible on their
tornado losses, and some, it was claimed, had even dropped
their insurance because of the deductible. On July 22, 1948, the
insurance agents in McKinney issued a release endorsing Rayburn because of Morris's support of deductibles.[134] Politically,
Morris's situation worsened.

As usual Rayburn's district tour took place in the last weeks
of the campaign. For example, on July 6 he visited in parts of
Fannin County, making stops at Ravenna, Mulberry, Ivanhoe,
Lamasco, Duplex, Tulip, Elwood, Telephone, Monkstown,
Selfs, Dial, Lannius, and Edhube. Visits were scheduled to last
from fifteen minutes to one hour and fifteen minutes.[135]

During the tour, press releases went out indicating that
Rayburn had pushed through the Revolving Fund for Purchase
of Natural Fiber Act. The fund made $150 million available to
the secretary of the army to purchase cotton (the major Fourth
District crop) and wool for Japan and Korea.[136] A campaign
letter pointing out that Rayburn had authored REA and backed
farm price supports, soil conservation, and farm-to-market roads
was sent throughout the district.[137] Royse City Rayburn supporters produced a pro-Rayburn handbill that showed he had
gotten Royse City a sidewalk grant of $7,016.73, a water filtra-
tion grant of $6,850.62, and a street pavement grant of
$169,281.35.[138]

Throughout the campaign, Rayburn kept in touch with what
was happening in the district and continually worked to build
organizational strength and strength with voters. He learned,
for example, that a newcomer had settled in Mabank, Kaufman
County. The newcomer's father had once been in the Texas legislature. As was his practice, Rayburn scribbled the information
on a slip of paper and later wrote the newcomer, "I remember
you as a boy and, of course, remember your father very well as
he served with me in the Texas House when I was Speaker. If
you have made as fine a man as your father was, which from reports you have, you are a worthy citizen." He then wrote of his
appreciation for the father's friendship.[139] Newcomers, Ray-

burn well knew, vote and he had established a bond with one of those new votes.

This is not to say that campaigning came easily to Rayburn. Cole, the 1948 campaign coordinater, recalled that "Mr. Rayburn hated worse than anybody I have ever seen to campaign. . . . A lot of people complained about him never coming down around the square, never seeing him. They complained about it; they didn't think he got out enough and mixed enough. That is why in the 1948 campaign we decided he was going to see them." It was Cole's opinion that Rayburn's legislative record was such that Mr. Sam did not think it necessary to beg for votes.[140] Rayburn was a surprisingly reticent man who had to be persuaded by staff members to attend many parties in Washington, but he usually enjoyed those he did attend.[141] John Nance Garner noticed Rayburn's shyness in Sam's first years in Congress and warned his friend Cecil Dickson that Rayburn would have to become more assertive if he was to be a successful legislator.[142] Sam obviously overcame the trait sufficiently to win twenty-five congressional elections, but asking for votes and socializing among large groups of people who were not close friends never became easy for him.

The 1952 Campaign

In 1952 remnants of the old Morris opposition united behind a new face. Reagan Brown was a well-liked, friendly young agricultural agent from Terrell in Kaufman County. Mr. Sam apparently saw young Brown as an irritation rather than as a serious political challenger. On one occasion, for example, he saw Brown in Royce City and told him: "I ain't got time to mess with you, you young whippersnapper. Why are you messing with me?" Brown responded with an appeal to Rayburn's sentimental side, saying he remembered how Mr. Sam had said that young people should get involved in politics, and, Brown recalled, "these great big tears came in his eyes and he gave me a hug."[143]

Brown ran an antiadministration campaign, counting Rayburn as a member of the administration.[144] His platform favored the exposure of communism, the elimination of waste, lower taxes, and equal representation of labor, industry, and agriculture. He was against bureaucracy and inflation and in favor of work. Most important, he was against rubber stamps for the administration.[145] In addition, Brown charged that Rayburn was too old, had been in office too long, and had grown rich in office, as evidenced by a large number of cattle. Brown also argued that Rayburn might be nominated for president in 1952, which would require that someone else, namely Brown, be elected to Congress.[146] Rayburn, incredulous at the last charge, recommended that his leaders point out how strange it was to suggest that he might be president and then to suggest that he be beaten for Congress.[147] The wealth-in-office charge was answered over the radio by Roland Boyd. Boyd noted that Rayburn had many accomplishments, whereas Brown had once been unsuccessful as a grocer. He went on: "Now there is a man that is running against him that cannot successfully sell pinto beans in a grocery store; he makes a complete failure. He cannot even count cattle," for Rayburn owned far fewer cattle than Brown had suggested. Boyd finished by telling his audience, "Now I'll tell you where the pasture is; you count them if you think this is not right."[148] The age and too-long-in-office charges were handled in the same way as always: he has done a good job for us and will continue to do so.

Rayburn worked within his usual volunteer organization and learned that Brown was not catching on, for he was an uninspiring speaker who did not attract large crowds.[149] Rayburn also learned that Brown seemed exceptionally weak in some counties in the district, especially Grayson, which was the district's most populous.[150] Of most interest to him, Rayburn learned that Brown's funding was not great.[151]

The intelligence network was working well. When an anti-Rayburn meeting was held in Greenville, Mr. Sam quickly learned of it.[152] His organization managed to infiltrate the meeting with four spies, a goodly number considering that only seventy-five or eighty people were present. He learned that the meeting was attended only by people from Greenville and Kaufman County, which indicated the opposition had not organized the entire district. Rayburn also received a list of the names of influential Greenville citizens who attended.[153]

When Brown visited Emory in Rains County, the Rayburn

county leader reported that Brown had given a speech on the square that attracted a crowd of only ten-to-fifteen people. When he finished speaking, he had put posters in all the buildings in town, but ninety percent were gone by the next day. Rayburn also learned that Brown had won the support of three young men. Leaving nothing to chance, the county leader had worked to convert the three to Rayburn's cause. By the time of the leader's report to Rayburn, one of the three had been converted, and efforts continued with the other two.[154]

From Denison Rayburn got a report that, when Brown placed his announcement of candidacy in the *Denison Herald,* he had asked for credit, it was refused, and he had then paid for the announcement with a personal check. In addition, Brown had as of late May purchased no time from either of the local radio stations.[155] Such things could reasonably be interpreted as signs of poor campaign funding. Although Brown had visited Denison at least three times by late May and had once gone store-to-store with his campaign, Rayburn's Denison leaders could find only one Brown supporter among the businessmen. That one businessman was displaying a Reagan Brown poster in his store, for which heresy it was reported that he was bound to "lose plenty of business." The Denison leader reported that he was making every effort to contact the businessman and convince him to mend his ways.[156]

Ward Mayborn reported that Brown apparently had, by mid-May, no plans for a campaign or any meetings in Sherman and that there was "no evidence yet of anyone sponsoring him up here."[157] Rayburn had organization members checking on Brown's meetings. Vernon Beckham, for example, reported that he went to Forrest Park in Denison to check on a scheduled Brown speech and "he stood all of the domino players up. No Brown made no speech, and outside of one or two eavesdroppers and eight domino players the park was wanting for an audience and speaker."[158] Little harm probably came to Brown as a result of the missed speech, for Denison was not to be persuaded to go against Rayburn. When Brown appeared there in late June, he was chased away from the front of the Labor Temple.[159]

Another report said that, when Brown appeared in Sherman, it was "to a very small group, who just happened to be in the park, maybe one or two more who had a listening ear. He told something of his family heritage, same stuff that he has in his pamphlet and ended up saying that Mr. Rayburn was in the Congress when he was born and he thought it was time to change for him."[160] Still another Rayburn observer noted that Brown had spoken twice in McKinney and that on both occasions he had attracted crowds of from eight to twelve people with no more than six of the listeners shaking hands with him after either speech. Collin County candidates had also been polled, with the conclusion that Brown's strength there was not great.[161]

Rayburn also received reports on individuals inclined toward Brown, for example, that the mayor of Frisco shared Brown's antiadministration views and that a visit from an old army friend had not persuaded him to support Rayburn.[162] Similarly, a report came in that the mayor of Terrell had given Reagan Brown cards to a resort operator.[163] On June 27 Brown paid for an ad with a fifty-dollar check issued to him by a Brownfield pharmacy. The check appeared to be a campaign contribution. That same day a letter went out bringing this probable contribution to Rayburn's attention.[164] When a Terrell real estate man tried to solicit funds for Brown, Rayburn also was notified.[165] When the Kaufman County Medical Society refused to contribute fifty dollars to the Brown campaign, this too was reported to Mr. Sam.[166] Rayburn received a report that a Smith from Farmersville was seen at a Brown meeting. Immediately, the word went out to check on the loyalty of the Farmersville postmaster, who was named Smith. Reports soon came back to Rayburn that postmaster Smith was absolutely loyal to him and the pro-Brown Smith was unrelated to the postmaster.[167] The Rayburn organization was very thorough in dealing with the Brown threat, minor though it was. One of Rayburn's leaders even visited with one of Brown's relatives in the hope that useful information on Brown could be gained.[168]

The Rayburn campaign followed the familiar pattern: friends and neighbors contacted by members of the Rayburn organization, speeches in his behalf by the leaders, and a return to Bonham by Rayburn at the end of the congressional session. After the homecoming, there was the usual open-home policy and hurried tour of the district, speaking at such places as a family reunion in Plano,[169] and the Royse City Cemetery Association and Annual Home Coming.[170] The campaign effort also included the use of radio and newspaper ads. There was the customary emphasis upon his integrity, his power, and his accomplishments, especially in benefiting argiculture and bringing projects to the district.

In 1952 the strategy worked again. Rayburn won overwhelmingly. He even won in Hunt County, probably aided there by his efforts to reactivate Majors Field in Greenville and by his success in getting Temco to locate there. Temco was at the time an industry with a ninety-thousand dollar weekly payroll and was described as a "life saver for Greenville."[171] Reagan Brown was to recall his race many years later: "I didn't have a bit of sense."[172]

The 1954 Campaign

The last year that Rayburn faced primary opposition was 1954, but after the 1948 primary election, his opposition was more of an irritation than a threat. In 1954 he was as politically secure within his district as any politician could be, but the race is of interest because it shows that Rayburn's style, organization, and intelligence network remained largely unchanged despite this political security.

Rayburn had suspected that Jack Finney, a baker from Greenville, would oppose him, with strong support from Gov. Allan Shivers, the conservative Democrat who disappointed Rayburn by supporting Eisenhower in 1952 and 1956. Rayburn believed that Shivers would put Finney in the race against him to keep Rayburn and his friends occupied with reelection. Thus, they would not have time to campaign against Shivers's own bid for reelection. But, Rayburn wrote Roland Boyd, Finney had been told that "no amount of money would beat Sam Rayburn."[173]

Finney did not run against Rayburn. Instead, to the surprise of many, A. G. McRae announced for Congress. He telegraphed Rayburn: "As a utility man my back has been sore for over twenty years. Do not believe in knowingly tolerating communist in any government position. Believe in state rights and farm support with surplus going to friendly nations instead of cash."[174] McRae had been a local manager of TP&L. Naturally, the utility company affiliation led many to believe that the old enmity between TP&L and Sam Rayburn was still alive, but TP&L officials were actually as stunned as many others in the community by McRae's decision. It was a decision that apparently was not even discussed with his father, A. L. McRae, who was deputy county clerk in Fannin County.

A. G. was a friend of Buster Cole, Rayburn's campaign manager in Fannin County and coordinator of his campaign throughout the district. Shortly before announcing for the office, McRae informed Cole of his intentions. When Cole could not dissuade McRae, who admitted that he was probably making a terrible mistake by running, Cole turned to McRae's father, but the senior McRae could do nothing to convince his son to withdraw. Cole then contacted TP&L vice president John Young and learned that the utility had no knowledge of McRae's decision. Realizing that Rayburn and his supporters would think that TP&L was backing McRae, Young was in frequent telephone contact with Cole and on February 5 sent a public relations man to Bonham to talk with Cole and clarify the company's position. Young even drove to Bonham himself, and for two hours Young, Cole, and McRae met. Cole and Young tried "to get him [McRae] to get out, go on and get a job and go to work."[175] They were unsuccessful.

McRae stayed in the race with the inevitable result: the public assumed because McRae was a former TP&L manager that the battle was between the company and Rayburn.[176] Texas Power and Light was so alarmed that the company's president, Bill Lynch, sent word that there was nothing to such rumors and "that if, when and where we wanted them to do anything they [TP&L] would do it." The company that was Rayburn's former arch enemy even attempted to locate McRae's financial backing for Cole.[177] By 1954 even TP&L had learned that it was best to remain in Speaker Rayburn's good graces.

Cole advised a strategy of keeping quiet and trying to ignore McRae, a strategy that seems to have been followed.[178] McRae, on the other hand, became increasingly insistent on running. People, he argued, were not only questioning his decision to run, but his *right* to run against a district-wide institution. Cole, however, tried to remain friendly with McRae on the theory that his behavior was perhaps not that of a well man.[179]

The best McRae could accomplish with his candidacy was to embarrass Rayburn. The story became widespread that Rayburn had gotten McRae to announce to prevent other possible opponents from filing out of fear of splitting the anti-Rayburn vote. It was said that McRae would withdraw from the race after it was too late for other candidates to file.[180] The quiet effort to get out the pro-Rayburn vote continued, with organization members all the while wondering why McRae was running and who was backing him. Then in May Rayburn received an interesting report on his opponent. Emmett Thompson, a businessman in Bonham with good connections in Forney, offered political aid to fishing friend Sam Rayburn and reported:

> Your opponent was in our office this morning and showed us Ten One Thousand dollar bills that he said was campaign expense money and that he could get some more when he needed it. He said he could not afford to put it in either bank here so he thought he would go put it in a bank in Sherman. He said he liked you and was not going to say a thing against you because he did not have a chance of even to get you interested in the campaign as a foe.[181]

Rayburn relayed this information to Cole but speculated that the money might have been phoney.[182] A display of phoney money could have been a ploy to indicate that the opposition was doing well with financial backing. Although a ten-thousand-dollar campaign donation was a substantial sum in those days, in the case of the Rayburn opposition, it was not unprecedented. Rayburn leaders Roland Boyd and R. C. Slagle were offered such sums to run against Rayburn but refused.[183] A local politician in Rockwall County who was friendly toward Rayburn also reputedly was "approached by some Dallas men who offered to pay him to run," but he, too, refused.[184] There were several very conservative, wealthy businessmen, mostly oil men in Dallas, who believed Rayburn too liberal and to whom sums of ten thousand dollars or more were trivial and well worth the investment for the possibility of an upset.[185]

It was said, for example, that in 1944 Houston oil millionaire Hugh Roy Cullen gave ten thousand dollars to G. C. Morris.[186] Cullen, known as the "King of the Wildcatters," was one of the richest men in the world, a self-made millionaire with only a fifth-grade education. Beginning in 1928 he made a series of extraordinary oil strikes, the greatest of which was the mile-deep billion-dollar pool of oil known as the Tom O'Connor field. After Cullen's son died in 1936, he began to give away large chunks of his fortune, over the next twenty years, $200 million. Opposed to a strong federal government and hostile to anticapitalist ideologies, he strongly opposed Franklin Roosevelt,[187] backed the Texas Regulars in 1944, and opposed Rayburn as an especially visible symbol of the New Deal.[188]

Rayburn found out about Cullen's donation to the 1944 Morris race and was deeply angered by it. He bided his time until 1946, when he had a meeting with Jack Porter, a close friend of Cullen's. Porter was then in Washington as president of the Texas Producers' and Royalty Owners' Association. He was interested in removing oil and beef from price controls. Porter recalled that Congress had passed a bill reducing the extent of controls but that the president had vetoed it. During the course of his lobbying, he visited Sam Rayburn:

> So we talked a little politics first, and one thing that was in his craw, Mr. Cullen had been sending ten thousand dollars up to his district—try to beat him. And so I said "Well, Mr. Speaker, I'll talk to Mr. Cullen and I think I can guarantee you that he won't send any more money up there and try to beat you. . . ." And he finally said to me—they had a bill in at that time to do away with price controls on oil and beef—he said, "I don't care what they do on that bill; we gave the President a good bill and he vetoed it."

Assured that Rayburn would not block the decontrol legislation, Porter "spread the word around and that bill sailed right on through." Porter did talk to Cullen. Cullen apparently got the message because in 1948 he provided no support to Morris. Judge Joe Ingraham, a friend of Porter's, thought the opposition received only a telegram from Cullen in 1948, rather than the sizable donation they might have expected in light of the 1944 donation.[189]

The Sun Oil group of companies is also said to have funded Rayburn's opposition over a period of many years.[190] Amounts of money are unknown, but the opposition seems likely in light of the political views of Sun's president, J. Howard Pew. When Pew died in 1971, he left a fortune estimated at $100 million. The Pew family fortune was at that time estimated at roughly $1 billion. Pew was president of Sun from 1912 to 1947, chairman of the board from 1963 to 1970, and chairman of the company executive committee until his death. Although in World Wars I and II he played a major role in directing the war effort of the petroleum industry, he was often the oil industry spokesman in opposition to governmental economic restraints and was known as an ultraconservative in politics, economics, and religion. Pew served on the editorial advisory board of the ultraconservative magazine *American Opinion* and was a stockholder in Robert Welch, Inc., the publication arm of the John Birch Society.[191] He was one of the chief financial contributors to the American Liberty League, an alliance of wealthy businessmen hostile to the New Deal who, in the midst of the Depression, supported free enterprise and nonintervention by the government in the economy. Its leading members besides Pew included several members of the duPont family, steel industrialist Ernest Wier, Texas cotton broker Will Clayton, General Motors president Alfred Sloan, Montgomery Ward's Sewell Avery, Baldwin Locomotive's George Houston, attorney-politician John W. Davis, and former New York Governor Al Smith. The members advocated social Darwinism and funded much anti–New Deal propaganda.[192] Pew had significant economic interests in Texas, had worked in Texas, and must have viewed Rayburn as a symbol of the hated New Deal. When the president of a Sun Oil subsidiary, the Crude Oil Company, took a major role in the 1944 Texas Regular movement, it was possibly on Pew's orders.[193]

These large donations to Rayburn's opponents began to dry up in 1948. After that campaign Rayburn's opponents were never able to obtain large campaign war chests. W. G. Hall, a long-time leader of the liberal wing of the Texas Democratic party, says it was clear there was no way Rayburn could be defeated in his district, so those rich donors hostile to him learned to live with him.[194] Rayburn was also by then so powerful in

Washington that it was unwise for major anti-Rayburn contributors with Washington interests to challenge Rayburn at home.

Some of Rayburn's leaders suspected that some of Rayburn's opponents took advantage of the ultraconservatives' hatred for Rayburn and used parts of their campaign donations for personal matters. Personal use of campaign funds would have been quite easy, especially given that large donations appear to have often been in cash. Texas campaign funding and expenditure laws are also notoriously lax, so much so that campaign funds can now legally be converted into personal use.[195]

In 1954, with no significant opposition funding, Rayburn and his organization produced their usual results: 30,003 votes compared with McRae's 10,123.

5. Rayburn in Bonham and Washington

THE ROLES OF FOURTH DISTRICT CONGRESS-man and Speaker did not always mesh, yet Rayburn filled these two roles in similar ways. The role agreements and conflicts are revealed in an examination of the advantages and disadvantages of Rayburn's high political visibility, his powers and responsibilities of leadership, and his behavior in reference to party loyalty, civil rights, and the oil depletion allowance.

High Political Visibility

It is easy to stay in Congress for many years by maintaining a low political profile. A congressman can accomplish this by staying out of leadership roles and focusing on such noncontroversial and politically rewarding activities as constituent service. Fiorina has suggested that such activity, which trades policy impact for political security, characterizes modern congressmen in contrast to those of an earlier generation, who were primarily policy-oriented.[1] Rayburn, however, was one of those earlier generation congressmen who did show an extraordinary dedication to constituent service.[2] He also showed a policy orientation unlikely to be surpassed by modern congressmen. It may be necessary to reconsider that relationship between policy making and constituent service in light of the Rayburn example. Some suggestions about that relationship are offered in the concluding chapter.

Rayburn chose a high political profile that opened up varying balances of policy impact and political security. There were times when the Speakership was of enormous value to him at the district level, others when it worked to his disadvantage. In the balance, though, the Speakership and his other high party

137

positions such as the majority leadership and the Democratic leadership were beneficial to him at the district level. Constituents, for example, took pride in electing not merely a congressman but a Speaker. As one associate described Rayburn's relationship with his district, "He was just next to the president and the Lord around here."[3] Another spoke of the ease in convincing people to vote for him: "Since he had served as long as he did as Speaker, it was pretty easy to campaign for an officeholder like that."[4] A third associate said that when he was campaigning for Rayburn, he would point out that the voters of the Fourth District were unique, for "we weren't just reelecting our congressman every two years; we were making it possible for the Speaker to go on, in effect, running the congress by returning him. He wasn't an ordinary congressman and hadn't been for so long."[5] The Fourth District congressman was regularly in the news. In 1948, 1952, and 1956, his visibility was even further enhanced by the media attention he received as chairman of the Democratic national conventions. Rayburn impressed many of his constituents with his broadcast handling of convention business.[6] At the same time, Rayburn's high visibility was sometimes at the expense of being tied too closely to unpopular actions of the national Democratic party, as when his close ties to President Truman led him to be identified in many constituents' minds with Truman's civil rights program. As the last chapter showed, it was an identification so strong that Rayburn ultimately had to campaign against Truman's program to insure that he would be returned to Congress.

Time and again Rayburn was faced with the charge that he was Speaker at the expense of representing the interests of his district. Though he was a moderate by national party standards,[7] many in Texas considered him far more liberal than his district. For a Democratic representative from a conservative state such as Texas, the danger was that the national party would diverge so much from local interests that an accommodation between the two interests would prove impossible. With only a few exceptions, however, Rayburn found he could work closely and cooperatively with Democratic presidents while also maintaining his district-level control. Nevertheless, his national leadership role seems to have pushed him somewhat more to the left than would have been considered expedient for a district-oriented congressman not in a leadership position.[8]

Rayburn depended on several mechanisms that allowed him to benefit from the high visibility of the Speakership and yet avoid the disadvantage of identification with unpopular policies. One was the vast reservoir of trust in his judgment, ability, and performance that his political style and his organization gave him. He had the flexibility to be a national Democrat when those policies might be opposed at the district level because so many of his constituents believed in him as a plain fellow who had known the hard life and could be trusted to do the right thing. The organization stood ever ready to put out brushfires of opposition that might emerge in spite of the smothering effects of the Rayburn style.

Another mechanism was the apparently successful explanation he developed for his behavior. In essence, he told his constituents that a leader must be a part of a team. Sometimes that team went against his wishes and the district's wishes, but it was necessary to go along on some distasteful policies in order to have impact on others. He also pointed out that some of those distasteful policies were a product of team compromise which he had been able to make less distasteful than they would have been without his influence. As Fenno has pointed out, it is often less important how a congressman behaves than how he explains his behavior to the district.[9] The team player and compromise explanations served Rayburn well with his constituents.

Rayburn's strong emphasis on bringing visible governmental projects to his district and his effectiveness in individual constituent service were also extremely important in giving him the flexibility to function as a national political leader. Constituents might not like his orientation as a national Democrat, but that was more than compensated for by a recognition that he got things done for his constituents and for the district. It was clear that Rayburn's contribution to an improved life style in the district was considerable. He could maintain his national Democratic stance because he had purchased district support by his constituency service.

The Speakership gave Rayburn enormous power. It enabled him to accomplish for the district more than could even the most senior congressmen. Farm-to-market roads, Lake Lavon, the McKinney and Bonham hospitals, and Perrin Field all stemmed from his power as Speaker. Yet the powers of leadership brought him responsibilities that caused district-level problems. During World War II, for example, he had to spend much of his time in Washington, preventing his usual fence mending in the district and prompting the strong attack by G. C. Morris. As Henry Jackson pointed out, when Rayburn assumed the powers of the Speakership, he also had to realize that he was more than a northeast Texas Congressman:

> He wore two hats: (1) representing his district, and (2) being a leader of a party that embraced diverse political views. He made a decision when he became Speaker. To the extent he wanted to stay as Speaker, it was his responsibility and duty to help other members who had problems other than agriculture, namely the cities. He wouldn't go to extremes. He sort of carved an independent course. He was supportive of aid to the cities. He was supportive of programs that essentially had an orientation in favor of the North. He was strongly supportive of Western interests in the field of irrigation, reclamation, the building of power dams, basic public resource development.

As Jackson recalled, "it was tough for him," and in 1944 he had a "hard campaign against him" because he was charged with being "too liberal" in that he supported programs as a national leader that a Bonham congressman would be disinclined to support.[10]

Party Loyalty

Throughout Rayburn's career he was a Democratic party loyalist. He argued that a Democrat should vote a straight Democratic ticket, from president on down to constable. The Democratic party, he claimed, was the party promoting the best interests of the people of Texas. To prove his point he spoke of the days of Republican domination during Reconstruction, and he pointed to the Depression and the lack of Republican efforts to improve conditions for people compared with Democratic efforts. If nothing else, he maintained that Texans should vote the

Democratic ticket out of appreciation for the party's efforts to improve their lives. He felt strongly about the party loyalty of Democratic officeholders, whom he considered obligated to support the Democratic ticket because they had gained office through their affiliation with the party.[11]

That Rayburn's belief in party loyalty was a long-standing one is evident from his campaign efforts in Texas for Democratic presidential nominee Al Smith. Smith was a candidate in 1928 and very unpopular in Texas for three reasons: (1) he was a Tammany man; (2) he was a wet; and (3) perhaps most important, he was a Catholic. Democrats and Democratic officeholders in Texas deserted Smith in droves and became Hoovercrats. Texas, for the first time since Reconstruction, moved into the Republican column and gave its electoral votes to Republican Hoover. It would have been easy for the young Congressman Rayburn to adopt a policy of silence and make no efforts in Smith's behalf. Instead he campaigned for Smith all over East Texas and often made joint campaign appearances with a young Dallas County politician, Sarah Hughes, who was later to become one of Texas's best-known federal judges.[12]

Of course strong support for the party's nominee would be a prerequisite for any future Speaker, and Rayburn was allegedly aiming for the Speakership from his first days in Congress. Indeed, late in life he claimed that achieving the Speakership was a childhood ambition.[13] Hal Horton, his first staff member, recalled to Rayburn in a letter:

> When I first went to work with you in 1913, you told me that your ambition was to some day be the Speaker of the House. Again, several years ago, when you had such strong opposition and the expense of your reelection was so burdensome, I again urged you to take a place on the I.C.C. You again said your ambition was to be Speaker. You told me that it was then in sight.[14]

Rayburn may have focused on the Speakership because he saw no avenue for political advancement except through the House of Representatives. Contrary to the general view that Rayburn was always totally oriented toward the House, he did have other ambitions. In his early years in the House, he wished to become a "state figure" but thought it unlikely that he could achieve that ambition. Rayburn's alliance with Joe Bailey, so beneficial to him in his earliest years in politics, haunted him. Bailey was, in the frustrated Rayburn's opinion, "as far as running for office is concerned . . . dead as hell," yet "everlastingly coming to the front as a candidate." Bailey's visibility reminded the people of his resignation and disgrace. It also reminded people of the close relationship between Rayburn and Bailey. Thus, Bailey, in effect, forced Rayburn to remain in the House.[15] D. B. Hardeman believed Rayburn in his later years could not have won a statewide race in conservative Texas.[16] Rayburn also considered himself barred from the presidency by Franklin Roosevelt: "I might have been President if Roosevelt hadn't wanted to stay in the White House forever. He'd be President today if he'd lived—yes, and in 1956 and 1960."[17] Rayburn's ambitions were thus channeled by circumstances toward achieving leadership in the House. That required a solid record of party loyalty.

Price Daniel suggested that another reason for Rayburn's strong feelings about party loyalty was that he reflected the attitudes of his generation.[18] He was, after all, born in 1882 when memories of the Civil War were still fresh. In fact, his father was a veteran of the Confederate army. Rayburn undertook some political risks in both 1952 and 1956 when he opposed Governor Shivers for being a Democratic supporter of Dwight Eisenhower for the presidency. Rayburn's campaigning for Adlai Stevenson was an especially lonely effort in 1952, when he was joined by very few elected officials and when little money was available for the Democratic campaign.

There was some risk to him in opposing Shivers because Shivers was one of the most able governors Texas has had.[19] In 1952 Shivers and Eisenhower were enormously popular in Texas. Rayburn, on the other hand, had to support a Democratic candidate who was, in Texas's mind, not only left wing but a supporter of the theft of the lands of Texas's schoolchildren. That charge involved the tidelands controversy, which pitted Texas against the national government. Both claimed the submerged lands off the Texas coast including mineral rights. The Texas claim was strongly supported by Texas voters, who saw the federal claim as an invasion of states' rights and who believed the possibly oil-rich lands contained the revenues for their children's education. When Truman vetoed pro-Texas tidelands legislation, he created an opportunity for Texans to flail the national Democratic party. Rayburn attempted a compromise between the state and national claims, but state Attorney General Price Daniel refused any attempts to reach a compromise and persisted with Texas's claim. Then Adlai Stevenson's stated intention to veto pro-Texas tidelands legislation provided the opportunity to bolt the Democratic party and support Eisenhower, who was supportive of the Texas tidelands claims.[20]

In the absence of a pro-Democratic state Democratic party, Rayburn attempted to build a Stevenson organization in Texas, but as Little has noted, it was "too little, too late,"[21] for Rayburn had delayed, hoping to reunite the badly divided state party at the September state convention.[22] Though he had been warned that Shivers would support Eisenhower in the election, he insisted that the governor would not do so.[23] When faced with a credentials dispute at the national convention between a Shivers-dominated delegation and a loyalist delegation, Rayburn supported the seating of the Shivers delegation. It may be that one unspoken reason was that the Shivers delegation supported Sen. Richard Russell of Georgia for the presidency. It has been claimed that Russell threatened to walk out of the convention if the Shivers delegation was denied seating.[24] Russell was a highly respected senator widely considered to be the leader of the South in the Senate. A walkout by Russell would have created chaos in the party in 1952, and it would have been in character for Rayburn to work to maintain party unity by supporting Shivers to prevent a walkout. Rayburn was to insist until his death that Shivers promised party loyalty in exchange for the seating of his delegation and that the governor lied to him.[25] Shivers claimed that he had merely promised to *try* to support the Democratic nominee and that he would make sure the nominee was listed on the election ballots in Texas. Shivers claimed he had complied with the agreement because he had successfully opposed an effort to deny Stevenson and Sparkman a place on the ballot. He had also met with Stevenson in an effort to get him to support the Texas position in the tidelands dispute. While Stevenson did express a willingness to support compromise legislation, he was unwilling to endorse the Texas position. As a result, Shivers felt justified in supporting Eisenhower for president.[26]

Whether or not Rayburn was misled, he had badly misjudged the situation. The split between the Shivers forces and the loyalists was clear long before the national convention. Shivers had been strongly critical of President Truman, the Democratic party, and Speaker Rayburn.[27] It may be, however, that Rayburn assumed Shivers was simply engaged in political posturing to put him in a conservative position against Tom Connally for the U.S. Senate.[28] Connally was hardly a liberal, but he was a Democratic party loyalist. He had not kept his fences mended in Texas and had lost touch with his base of support. By the early 1950s age was affecting Connally, and he was politically vulnerable.[29] Shivers may well have entertained thoughts of running for Connally's seat. He did run a survey to determine if Connally could be beaten and found him an easy target.[30] Attorney General Price Daniel had also apparently thought that Shivers entertained ambitions for the Senate and was disappointed when Shivers told him he would run for reelection as governor and that Daniel should run for the Senate against Connally.[31] Lyndon Johnson, who also appears to have thought Shivers had Senate ambitions, was only quietly and inactively for Stevenson in 1952 in order to curry Shivers's favor and prevent a Shivers challenge when he stood for reelection in 1954. Johnson had only won election to the Senate by eighty-seven questionable votes and so felt far from secure against a challenge by the popular Shivers.[32] Rayburn, Johnson, and Daniel were all fooled, however. Shivers remained in the governor's office through 1956 and led the state into the Republican fold in both 1952 and 1956.

Had Rayburn not been Speaker, he could have promoted his political security by voting for Stevenson, perhaps giving a few speeches in Stevenson's behalf, but generally maintaining a low political profile. Such behavior would have protected his seniority in the House by insuring that he would have been recognized as a loyal Democrat. In Texas he could appeal to both the Democratic loyalists and the Shivers faction. To the loyalists, he could point to his vote and speeches for Stevenson; and to the Shivers faction, he could stress his low political profile. But

Rayburn was not just a senior Democratic congressman; he was Speaker, a powerful and visible symbol of the national Democrats. The Speakership provided a strong incentive for him to challenge the Shivers move. It was a challenge that insured the continued support of his leadership by scores of congressmen from all over the country, especially those from competitive districts who saw Shivers's actions as leading to the destruction of the Democratic party.[33]

That Rayburn's efforts against Shivers were not without political risks is evident by efforts within the Shivers faction to redistrict Rayburn and give him part of Dallas County.[34] The Shivers faction also promoted the candidacy of a man they claimed would run first for state senator in a district within Rayburn's congressional district, gain experience as a senator, and then run against Rayburn. Ray Roberts recalled that he ran for state senator as the Rayburn organization candidate and that his entry into the race was primarily due to a perceived need to meet this challenge to Rayburn. Roberts recalled that the Shivers faction was saying of the state senate candidate, "The senate now and Congress in two years from now. The Rayburn people met . . . Rayburn decided . . . that we had to have somebody, that we just couldn't let the guy run free."[35]

Although Rayburn's commitment to party loyalty was personal and deeply held, it was his party leadership role that encouraged him to be so deeply committed that he attacked a figure as powerful as Shivers. Privately, he understood the political value of opposing Stevenson in Texas. He remained angry for several years with Price Daniel, who, as Texas attorney general, had supported Eisenhower in 1952; yet he privately told Mrs. Price Daniel, "I have gotten after old Price a lot about supporting Eisenhower. I know why he did it. If I had been Attorney General of Texas, I would have done the same thing."[36] Publicly, however, he had to castigate those disloyal to the party.

Rayburn's pragmatism, however, is indicated by his behavior in 1956. Rayburn and the loyalists of 1952 were joined by Lyndon Johnson in a fight against Shivers for control of the party in Texas. In 1956 Johnson was in a leadership role in the Senate, had four more years before running for reelection, had won a strong victory in 1954, and had presidential ambitions. Shivers, on the other hand, was retiring from office with his administration shaken by scandal. It was a propitious time for Johnson to make a move for leadership of the Texas Democratic party.[37]

The fight for control of the party ended with a defeat for Shivers and a victory for the Johnson-Rayburn-loyalist alliance. It was a victory that soon turned sour for many loyalists, who promptly found that Johnson and Rayburn joined with Price Daniel, who had supported Eisenhower in 1952, and other Texas conservatives to keep liberal loyalists from power in the party.[38] It was neither Johnson's nor Rayburn's finest moment. The bitterness of the liberals over the "big steal" of the September 1956 state convention by Johnson, Rayburn, and Daniel was to last for years.[39]

At the May convention, Johnson and Rayburn should have been savoring their victory over the Shivercrats; instead they were having second thoughts about their partners in the overthrow. The liberal-loyalist wing of the party was proving troublesome. They refused to be dominated by the senator and the Speaker. Johnson, for example, proposed Mrs. Lloyd Bentsen as the Democratic national committeewoman. In this move he was opposed by the liberal-loyalists, who favored Mrs. R. D. Randolph, one of the state's most influential liberal leaders. Johnson was unable to control the convention, and Mrs. Randolph was elected committeewoman. The liberals wished to reconstitute the party along liberal lines. Johnson and Rayburn viewed the liberals as extreme leftists who would frustrate not only their goal of party control but their goal of a broad, moderate coalition.[40]

After the May convention Johnson was disgusted with the liberals and approached his Senate colleague Price Daniel, who had just received the Democratic nomination for the governorship in a close race against liberal-loyalist Ralph Yarborough.[41] Daniel was a conservative with many of the same financial backers and supporters as Shivers, though he and Shivers had never been personally close.[42] Johnson had developed a good relationship with Daniel during Daniel's brief service in the Senate.[43] He suggested to Daniel that an alliance be formed among Johnson, Rayburn, and Daniel to control the state Democratic party. Daniel was faced with a revolt of the powerful liberal-loyalist forces, who felt the election had been stolen from Yarborough.[44] As a result, Daniel would have been unable to control the party without the alliance, so he was agreeable.

Rayburn, on the other hand, was uncomfortable about joining with Daniel, for he was still unhappy about his disloyalty in 1952.[45] Daniel had split with the party primarily over the tidelands issue, however, and that issue had for the most part been settled with Eisenhower's support for federal quit-claim legislation. Daniel expressed a willingness to support the Democratic nominee.[46] Rayburn argued that Daniel should wholeheartedly endorse Stevenson at the September state convention,[47] but Daniel chose to wait until afterward. Believing that Daniel would be loyal in 1956, Rayburn agreed to the alliance, and the three worked together to decide key credentials disputes against the liberal-loyalists. Johnson and Daniel were the key figures in the fight. Rayburn only controlled the Fannin County delegation, but he had supporters in other delegations throughout the state. The alliance crushed the liberal-loyalists who had seemed so much in control of the May convention.[48]

Rayburn personally disliked some of those liberal-loyalists, mainly because he believed them lacking in the pragmatism necessary for success in Texas politics. But Rayburn did not share Johnson's burning hatred of the liberals, nor was he hated by liberals as they hated Johnson.[49] For Rayburn, the removal of the liberal-loyalists from power was a cold, calculated political decision. He concluded that they were losers, that they would not be victorious in Texas politics, and he sided with the winners, in the alliance with Johnson and the Daniel forces. If the Democratic party were purged of the conservatives, Rayburn foresaw that they would align with the Republicans to create a winning party. The liberals, on the other hand, had no place to go. Rayburn believed they would remain in the Democratic party with or without power. In this assumption, Rayburn eventually was to be proved wrong. The liberals did have somewhere to go. That was to stay home when Democratic nominees were too conservative for their tastes. That liberal inactivity, for example, led to the election of Republican John Tower to the U.S. Senate in 1966 over his conservative Democratic challenger Waggoner Carr.[50]

The alignment did allow Johnson, Daniel, and Rayburn to control the state Democratic party. Inasmuch as Daniel's Democratic party loyalty was the price for joining with Johnson and Rayburn, the result was a loss of power as well by conservative Democrats who wanted the party to be pro-Eisenhower. The alignment did keep many conservative Democrats in the party, however. Because a leadership role for Rayburn in the state was assured by the alignment, he was able to protect his district from reapportionment efforts. Finally, matters in Texas were kept under control as Rayburn and Johnson worked their will in Washington. As Rayburn explained his behavior to W. G. Hall:

> The only man up here that I know of that is in the unique position where he can be effective both on a state level and a national level is Harry Byrd of Virginia. He runs Virginia. He can do what he pleases here or there, but the rest of us have to look at our congressional district or our states as a base of operation in order to perform on a national level. We can't be having too many frictions back home or be spending too much time putting out fires back home. We have to feel that we are safe back there in order to be effective in Washington. Therefore we try to keep safe back home and not have effective factions develop that we have to contend with.[51]

Civil Rights

As Speaker, Rayburn had to consider the interests of the national party as well as those of his district. It is probable that the conflict between national and district roles was never greater than in reference to racial equality. As World War II ended, it became increasingly clear that black political power, especially in the northern cities, could be an important political asset for the Democratic party if it could be harnessed through the party's support of civil rights legislation. The effort to achieve racial equality, however, met with enormous opposition in the Fourth Congressional District, a district that shared the racial values of the Old Confederacy.

Whereas Rayburn's constituents' values might incline him to depart from the national party on this issue, as Speaker he had to try to remain within the party mainstream. Often he could work quietly behind the scenes protecting his local interests while at the same time functioning in his national leadership role, but he had always to be prepared for open conflict between his two roles. When conflict arose, Rayburn, like any political actor, tended to protect his reelection interests, as he did with Truman's civil rights program.

Initially Rayburn tried to handle this role conflict by adopting a policy of silence, saying as little as possible about the civil rights program. When Truman proposed his legislation, Rayburn quietly worked to keep his state delegation from joining the general southern chorus criticizing Truman. It was only after the 1948 Morris threat became severe that he openly criticized the Truman program. By 1948 civil rights may well have been the only issue that could have meant political destruction for him.

In 1956 and again in 1957, however, Rayburn quietly offered help to the liberal Democratic leaders who were attempting to pass a civil rights act. But again in the late 1950s he almost was forced to oppose the civil rights bill openly. Drew Pearson discovered his behind-the-scenes work in favor of the bill that ultimately emerged as the 1957 Voting Rights Act. As Richard Bolling recalled, Rayburn stated in private that he did not object to the Counter Southern Manifesto, which was prepared by McCarthy's Marauders, later to become the Democratic Study Group. The Counter Southern Manifesto included a voting rights act. Drew Pearson learned of Rayburn's statement and was about to publish a column about Rayburn's support for civil rights. Bolling learned of the forthcoming column and told Pearson, "I'm going to ask a newspaper man something I have never asked before. I'm going to ask him to suppress a fact." Knowing Pearson was pro–civil rights, Bolling told him that his information was accurate, but "if you run this God damn column, Rayburn's going to have to deny the position because those people in his district are not going to be for that." Pearson did not publish the column, and Rayburn did aid in passing the House civil rights bill in 1956 and the act in 1957. Bolling noted that neither could have been passed without Rayburn's help. "Rayburn," he said, "was educating me as we went along into some of the tricks that would be pulled to try to defeat us."[52]

The 1957 act was weak in results. It applied only to voting. The bill created a civil rights division in the Department of Justice and also the Civil Rights Commission. Most important, it created an equitable remedy for attempted deprivation of voting rights: the federal government could bring civil actions for injunctive relief where discrimination denied or threatened to deny the right to vote. Between 1957 and 1960, however, only three cases were filed under the act, and they moved slowly through the legal process. One explanation for the act's weakness was lax enforcement, due in part to the lack of manpower committed to enforce the act's provisions. Another explanation was that the defendant in a criminal contempt proceeding arising from the violation of a federal voting rights injunction could demand a jury trial unless the fine was three hundred dollars or less or the jail sentence was forty-five days or less; it was widely believed that southern juries would not vote for conviction. As a result, the act could provide little more than a slap on the wrist to violators.[53]

The House-passed bill was a more stern version than the Senate version of the legislation that was to become the 1957 act. It was southern senators who greatly weakened the bill by using the threat of a filibuster, which could have killed the chance for any bill. One can argue that Rayburn did little for civil rights in supporting such a bill, yet it must also be stressed that it was the first civil rights act in eighty-two years. It was also a law that could have easily been defeated in the House Rules Committee if Rayburn had not chosen to support it.[54]

Carl Albert recalled civil rights as a cause of conflict between Rayburn's role as a district representative and his role as Speaker. Albert characterized Rayburn as "sensitive to the pressures of his district" and civil rights as an issue about which he was particularly sensitive. He had received considerable criticism from his district for being too favorable to civil rights, and Albert thought it was criticism that bothered him. On one occasion when a civil rights bill was being considered, Albert said:

> [Rayburn] made up his mind that we had to go with civil rights—that the time was past due. He really had a feeling. He told me . . . "We've got to support that bill." I said, "Well, it's certainly going to help the party." He said, "It will not just help the party. These people are entitled to this. . . ." Well, Mr. Rayburn knew me. He knew that my district was a whole lot like his. In fact, probably a third of the people in this [Albert's] district grew up or were sons and daughters of people in his district. He

knew my district. . . . He said, "We've got to have John McCormack back here. . . ." It [civil rights] was no problem in his
[McCormack's] district.

As a result, Rayburn contacted McCormack and asked him to
return from a trip he had taken with his wife because he was a
member of the leadership who could take an open pro–
civil rights position without concern for the response from
his district.[55]

The Oil Depletion Allowance

Sam Rayburn was known as one of the strongest House supporters of the oil depletion allowance. One of the most controversial of all tax provisions, the allowance was a boon to oil
men. In essence, it provided oil producers with 27½ percent of
their income tax free. So strongly was Rayburn in favor of the
allowance that it was said he would hold interviews with prospective members of the Ways and Means Committee so he
could stress the importance of maintaining the allowance and assure himself that prospective members supported it.[56] Only if a
majority of the committee supported the allowance could it be
prevented from coming up for a vote on the floor of the House.
As Rayburn said, "Let it out of committee and they'd cut it to
fifteen, ten, five percent—maybe take it away altogether. Do
you think you could convince a Detroit factory worker that the
depletion allowance is a good thing? Once it got on the floor, it
would be cut to ribbons."[57] Along with Lyndon Johnson in the
Senate, Rayburn diligently protected the allowance.[58]

Johnson's support is readily explainable. It was a provision
that greatly benefited Texas and Texans. Johnson, after all, was
Texas's senator and a politician who recognized that oil men
would show their appreciation for his efforts by providing campaign support. Rayburn's support is less easily explained. The
Fourth Congressional District was not an oil district; only Grayson County had any significant production. Some of his friends
have suggested that Rayburn supported the allowance because it
benefited Texas.[59] He never apologized for his support.[60]
Since early in the century oil has played a major role in Texas

and Texas politics, so much so that in 1947 the chairman of the Democratic State Executive Committee, Robert W. Calvert, said, "It may not be a wholesome thing to say, but the oil industry today is in complete control of the state government and state politics."[61] Since the 1901 Spindletop oil strike, Texas has been the center of domestic oil production. At the time of Rayburn's death, Texas produced thirty-eight percent of the country's oil and had about half of the country's oil reserves. Of the state's 254 counties, 195 produced oil from nearly two hundred thousand wells. One out of eleven Texas workers was employed by the oil business. That translated into 225,000 jobs. Oil paid more than twenty-five percent of the state's taxes.[62] Rayburn could become quite angry with congressional friends such as Henry Jackson who were critical of the allowance. Mr. Sam insisted that it was necessary to protect the independent oil producer and that it stimulated the exploration necessary to maintain high petroleum production.[63]

Support for the allowance also had political advantages for Rayburn. He used it as a weapon against oil men, threatening its loss if they did not remain in the Democratic column.[64] Rayburn as Speaker was also closely associated with Roosevelt, Truman, and Stevenson. These men and the policies they espoused were anathemas to a considerable number of conservative oil men, who were of course unhappy with Rayburn because of his national Democratic leanings. With such men, support for the oil depletion allowance bought him flexibility. He might campaign for liberal Democratic presidential nominees and function as a national Democratic leader, but he also protected the interests of oil and did so very effectively. Many conservative oil men, well aware of the benefits of the depletion allowance and Rayburn's efforts on their behalf, were thus willing to forgive Rayburn for his liberalism.

It is important to keep in mind that oil men in Texas are not of one ideology. Some, like J. R. Parten, are national Democrats and civil libertarians. Others, such as E. B. Germany, were Texas Regulars and ultraconservatives. Political conservatism has, however, been particularly prevalent among Texas oil men. Some hated Rayburn for his liberalism enough to ignore his work in behalf of oil's interests, but a large number of even the most conservative were inclined to be friendly toward Rayburn.

Oil money did regularly appear in the hands of Rayburn's opposition, but it came from the extremists. On the whole, Rayburn
was safe from an avalanche of oil money funding his opposition.

Even in the 1944 campaign, one of his toughest, against an
opponent who was talented and well funded, Rayburn maintained the support of influential and wealthy Texans. James
Elkins of Houston was one of the major behind-the-scenes oper-
ators in Texas politics. He was very conservative, anti–New
Deal, and a lawyer with far-flung banking and oil interests.
Elkins was a member of the "8-F Crowd," a group of million-
aires that wielded enormous political power in Texas in the
1940s and 1950s. This group met regularly for cards and political
discussions in Herman Brown's hotel room, numbered 8-F, in
Houston's Lamar Hotel. Members included Brown and Root's
George and Herman Brown and builder, publisher, banker, and
political operator Jesse Jones, a leading force in the creation of
Texas Commerce Bancshares and Tenneco. Gus Wortham, the
founder of the largest insurance company in the South, was a
regular, as were railroad millionaire William Smith, retailer Leo-
pold Meyer, and oil man James Abercrombie, a close friend of
Mr. Sam's.[65] Rayburn was assured that Elkins was working to
keep the Establishment behind him. In late 1943 Rayburn received a letter stating: "You will remember the little conversation we had several months ago one night at Lyndon Johnson's
home in Washington. My old friend Jim Elkins, of Houston,
told me recently that he sincerely hoped you would have no opposition in your District next year, and that he would do everything possible to keep down any that might show up."[66]

Rayburn's support for oil also provided protection for his district. He never faced any coordinated effort by oil men to redistrict him. His support for the allowance was probably also appreciated by Texas legislators who would ordinarily be
unfriendly toward national Democrats and perhaps inclined to
tamper with their district.

Support for the allowance must also have inclined many oil
men toward providing financial help to Rayburn, but he was
not a man who cared about accumulating wealth. Had he been
interested, his close association with oil men such as James
Abercrombie and Sid Richardson, who were among the world's
richest people, would have provided opportunities for very re-

warding investments. Rayburn's district, his campaign style, and his organization were such that campaign money was largely unnecessary, and most of what he did spend came from his own pocket or from the district.

Rayburn did, however, obtain substantial contributions from oil men and other wealthy individuals to support the Democratic party and Democratic candidates.[67] Dugger, for example, noted that Rayburn and Johnson were working as early as 1940 to collect money for Democratic candidates for the House. They were said to have collected sixty thousand dollars, though there are also reports of donations from Richardson alone amounting to one hundred thousand. Richardson claimed he was a "big factor in raising $70,000" for Democrats. Johnson in that year, raising money for Democratic congressional campaigns, was hard at work getting Texans to donate money, and Rayburn was active in Dallas in soliciting funds.[68] Such fund-raising efforts aided in gaining the Democrats six seats in the 1940 House elections. Rayburn was also called upon by Johnson in 1948 to get Abercrombie active in the Johnson Senate campaign against Coke Stevenson. Abercrombie, known to have sold his oil properties for $450 million,[69] was known as Rayburn's friend and as a major contributor to the Democratic party.[70] Such contacts and money raising abilities must have enhanced Rayburn's influence in the party; yet there were times when Rayburn was angry with many of the oil men because he believed his work in behalf of oil had not been adequately appreciated and because he believed the Democratic party had done more for oil than oil had done for the party.[71]

Rayburn also sent substantial cash contributions to congressmen who were having election difficulties and whom he thought should be returned to Congress. Little has noted that in gratitude for protecting oil's interests, Rayburn received money from oil.[72] He has also noted that on one occasion Rayburn privately distributed amounts of 250 to 500 dollars to twenty-five Congressmen.[73] On October 6, 1960, in time for use before the November election, Rayburn mailed cash to several Democratic congressional candidates who were experiencing reelection difficulties. The source of these moneys is unknown, but given Rayburn's contacts and Little's findings, it seems likely that the money came from oil men.[74]

Thus, support for the oil depletion allowance was of enormous political value to Rayburn. His power as Speaker was recognized as important for the maintenance of the allowance. Those with more conservative views were generally willing to accept his New Deal tendencies because he could protect the interests of oil as long as he remained in a leadership role.

The Washington Rayburn and the Bonham Rayburn

Rayburn was far more relaxed, informal, and unpressured in the district than in Washington. These are the primary differences between the Bonham Rayburn and the Washington Rayburn. There are also several significant similarities in the behavior of Rayburn in his two environments, one of the greatest being his use of intelligence networks. Just as he relied on a vast number of contacts with friends and associates as well as published news to gain information about virtually anything of political relevance in his district and used this knowledge to build support through personal relationships with constituents, Rayburn used a similar intelligence network in the House. According to Frank Ikard, a former Texas congressman who was one of his closest friends:

> He [Rayburn] and Lyndon Johnson had the two best intelligence systems that have ever been devised by the human mind. If somebody was having trouble, of whatever kind, Rayburn knew about it. . . . [The Board of Education] was part of the intelligence network. It was not all of it. He had staff people, for example. Also, he wandered around. He knew more people in the House and more staff people than you can imagine. He picked up little bits of information. That was how he gathered intelligence. It wasn't because he was trying to snoop on people. Instead, he did it because he was genuinely interested. That is the reason his intelligence was so good. People knew he was interested in what was going on.[75]

The Washington network provided him with information in much the same way as the Bonham network. He knew if members were having political problems, if they desperately needed a dam or a federal courthouse in their districts, or if they were having personal or domestic problems.

In Washington as in Bonham, the intelligence network was central to Rayburn's political power. In both places his power was based on a very personal approach rather than on some formal structure, ideology, or issue positions, and information was necessary with which to build his personal ties with both members and constituents. Rayburn had to show that he cared enough to know about important events in people's lives, to offer aid, congratulations, or condolences when necessary. He also had to know when an offer of help on a project, whether it be for a farm-to-market road back home or a post office appropriation for a member, would be appropriate to build political support for himself in future years.

The foundation of his power in both Washington and Bonham was his ability to use information networks to build personal loyalties. Loyalty to Sam Rayburn was a characteristic of his leadership in the House and in the district. That loyalty was based on admiration for Rayburn as a person, for his character, his integrity, his lack of vindictiveness, and his ability. It was also loyalty based on his ability to do favors.[76] He could place a member on select committees that might be important to that member, arrange for White House invitations for a member, provide campaign funds, aid in getting legislation passed, and perhaps most important, aid a member in getting a good committee assignment. With constituents he was very successful both in negotiating in their behalf with the bureaucracy and in obtaining projects for the district. Constituents who were his leaders or most active supporters could also rely on Rayburn for such special favors as political appointments, special access to important officials, and delegate positions at national conventions. Friendship is often a complex blend of affection, respect, and favors or the potential for future favors.[77] Many such friendships made up the Rayburn organization in the district and made Rayburn the powerful Speaker of the House of Representatives.

Another important aspect of the Rayburn style found in Washington as well as Bonham was his skill in cultivating the support of younger generations. It is important in explaining his quarter of a century of political leadership in the House as well as his political longevity in the district. His recruiting of young leaders, thus keeping his organization multigenerational, with the younger gradually replacing the older, insured him against the danger of being an elderly leader with a following decimated by old age. Cultivation of the younger generation also limited the possibility that an ambitious youngster could challenge an old man no longer in touch with modern realities.[78] Carl Albert recalled that Rayburn had been very worried about the challenge from Morris in 1948 but told him he had been able to overwhelm Morris because "the young people came to my rescue. I had the support of young people better than anytime since I was a young man myself."[79]

Likewise in the House, while being careful to retain the friendship of the politicians of his generation, such as Hatton Sumners, Marvin Jones, and Carl Vinson, he was also open to developing strong personal bonds with younger members. At times there was even competition and jealousy over which of Sam Rayburn's "boys" was his favorite.[80] His network of youthful protégés reads like a who's who of major political figures, for example, Lyndon Johnson, Hale Boggs, Carl Albert, Henry Jackson, Frank Ikard, Wilbur Mills, Homer Thornberry, and Richard Bolling. Rayburn became their close personal friend and aided their careers; they became his arms, his eyes, and his ears in the conduct of House business. They were ambitious men and very able, but rather than being rivals for his power from another generation, they were solidly in the Rayburn camp.

According to Bolling, it was a southern practice for older congressmen to be the mentors of younger ones.[81] Rayburn, for example, had once been the protégé of Bailey. Rayburn benefited from Bailey's support and advice, while Bailey used Rayburn as an important lieutenant in Texas politics. When Rayburn was Speaker of the Texas House, for example, Bailey had great influence over who benefited from the patronage associated with Rayburn's position.[82] When Rayburn served in Congress, a mentor–protégé relationship existed with Garner.[83] Rayburn continued such relationships through the years, but age, power, and experience transformed his role from protégé to mentor.

Rayburn was also inclined both in his position as Speaker and in Bonham to avoid alienating the opposition. His view was that, as an opponent on one issue could become a friend on another, it was wise to avoid vindictiveness and efforts to punish enemies. It was a lesson Rayburn claimed to have learned from Joe Bailey, who was known for his vindictiveness. Bailey once wrote young Sam that he wished to return to Texas so that he could "smite his enemies hip and thigh,"[84] but he also advised the young congressman not to "make the mistake of thinking that just because someone is on the other side of a political matter that he is a son of a bitch. Likely as not, you will discover that he ain't."[85]

Rayburn's interest in cultivating friendly relationships with opponents is evident in the close personal relationship he developed with the fiery, ultraconservative southern coalition leader Eugene Cox. Rayburn skillfully cultivated this personal relationship and could often use it to cause Cox to release a bill from the Rules Committee, where he served for years and had great influence.[86] Similarly Rayburn was able to establish a strong personal bond with Joe Martin, the Republican leader, which led to considerable cooperation with the Republican side.[87] The Speaker had a way of avoiding turning political disagreements into long-term personal conflicts. The widely publicized battle between Howard Smith and Rayburn over the Rules Committee in 1961, for example, has been treated as a personal battle between two congressional powers, but the personal tensions have been greatly exaggerated.[88] One of Rayburn's secretaries, loyal like all the staff, recalled times during disagreements between Rayburn and Smith when she felt like "throw[ing] Howard Smith out of the window." Yet, when it seemed their disagreements were in their most bitter state, "the first thing you would know, here they would come in together, Mr. Rayburn and Howard Smith as if nothing ever happened."[89]

Rayburn kept Omar Burleson from obtaining a seat on the Ways and Means Committee, explaining that although they agreed on the oil depletion allowance, Burleson was too conservative for the committee. Burleson very much wanted the assignment, but because the denial was not personal, he and Rayburn continued to fish and eat out together.[90] The friendship with Joe Kilgore was another that remained firm even though on one occasion Rayburn found it necessary to deny Kilgore a seat on the Democratic National Committee because he had voted for Eisenhower in 1952.[91]

In the district, Rayburn evidenced similar behavior. His leaders and friends frequently described him as not vindictive and as one who did not exacerbate troubles or expand political difficulties. As a result, Rayburn's former Democratic primary opponent Morrison became his supporter, and one of Morrison's supporters, Bob Dunn, even became one of Rayburn's leaders in Denison.[92] In Hunt County, a politically ambitious Morris supporter switched to supporting Rayburn in later elections and became a leader.[93] A Morris supporter in Point in 1944 became a Rayburn supporter in 1948 owing to the kindness Rayburn displayed toward him during a visit he and his family made to Washington.[94] Such illustrations show that the Bonham Rayburn, like the Washington Rayburn, acted to build rather than alienate support.

Both the Bonham and the Washington Rayburn did business through trusted friends. Just as in Bonham Rayburn relied heavily on his organization, especially his campaign managers, to promote his interests and make up his intelligence network, in Washington he also used friends to accomplish his purposes. He told Cecil Dickson that he tried to have at least two friends on every major committee who would represent his interests and keep him informed of the committee's activities.[95] Those friends included John Lyle and Homer Thornberry. Rayburn moved Lyle from the Post Office and Civil Service Committee to the Rules Committee, where Lyle was recognized as having special access to Rayburn and was treated as his representative. He was frequently approached by the committee members with requests for help in negotiating with Rayburn. Rayburn, in turn, relied on Lyle to present his views to the committee members.[96] A few years later Rayburn moved Thornberry from the Interstate and Foreign Commerce Committee to the Rules Committee to perform the same function.[97]

Frank Ikard was one of Rayburn's representatives on the Ways and Means Committee, where he was recognized as having especially strong ties to the Speaker. Ikard's rise to Ways and Means and to power in the House was indeed rapid. He moved ahead of fellow Texan O. C. Fisher, who wanted a place on the committee. Fisher was far more senior than Ikard but lacked friendship and the willingness to work closely with Rayburn.[98] Ikard served as Rayburn's primary Ways and Means contact. In those days the Democratic members of Ways and Means functioned as the Democratic Committee on Committees. When committee assignments were being made, Ikard met daily with Rayburn. In this way, contact between the committee and the Speaker was maintained, and Rayburn's wishes were made known to committee members.[99]

Fenno has speculated that there may be a linkage between the methods of operation for congressmen at home and in Washington, and in Rayburn's case there clearly is.[100] The Fourth Congressional District created the pattern of behavior that proved successful not only for the district-level politician but for the Speaker of the House of Representatives.

6. Conclusion

Leadership and Political Longevity

SAM RAYBURN HAS BEEN DESCRIBED AS A HOUSE insider concerned with legislative specialization, substantive expertise, procedural manipulation, and party leadership.[1] Insiders usually stand in contrast to legislators who try to reflect the needs or wishes of particular constituencies. Rayburn, though he was the great legislator and party leader, saw himself as the representative of a constituency.[2] He tried not to let constituency pressures dominate his behavior, but his constituency occupied a very crucial place in his concerns.

Rayburn had no respect for the congressman who was afraid of his district, the congressman who was overly fearful of defeat and always trying to determine if his vote was politically acceptable to the district.[3] He did respect congressmen who recognized that, above all else, they needed to take care of the electorate who put them in office. Rayburn advised new congressmen to "go along to get along," meaning that freshmen should try to cooperate and vote with the leadership in order to have effectiveness in the House,[4] but that was not all. He also told them to "take care of your constituency," for the basis of political power in the House is usually a secure political base at home, which must be constructed by the House member.[5] His combination of the extreme House insider and representative roles is striking. Davidson has noted that there are congressmen who combine elements of both roles,[6] but the Rayburn combination is most unusual.

Rayburn's secure political base in the district was the result of three things—the political stability and security of the Fourth District, the Rayburn organization, and the Rayburn style—all interrelated. The stability and security of the district encouraged the growth of a strong Rayburn organization. The highly personal Rayburn style could best thrive in a small district where long-term friendships and alliances were common. The Rayburn style was also useful in creating his organization. The district was a compact size for a rural Texas district, and it had a small population of less than one-quarter million.[7] That smallness made possible the organization that emphasized friends-and-neighbors politics rather than high budget campaigns with extensive media use.[8] The voters knew and trusted Rayburn and voted for him, or they knew his family and so voted for Rayburn, or they knew and trusted a Rayburn organization member and so voted for him.

The Fourth District was throughout Rayburn's career a kind of political anachronism, with its small-town life style that provided a sense of community so central to Rayburn's political longevity. Wiebe, in writing about the United States in the late nineteenth century, captured much that was true of the Fourth District in the first six decades of the twentieth century. Society could be thought of as numbers of individuals. "Year after year townspeople watched each other labor and idle, save and spend, help and cheat, attend church and frequent saloons."[9] People were known, or "people at least thought they knew all about each other after crossing and recrossing paths over the years."[10] In such a district, when Rayburn appointed someone as postmaster or helped a veteran get a pension or got funding for a lake, that too became known to the members of the community. Rayburn was, in a sense, the Fourth District's tie to the outside world. He was not an outsider. He reflected the common sense of rural America, yet he could contest with forces outside the Fourth District and win. The enemies were the railroads, the Wall Street bankers, the utility holding companies, and the city slickers. He could defeat them and improve the lives of his primary core of supporters, the black-land small farmers and the small businessmen dependent on agricultural prosperity.

In the Fourth District, as in Wiebe's late-nineteenth-century America, small-town power was "an eminently human network of relations,"[11] and Rayburn's highly personal style made him adept at its management. There were social divisions not obvious to outsiders, as Wiebe has noted. At the apex of community society were the influentials who controlled wealth or access to it. These persons were known and respected because of their wealth, position, family name, or personality. Such people were not merely called by their first names; like Rayburn, they were called "Mister" Sam or "Mister" Tom or "Major" Jim.[12] These were the core of the Rayburn political organization.

It is noteworthy that a congressman from a rural, rather isolated district was primarily responsible for trying to hold together the loose congressional coalition first formed by Franklin Roosevelt's election in 1932.[13] That coalition included urban and rural interests, labor and capital, northerners and southerners, racists and minorities. Perhaps only Rayburn could have been so successful in building requisite legislative coalitions from such diverse interests.[14] His skill was premised on the political flexibility his district gave him. He was usually free of any demand that he account for his legislative actions, so he could maneuver to achieve the political compromises needed to accomplish a legislative objective. The district was an ideal environment for his constituency orientation that won for him the flexibility necessary to build legislative majorities in the post-1932 Democratic party.

Davidson and Oleszek have suggested that constituency service may be used by a congressman to gain breathing room to take legislative stands that differ from district norms.[15] Rayburn developed such a strong and successful constituency orientation that he could win elections by stressing style, personality, and constituency service rather than controversial political issues. Without those election victories, Rayburn could not have gained the necessary seniority for leadership in the Congress. Once he did gain leadership positions, especially the Speakership, he continued to stress his constituency orientation in order to function well in the leadership. His Fourth District constituency had to be kept satisfied to provide the flexibility to lead the congressional constituency that elected him Speaker. That congressional constituency was so diverse that Rayburn needed to maneuver to find the middle ground necessary for congressional policy making. That was a tedious effort that required him to delay committing himself on some issues, conduct negotiations rather than take public stands on others, and even take stands unpopular in the district on some issues.[16]

Richard Bolling, for example, recalled a situation in which Rayburn was subject to a barrage of criticism for delaying referral of a labor union reform bill to committee. In spite of the outcry Rayburn delayed for six weeks until the committee reported out a pension management bill. The public clamor for rapid referral bothered Rayburn little. As Speaker he considered it necessary to delay referral because immediate referral would block action on the pension reform bill.[17] He could take such a stand, in spite of public outcry, because he had a secure base of support in the district anchored not by issue positions but by his constituency orientation. Thus, he could maneuver on issues in Washington without fearing political reprisals at home.

Similarly, Rayburn opposed the Taft-Hartley Act and the Landrum-Griffin Act even though they would probably have been popular antilabor laws in his district. The South, for example, was solidly in favor of Taft-Hartley. Rayburn was the exception. As the *New York Times* reported, Rayburn was in the forefront of opposition to Taft-Hartley because his position as Democratic leader gave him a special responsibility to present the party position.[18] It was a task requiring a district that granted its congressman great issue flexibility even on major issues. In opposing Landrum-Griffin, Rayburn was joined by only four of the twenty other Texas congressmen, yet on this issue, too, he could safely reflect the party position and remain secure in his district.[19]

Only on civil rights did the district refuse to allow Rayburn much issue flexibility. Given his experience in the 1948 campaign, it appears that civil rights was the one issue that could have resulted in his defeat in the latter stages of his career. District feelings on the racial question were strong enough to preclude an overtly pro–civil rights position, yet even on this issue, it was unnecessary for Rayburn to engage in shrill attacks on the Democratic administration as did so many of his southern colleagues.[20] He could satisfy the voters' concerns by quietly reaffirming his beliefs in southern racial values and his long-standing opposition to civil rights.

The Old Politics

Just as the Fourth District was a microcosm of rural nineteenth-century America, Rayburn was a product of the nineteenth century. His personal political style was old fashioned, and he realized he was among the last of the politicians who could successfully rely on personal contact with constituents, friendship, honor, and mutual trust between voters and politician. Halberstam has noted that Rayburn detested the new, big-money, media-oriented politics.[21] Much has been lost in politics since Rayburn's day, but the biggest loss has been a politics of intimacy between candidate and voter. Now it is increasingly difficult for a congressman even to remain in touch with constituents.

For one thing, it is becoming more difficult to find constituents. Rayburn could attract groups of several hundred and even several thousand to political rallies, for politics was then a form of recreation, the television of the pretelevision era. Politics is no longer viewed as a pleasant diversion. A busier life style and distractions such as television make audiences more difficult to attract. Rayburn could always be assured of a good crowd on the town square or near the courthouse, especially on Saturday, traditionally the day farmers came to town to shop. Today's congressmen must contend with decentralized shopping and the anomie of urban and suburban life, both of which make it hard to gather a crowd.[22]

Rayburn knew many of the people in the district or at least their families. Rural and small-town life makes it easy to know people, their relations, their beliefs, and their problems. Anonymity in such an environment must be obtained with a considerable effort. The breakup of the extended family, not to mention the nuclear family, increased mobility, and the growth of cities and suburbs have made anonymity more the norm than the exception today. It is increasingly difficult for a politician to know and be known.

The Rayburn era was also, as Bolling has pointed out, a time when people, especially congressmen, had more time.[23] Rayburn could stay in touch with constituents even though he might only visit the district a few times a year. Congressional sessions were generally of less than a year's duration. Rayburn's associates recall that he often was in the district for several months. The length of congressional sessions increased dramatically of course with the coming of World War II, but for much of his congressional career, Rayburn had months to be in Bonham, visiting with constituents, getting to know, and becoming known.[24] That huge allotment of time for political activities is unknown to the contemporary congressman, who has year-long sessions and only recesses and weekends for district contacts. Even dozens of weekend trips home cannot substitute for months of uninterrupted political effort.

Rayburn also had the enormous political advantage of serving the same population over the length of his career. Since the Supreme Court's reapportionment decisions of the 1960s, congressmen are virtually certain to have district boundaries redrawn at least every decade, making it more difficult to maintain constituent contact as boundary changes remove old constituents and add new ones. Rayburn also benefited from malapportionment in that his district had a very small population. Personal contact with constituents is much easier in a district of less than one-quarter million than in a district that reflects the Court's one person–one vote doctrine. A modern congressman trying to establish personal contacts faces a district with twice the population of Rayburn's.

The Rayburn organization so crucial to his political longevity also grew from the continuity and stability of the old politics. The contemporary congressman has a much harder time building and maintaining an organization with today's high mobility. Organization leaders are more likely to move out of the district, and in-migration makes community leadership unsettled. Mobility also makes it unlikely that leadership will be easily transferred from one generation to another. Nor can the modern organization provide the effective intelligence network it did in Rayburn's day. As population increases, so does lack of knowledge of the kind of events that can be used to political advantage. This lack of knowledge is due to the anonymity of life where there are population concentrations and to such factors as the tendency of larger papers and radio stations to avoid the publication or broadcasting of hospital stays, illnesses, births, and much of the chit-chat found in weeklies, small-town dailies, and small-town radio broadcasts. The contemporary congressman might have more and larger radio and television stations and larger newspapers than Rayburn, yet less intelligence useful to the maintenance of constituent relations.

Of course it is not impossible for a contemporary congressman to have the political longevity of Rayburn, though his years of service are rarely matched in American congressional history. Nor is it impossible for a politician with a Rayburn method of operation to be victorious in a contemporary congressional election, but the personal relationships he maintained with constituents would be much more difficult for a congressman to achieve today. The tools of modern campaigns—professional public relations and television—by their very nature reduce the personal interaction that to Rayburn was the essence of representation. Today's congressman is likely to be a far more distant, prepackaged personality engaged in a one-sided media-based conversation with the constituency.

Home to Die

Sam Rayburn returned to Bonham to die, as he said, among "those friends and neighbors who for so long have given me a love and loyalty unsurpassed in any annals."[25] There, he granted his last interview to W. B. Ragsdale, a reporter from *U.S. News and World Report* and an old friend from the days of John Nance Garner and Nicholas Longworth's Board of Education meetings (where Garner would "strike a blow for liberty" by serving whiskey to those in attendance). Ragsdale recalled that Garner had then expressed his appreciation for Rayburn as one who stayed "hitched." On Ragsdale's first visit he found Rayburn too weak to be interviewed and had to return for a second visit. By that time, Rayburn's pain was very severe, and his physical appearance showed it. As Ragsdale waited to interview Rayburn, Mr. Sam received several constituents, each of whom he treated as "a friend, neighbor, advisor on all kinds of affairs." He also answered phone calls: one from the Republican leader, Charles Halleck, who wished him well; one from an elderly woman who wanted advice about the upbringing of her grandson; one from a man being ordered into active military service; and another from a House committee chairman seeking advice on a legislative matter.[26] On November 16, 1961 Sam Rayburn died, the Fourth District congressman to the last.

Appendices
Notes
Index

Appendix A

List of Persons Interviewed

Name	Relationship with Rayburn
1. Carl Albert	Congressman
2. Robert Allen	Political reporter
3. Vernon Beckham	Rayburn leader in Denison
4. Lindley Beckworth	Congressman
5. Lloyd Bentsen	Congressman
6. Lindy Boggs	Friend
7. Richard Bolling	Congressman
8. Roland Boyd	Rayburn leader in north Collin County
9. John Brademus	Congressman
10. Robert Bradshaw	Staff member
11. Omar Burleson	Congressman
12. Elizabeth Carpenter	Political reporter
13. E. B. Chapman	Rayburn leader in Grayson County
14. Buster Cole	Rayburn leader in Fannin County
15. Fred Conn	Rayburn leader in Denison and publisher of the *Denison Herald*
16. Price Daniel	Texas attorney general, senator, and governor
17. Cecil Dickson	Political reporter
18. H. G. Dulaney	Staff member
19. Martha Dye	Rayburn's niece
20. Clarence Elkins	Friend
21. Kate Estes	Friend
22. J. W. Fulbright	Congressman and senator
23. Ed Gossett	Congressman
24. Levis Hall	Rayburn leader in Grayson County
25. W. G. Hall	Texas Democratic party leader
26. Paul Hardin	McKinney civic leader
27. G. C. Harris	Rayburn leader in Hunt County
28. John Holton	Staff member
29. Sarah Hughes	Judge
30. Frank Ikard	Congressman
31. Dan Inglish	Staff member
32. Henry Jackson	Congressman and senator
33. Lady Bird Johnson	Friend
34. Joe Kilgore	Congressman
35. Rene Kimbrough	Staff member
36. Oscar Lowry	Nephew in law
37. John Lyle	Congressman
38. George Mahon	Congressman
39. Aubrey McAlester	Publisher of the *Bonham Daily Favorite*
40. John McCormack	Congressman
41. Dale Miller	Lobbyist

42. Ed Nash — Rayburn leader in Kaufman County
43. J. R. Parten — Texas Democratic party leader
44. Ray Peeler — Rayburn leader in Fannin County
45. Bob Poage — Congressman
46. W. B. Ragsdale — Political reporter
47. Ray Roberts — Staff member, Rayburn leader in McKinney, and state senator
48. Pete Rodes — Rayburn leader in Rains County
49. J. T. Rutherford — Congressman
50. Fred Schwengel — Congressman
51. Hugh Scott — Congressman and senator
52. Grover Sellers — Judge
53. Matt Sheley — Publisher of the *Greenville Herald Banner*
54. Byron Skelton — Texas Democratic party leader
55. R. C. (Bob) Slagle, Jr. — Rayburn leader in Grayson County
56. Truett Smith — Rayburn leader in south Collin County
57. Homer Thornberry — Congressman
58. D. M. Tunnell — Rayburn leader in Kaufman County
59. Bill Wilcox — Staff member
60. Ann Worley — Friend
61. Jim Wright — Congressman
62. Ted Wright — Staff member

Appendix B
Tables

Table 1. Characteristics of Texas and the Fourth District

	Texas	Fourth District
Population and racial composition		
Total in 1960	9,579,677	216,371
Percentage black	12.4%	14%
Percentage Spanish	14.8%	1.6%
Extent of urbanism[a]		
Population per square mile in 1960	36.4	45.6
Percentage urban in 1960	75.0%	52.9%
Occupational breakdown		
Percentage employed in agriculture in 1960[b]	8.7%	14.4%
Number of commercial farms in 1959	137,512	6,941
Percentage of commercial farms growing cotton in 1959	37.4%	44.5%
Percentage employed in white-collar occupations in 1960[c]	41.1%	33.0%
Number of manufacturing and mineral establishments with 20 or more employees in 1958	4,237	95
Income and education		
Family median income	$4,884	$3,854
Median education for those over 25 years	10.4	9.5

SOURCE: Bureau of the Census, *Congressional District Data Book* (Washington, D.C.: Government Printing Office, 1963), 483–489.
[a]*Urban* is defined as places of twenty-five hundred or more inhabitants.
[b]Percentage employed in agriculture is obtained by dividing the number employed in agriculture by the number employed.
[c]White collar occupations are professional, technical and kindred workers, managers, officials, and sales.

Table 2. Population of the Fourth, Fifth, and Average Texas Congressional Districts

	1950 census	1958 census
Fourth District	227,735	216,371
Fifth District (Dallas County)	614,799	951,527
Mean population of all districts in Texas	350,509	435,440

SOURCE: Bureau of the Census, *Congressional District Data Book* (Washington, D.C.: Government Printing Office, 1963), 483–492.
NOTE: Mean population is the state population divided by the number of districts excluding at-large districts.

Table 3. Votes Cast in Presidential Elections by Texas and by the Fourth District

Year	Texas			Fourth District		
	Democrats	Republicans	Third party[a]	Democrats	Republicans	Third party
1944	821,605	191,425	135,439	36,426	4,402	4,117
	71.5%	16.7%	11.8%	81.0%	9.8%	9.2%
1948	750,700	282,240	106,909	32,886	6,069	3,506
	65.9%	24.8%	9.4%	77.4%	14.3%	8.3%
1952	969,228	1,102,878		32,182	23,552	
	46.8%	53.2%		57.7%	42.3%	
1956	959,958	1,080,619		27,057	21,543	
	44.3%	55.7%		55.7%	44.3%	
1960	1,167,932	1,121,699		28,098	20,875	
	51.0%	49.0%		57.4%	42.6%	

SOURCES: For 1944, Alexander Heard and Donald Strong, *Southern Primaries and Elections, 1920–1949* (Freeport, N.Y.: Books for Libraries, rep. 1970), 185–186. For 1948, *Texas Almanac 1949–1950* (Dallas: Dallas News, 1950), 476–477. For 1952, 1956, and 1960, Bureau of the Census, *Congressional District Data Book* (Washington, D.C.: Government Printing Office, 1963), 483.

[a]In 1944, the third party was a conservative, anti-Roosevelt party known as the Texas Regulars; in 1948, the third party was a conservative southern party opposed to the Democrats' position on civil rights. It was known as the States' Rights party.

Table 4. Rayburn's Contested Democratic Primary Elections

Year	Number of opponents	Rayburn's percentage of the total vote[a]
1912	7	23[b]
1914	1	68
1916	2	55
1918[c]	1	81
1920[c]	1	60
1922	1	52
1924	1	62
1928[c]	3	57
1930[c]	2	51
1932	2	51
1934[d]	1	59
1936	2	65
1940	2	85
1942	1	78
1944	2	55
1948	2	63
1952	1	66
1954	1	75

SOURCE: Calculated from mimeographed paper titled "Rayburn's Contested Primaries," SRL.

[a]Rounded to the nearest percentage point.

[b]Rayburn won this election because of a state law that declared the primary winner the candidate with the greatest number of votes. Rayburn received 4,983 votes; the next-highest vote total was 4,493, for candidate Tom Perkins. Perkins ran as Rayburn's only opponent in 1914 and received only one-third of the total votes.

[c]Statistics on Rains County unavailable.

[d]Beginning in 1934 Kaufman and Rockwall counties were added to the district and are included in the calculations.

Table 5. Voting in Selected Fourth District Democratic Primary Elections

Year and total votes	Candidates	Percentage of the total vote[a]							
		Collin	Fannin	Grayson	Hunt	Rains	Kaufman[b]	Rockwall[b]	Total district
1916	Rayburn	50	68	43	61	66			55
	A. Randell	37	31	52	37	31			40
	T. Wiley	13	1	4	3	3			5
(Total votes)		(5,624)	(4,988)	(7,001)	(5,655)	(700)			(23,968)
1944	Rayburn	54	66	66	37	40	55	47	55
	G. Morris	44	33	34	58	53	43	53	43
	G. Balch	2	1	1	4	7	2	1	2
(Total votes)		(7,941)	(7,689)	(11,418)	(8,517)	(1,258)	(5,351)	(1,737)	(43,911)
1948	Rayburn	62	79	71	41	63	56	47	63
	G. Morris	29	15	11	50	23	31	31	25
	D. Brown	9	6	18	9	14	13	22	12
(Total votes)		(8,665)	(9,938)	(13,751)	(7,815)	(1,566)	(6,319)	(2,157)	(50,211)
1952	Rayburn	74	81	73	57	63	39	56	66
	R. Brown	26	19	28	43	38	61	45	34
(Total votes)		(7,187)	(8,177)	(13,049)	(7,335)	(1,302)	(6,285)	(1,851)	(45,186)
1954	Rayburn	79	85	82	63	66	66	68	75
	A. McRae	21	15	19	38	34	34	32	25
(Total votes)		(7,294)	(7,193)	(11,315)	(7,846)	(1,210)	(4,831)	(1,237)	(40,926)

SOURCE: Calculated from mimeographed paper titled "Rayburn's Contested Primaries," SRL.
[a]Rounded to the nearest percentage point.
[b]Not part of the Fourth District until 1934.

Notes

Preface

1. C. Dwight Dorough, *Mr. Sam* (New York: Random House, 1962); Alfred Steinberg, *Sam Rayburn: A Biography* (New York: Hawthorn, 1975); H. G. Dulaney, Edward Hake Phillips, and MacPhelan Reese, eds., *Speak Mr. Speaker* (Bonham, Tex.: Sam Rayburn Foundation, 1978).

2. Richard F. Fenno, Jr., *Home Style* (Boston: Little, Brown, 1978).

Chapter 1

1. Roland Boyd speech, Sam Rayburn Memorial Day, January 6, 1977.

2. Demographic data in this chapter are from: *1931 Texas Almanac* (Dallas: Dallas News, 1931); *1941–1942 Texas Almanac* (Dallas: Dallas News, 1941); *1961–1962 Texas Almanac* (Dallas: Dallas News, 1961); Bureau of the Census, *Congressional District Data Book* (Washington, D.C.: Government Printing Office, 1963).

3. H. G. Dulaney interview, August 15, 1980; Levis Hall interview, May 29, 1980; E. B. Chapman interview, May 28, 1980; Fred Conn interview, March 10, 1981; Vernon Beckham interview, December 17, 1980. [Unless otherwise noted, interviews are on file at the Sam Rayburn Library (SRL).]

4. Cecil Dickson interview, December 17, 1980; Beckham, December 17, 1980; Alfred Steinberg, *Sam Rayburn: A Biography* (New York: Hawthorn, 1975), 71–72.

5. Alexander Graham Shanks, "Sam Rayburn and the New Deal, 1933–1936" (Ph.D. diss., University of North Carolina at Chapel Hill, 1964), 224.

6. Matt Sheley interview, May 3, 1981.

7. W. M. Rodes interview, May 9, 1980.

8. Ibid.; Ed Nash interview, June 5, 1980; Rodes, May 9, 1980; Chapman, May 28, 1980; Truett Smith interview, May 16, 1980; Hall, May 29, 1980.

9. Oscar Lowry interview, October 2, 1981.

10. Dulaney, August 15, 1980; Ray Peeler interview, February 25, 1981; Smith, May 16, 1980.

11. Beckham, December 17, 1980.

12. H. G. Dulaney interview, June 12, 1981 (interview not available from the SRL).

13. Ibid.

14. Peeler, February 25, 1981; Roscoe Martin, *The People's Party in Texas* (Austin: University of Texas Press, 1970).

15. Smith v. Allright, 321 U.S. 649 (1944).

16. The poll tax for federal elections was outlawed by the Twenty-fourth Amendment to the Constitution. The poll tax for state elections was declared unconstitutional in Harper v. Virginia State Board of Elections, 383 U.S. 663 (1966).

17. "Speech Opening Campaign of Hon. Sam Rayburn for Re-election to Congress," *Bonham Daily Favorite,* June 6, 1922, 4.

18. Typewritten copy of news article titled "Rayburn Reviews Work Flays GOP in Campaign Opener Denies FEPC Will Destroy Texas Segregation Laws," *Bonham Daily Favorite,* June 30, 1944. In SRL, 1944 Texas and District Politics File. [File is given for items in SRL that cannot be located by date.]

19. Conn, March 10, 1981.

20. Dwayne L. Little, "The Political Leadership of Speaker Sam Rayburn, 1940–1961" (Ph.D. diss., University of Cincinnati, 1970), 9, 159–160, 357.

21. G. C. Harris interview, May 21, 1980; Nash, June 5, 1980.

22. Dwight Dorough, *Mr. Sam* (New York: Random House, 1962), 402, 576.

23. H. G. Dulaney, Edward Hake Phillips, and MacPhelan Reese, eds., *Speak Mr. Speaker* (Bonham, Tex.: Sam Rayburn Foundation, 1978), 253.

24. Martha Freeman interview, January 6, 1982.

25. Carl Albert interview, December 6, 1979; Peeler, February 25, 1981.

26. Dorough, *Mr. Sam*, 111–112; Robert Caro, *The Years of Lyndon Johnson: The Path to Power* (New York: Knopf, 1982), 314.

27. Sam Rayburn to R. W. Wortham, December 7, 1932. [Unless otherwise noted, correspondence is on file at the SRL.]

28. Wortham to Sam Rayburn, November 12, 1932.

29. Sam Rayburn to Claude Isbell, June 20, 1933.

30. Sam Rayburn to Joseph Nichols, May 14, 1933.

31. Dick Rayburn to Sam Rayburn, May 24, 1933.

32. Ibid.

33. Sam Rayburn to Dick Rayburn, May 27, 1933; for details of an agreement among Texas congressmen on handling patronage problems resulting from the redistricting, see Robert A. Caro, "The Years of Lyndon Johnson," *Atlantic,* October 1981, 65–66.

34. Sam Rayburn to Isbell, June 20, 1933.

35. Dick Rayburn to Sam Rayburn, May 24, 1933.

36. Sam Rayburn to Joseph Nichols, May 24, 1933.

37. Isbell to Sam Rayburn, June 16, 1933.

38. Sam Rayburn to Isbell, June 20, 1933.

39. Walter D. Adams to Sam Rayburn, May 19, 1933.

40. Dorough, *Mr. Sam,* 453. See also Peeler, February 25, 1981; Albert, December 6, 1979. Parmet wrote: "Also a threat, one that could have ended his national career, was the frequently mentioned possibility that Shivers might undertake some deft and justifiable redistricting. Both the interests of equitable representation and Rayburn's demise could have been promoted by joining the Speaker's constituents with the much more populous and heavily conservative suburbs of Dallas"; Herbert S. Parmet, *The Democrats* (New York: Macmillan, 1976), 118.

41. Shanks, "Sam Rayburn," 22. See also Albert, December 6, 1979. Dallas's congressman was unusually ineffective but extremely conservative. Congressman Alger in 1958 obtained the distinction of being the only congressman who voted against free milk for schoolchildren. From 1959 until the Kennedy assassination, Alger lost eight federal agencies in his district and six-and-one-half million dollars in federal payroll money. See George Norris Green, *The Establishment in Texas Politics* (Westport, Conn.: Greenwood, 1979), 165; idem, "The Far Right Wing in Texas Politics, 1930s–1960s" (Ph.D. diss., Florida State University, 1966), 258–259. An interesting treatment of Alger is in the Earl Cabell interview by Ronald E. Marcello, March 21, April 3, June 14,

October 2, 9, and 16 of 1974, North Texas State University Oral History Collection. The *Dallas News*, according to *Business Week*, was the major source of opposition to Rayburn in North Texas; see "Sam Rayburn: Using 42 Years," *Business Week*, December 4, 1954, 168.

42. Little, "Political Leadership," 228–229. See also R. C. Slagle interview, October 17, 1980; Homer Thornberry interview, January 4, 1980.

43. "Record for Service Snapped by Rayburn," *Houston Post*, March 5, 1959, III-6. Rayburn also said, "Any town big enough to have a Chamber of Commerce is beyond saving"; see Jerry Flemmons, *Amon: The Life of Amon Carter, Sr. of Texas* (Austin: Jenkins, 1978), 102.

44. A. M. Aikin speech, Sam Rayburn Memorial Day, Bonham, Texas, January 6, 1978.

45. Ibid.

46. Ibid.

47. Ibid.

48. Sam Rayburn to John B. Shepperd, February 6, 1953.

49. Compare the security and stability of Rayburn's district with his friend Cong. Marvin Jones's district. In 1915 when Jones first announced for Congress, the district in which he ran consisted of forty-eight counties and 338,333 people. It ran from north central Texas with Rayburn's Grayson County at its eastern border to New Mexico at its western boundary. Jones's district became smaller over the years owing to redistricting, but it never approached Rayburn's Fourth District in small size, compactness, small population, or lack of in-migration. See Irvin M. May, Jr., *Marvin Jones: The Public Life of an Agrarian Advocate* (College Station, Tex.: Texas A & M University Press, 1980), 22, 25–26.

50. George B. Tindall, *The Disruption of the Solid South* (Athens: University of Georgia Press, 1972).

51. Dwayne L. Little, "The Congressional Career of Sam Rayburn, 1913–1961" (M.A. thesis, University of Cincinnati, 1963), 165.

52. Carl Albert interview by Deward C. Brown, July 1969 (no specific date); Dorough, *Mr. Sam*, 574–575. One should not overemphasize the religious issue, however. Weeks has noted: "The Kennedy farm program and traditional loyalty to the Democratic Party carried more weight than religious considerations"; see O. Douglas Weeks, *Texas in the 1960 Presidential Election* (Austin: University of Texas, Institute of Public Affairs, 1961), 70.

Chapter 2

1. Erving Goffman, *The Presentation of Self in Everyday Life* (New York: Doubleday, 1959); Richard F. Fenno, Jr., *Home Style* (Boston: Little, Brown, 1978).

2. Richard Bolling interview, June 26, 1980.

3. Truitt Smith interview, May 16, 1980.

4. C. Dwight Dorough, *Mr. Sam* (New York: Random House, 1962), 120.

5. R. C. Slagle interview, October 17, 1980.

6. Rayburn's informality at home was stressed in the Ed Nash interview, June 5, 1980; the Grover Sellers interview, October 6, 1979; the H. G. Dulaney interview, August 15, 1980; the Rene Kimbrough interview, November 23, 1980; the Robert Bradshaw interview, May 11, 1981; the Paul Hardin interview, November 5, 1980; and the Kate Reed Estes interview, February 13, 1981.

7. Estes, February 13, 1981; Ray Peeler interview, February 25, 1981.

8. Peeler, February 25, 1981; "Rayburn Formally Opens Campaign for Re-election," *Bonham Daily Favorite,* June 24, 1948, 1; "Million Dollar Rain Hits Fannin County Late Wednesday," *Bonham Daily Favorite,* June 24, 1948, 1.

9. Estes, February 13, 1981.

10. John Brademas interview, June 24, 1980. Ripley has noted that Rayburn earned a reputation as an "incomparable legislative wizard when faced with unfavorable odds." His method of operation was very centralized and highly personal. His leadership of the House was one in which he was in control. Rayburn did consult with others, but on his own terms. See Randall B. Ripley, *Party Leaders in the House of Representatives* (Washington, D.C.: Brookings Institution, 1967), 92–93.

11. For example, Robert A. Caro, "The Years of Lyndon Johnson: Lyndon and Mister Sam," *Atlantic,* November 1981, 45.

12. Lindy Boggs interview, June 12, 1980; Jim Wright interview, June 23, 1980.

13. Dulaney, August 15, 1980.

14. Vernon Beckham interview, December 17, 1980; Dulaney, August 15, 1980; Estes, February 13, 1981.

15. Oscar Lowry interview, October 2, 1981. Hardeman noted that the stock was worth one thousand dollars and was in Kirby Petroleum; D. B. Hardeman, "Sam Rayburn and the House of Representatives," in William S. Livingston, Lawrence Dodd, and Richard Schatt, eds., *The Presidency and the Congress* (Austin: LBJ School, 1979), 246.

16. Robert Bartley interview, January 6, 1982.

17. Caro, "Years of Lyndon Johnson," 50.

18. Lowry, October 2, 1981.

19. Cecil Dickson interview, June 29, 1980.

20. Several wealthy oil men were invited guests at the Library dedication. See W. H. Kittrell, Jr., "Pay Tribute to Mr. Sam," *Longview News,* undated and unpaginated. In the Sam Rayburn Library news clipping scrapbook titled "Dedication of the Sam Rayburn Library, October 9, 1957." [All news scrapbooks are on file in the SRL.]

21. See Lewis Nordyke, "A Tribute to 'Mr. Sam,'" *New York Times Magazine,* undated and unpaginated; scrapbook titled "Dedication of the Sam Rayburn Library, October 9, 1957."

22. Slagle, October 17, 1980. Yarborough won that race, his first statewide victory.

23. Dwayne L. Little, "The Political Leadership of Speaker Sam Rayburn, 1940–1961" (Ph.D. diss., University of Cincinnati, 1970), 376–378.

24. George Norris Green, *The Establishment in Texas Politics* (Westport, Conn.: Greenwood, 1979), 202. R. C. Slagle arranged the timing and form of the Rayburn endorsement of Yarborough. The strategy was to maximize the impact of the endorsement without making it appear that Rayburn was trying to dictate to voters how to vote. Slagle worked with Rayburn on these arrangements because he was a friend of Rayburn's as well as one of Rayburn's leaders. He was also a major figure in the Yarborough campaign and was probably the most visible Rayburn leader supporting Yarborough. See Slagle, October 17, 1980.

25. Bill Wilcox interview, August 22, 1980 (this aspect of the interview unrecorded).

26. Richardson paid thirty-five hundred dollars for the two Porfiro Salinas paintings he gave to Rayburn, a trivial sum for a man of his wealth. In 1935, for example, Richardson discovered the Keystone Field in West Texas. It proved to contain a billion dollars in oil reserves. Of 385 wells drilled, only 17 were dry; see John Bainbridge, *The Super-Americans* (Garden City, N. Y.: Doubleday, 1961), 93–94. In 1962 John Connally

estimated the size of the Richardson estate at $100 million. In 1948, however, *Fortune* magazine had estimated Richardson's fortune at over $150 million. Some estimates of the worth of the estate have been as much as $800 million; see Ann Fears Crawford and Jack Keever, *John B. Connally: Portrait in Power* (Austin: Jenkins, 1973), 59.

27. Bailey's numerous business deals and ethical conflicts, including the famous Waters-Pierce Oil Company loan, are carefully examined in Bob Charles Holcomb, "Senator Joe Bailey, Two Decades of Controversy" (Ph.D. diss., Texas Technological College, 1968).

28. Caro, "Years of Lyndon Johnson," 45.

29. "To the Voters of the Fourth Congressional District," campaign leaflet, 1932 Texas and District Political File, Sam Rayburn Papers. Another illustration of the political use of Rayburn's honesty is a political advertisement published during the 1948 campaign: "Did it ever occur to you that Sam Rayburn has served this district for thirty-six years without getting rich. He has had the power and the intelligence to have feathered his nest with millions, and today is no richer in this world's goods than the rest of us. You can name others who have not been up there over six years that have retired with a fabulous fortune, and they were men without the ability of Sam Rayburn"; see "Let's Give Sam a Fair Deal," *Bonham Daily Favorite,* June 16, 1948, unpaginated; in "Scrapbook 1935–1954."

30. Robert L. Peabody, *Leadership in Congress* (Boston: Little, Brown, 1976), 473.

31. Levis Hall interview, May 29, 1980.

32. Homer Thornberry interview, January 4, 1980.

33. Lloyd Bentsen interview, June 18, 1980.

34. For example, Henry Jackson interview, June 12, 1980; Hugh Scott interview, June 23, 1980; H. G. Dulaney interview, June 12, 1981 (not available from the SRL).

35. Jackson, June 12, 1980.

36. Roland Boyd interview, May 22, 1980.

37. Dickson, June 29, 1980. Though Rayburn died with a larger estate than Vinson, former Cong. Ed Gossett also considered the two men to have had the same ethical code. Both men wielded great power, claimed Gossett, but neither made money as a result of it; Ed Gossett interview by H. W. Kamp, June 27 and August 1, 1969, North Texas State University Oral History Collection.

38. Hall, May 29, 1980.

39. Estes, February 13, 1981.

40. Hall, May 29, 1980.

41. Estes, February 13, 1981.

42. Beckham, December 17, 1980. Bradshaw, May 11, 1981, provides an interesting illustration of this technique.

43. Beckham, December 17, 1980. Hardeman wrote that he once heard Rayburn quote a long, involved part of Hugo's *Les Miserables,* a book Rayburn had last read forty years before; Hardeman, "Sam Rayburn and the House," 249. Dorough wrote that, after nearly thirty years, Rayburn remembered the name of a man he had met only once, remembered where they had met, and the exact date and circumstances of the meeting; Dorough, *Mr. Sam,* 407. The political value of Rayburn's ability to remember names is well illustrated by Thad Omahundro, "Rayburn Has But One Aspiration—To Be Reelected," *Bonham Daily Favorite,* March 31, 1944, 1. The reporter for this article apparently lived in California but had Fourth District ties and was hired by the Bonham paper to cover a political meeting in Los Angeles. Rayburn was there and held a press conference. When the reporter mentioned his name, a Grayson County name, Rayburn suddenly stopped the press conference and said, "How are your folks?" The reporter replied that his mother now lived in Long Beach with his brother Sam. He also mentioned that brother Sam had married Nina Cantrell of Greenville. Rayburn said, "Why, of course, I knew her father and her Uncle Will Cantrell who was active in supporting my first race for Congress in 1912. So Sam married Cantrell's daughter. Well, well." The reporter was so impressed with this recognition that not only was it published in the article but the remainder of the article effusively praised Sam Rayburn.

44. Martha Freeman interview, January 6, 1982.

45. Dan Inglish interview, March 13, 1981.

46. Beckham, December 17, 1980; Slagle, October 17, 1980.

47. Dulaney, June 12, 1981.

48. Beckham, December 17, 1980.

49. For example, Inglish, March 13, 1981.

50. Tony Slaughter, "Great Event Near in Life of Mr. Sam," *Ft. Worth Star Telegram,* October 6, 1957, unpaginated; scrapbook titled "Dedication of SRL, October 9, 1957."

51. Dulaney, August 15, 1980.

52. Ralph Hall speech, Friends of Sam Rayburn Barbecue, Bonham, Texas, June 13, 1981.

53. Hardeman, "Sam Rayburn and the House," 231.

54. W. B. Bruce to Sam Rayburn, July 19, 1948.

55. Kimbrough, November 23, 1980; Peeler, February 25, 1981.

56. Kimbrough, November 23, 1980; Dulaney, August 15, 1980. See also Alexander Graham Shanks, "Sam Rayburn and the New Deal, 1933–1936" (Ph.D. diss., University of North Carolina at Chapel Hill, 1964), 21; "Sam Rayburn: Using 42 Years," *Business Week,* December 4, 1954, 168.

57. Peeler, February 25, 1981.

58. G. C. Harris interview, May 21, 1980.

59. Kimbrough, November 23, 1980. See also Albert D. Cover and Bruce S. Brumberg, "Baby Books and Ballots: The Impact of Congressional Mail on Constituent Opinion," *American Political Science Review* 76 (June 1982): 347–359.

60. Smith, May 16, 1980.

61. Elizabeth Carpenter, "History Likely to Repeat for Rayburn," *Houston Post,* May 24, 1953, II-1, II-7.

62. For example see Bradshaw, May 11, 1981; Hardin, November 5, 1980; Nash, June 5, 1980; D. M. Tunnell interview, November 21, 1980; Harris, May 21, 1980.

63. W. M. Rodes interview, May 9, 1980.

64. R. C. Slagle interview, October 17, 1980.

65. E. B. Chapman interview, May 28, 1980; Fred Conn interview, March 10, 1981.

66. Texas Historical Commission, "Sam Rayburn House," a brochure available from the Sam Rayburn House, Bonham, Texas.

67. Dulaney, August 15, 1980.

68. David Halberstam, *The Powers That Be* (New York: Knopf, 1979), 4.

69. Lowry, October 2, 1981.

70. Dulaney, August 15, 1980; Kimbrough, November 23, 1980; Wright, June 23, 1980.

71. Beckham, December 17, 1980; Bradshaw, May 11, 1981.

72. For example, Caro, "Years of Lyndon Johnson," 45–46, 55–58.

73. Dulaney, August 15, 1980.

74. Beckham, December 17, 1980.

75. Clarence Elkins interview, February 20, 1981.

76. Smith, May 16, 1980; Hardin, November 5, 1980.

77. Beckham, December 17, 1980. For other examples of the problems of constituent visitors, see Alfred Steinberg, *Sam Rayburn: A Biography* (New York: Hawthorn, 1975), 204.

78. Tunnell, November 21, 1980.

79. Fred Schwengel interview, June 16, 1980.

80. Levis Hall interview, May 9, 1980; Dulaney, June 12, 1981. The atomic bomb research was enough of a secret that not even Cong. Paul Kilday of the Committee on Military Affairs knew of it; see Paul J. Kilday interview by H. W. Kamp, August 28, 1965, North Texas State University Oral History Collection. Burns has noted, however, that some Congressmen were suspicious of the research activities and even proposed inquiring visits that would have endangered the project's secrecy. They were kept from further probing by colleagues, General Marshall, and Secretary Stimson. See James MacGregor Burns, *Roosevelt: The Soldier of Freedom* (New York: Harcourt Brace Jovanovich, 1970), 456.

81. Some of the Rayburn style in Bonham is captured in Walter C. Nash, "Sam Rayburn the Congressman of the Fourth District of Texas" (M.A. thesis, East Texas State College, August 1950), especially 57–64.

82. Rodes, May 9, 1980.

83. Caro, "Years of Lyndon Johnson," 45–46.

84. Dulaney, June 12, 1981.

85. Ray Roberts interview, June 16, 1980. Roberts also said, "Rayburn had a tremendous influence. He didn't often throw his feet out or make a hard and fast recommendation, but when he did, they [government officials] didn't question it; it was done"; Ray Roberts interview by Michael L. Gillette, June 9, 1975, Lyndon Baines Johnson Library.

86. For example, Slagle, October 17, 1980; Estes, February 13, 1981; Carl Albert interview, December 6, 1979; Wright, June 23, 1980; Bolling, June 26, 1980.

87. Brademas, June 24, 1980; Lindley Beckworth interview, October 14, 1979; Omar Burleson interview, December 18, 1979; J. T. Rutherford interview, June 18, 1980.

88. For example, Estes, February 13, 1981; W. G. Ragsdale interview, June 27, 1980.

89. Dorough, *Mr. Sam,* 254.

90. Ibid., 376–377.

91. Quoted in H. G. Dulaney, Edward Hake Phillips, and MacPhelan Reese, eds., *Speak Mr. Speaker* (Bonham, Tex.: Sam Rayburn Foundation, 1978), 158.

92. Ibid.

93. Ibid.

94. Ibid., 159.

95. Martha Rayburn Dye interview, December 2, 1980; Dulaney, August 15, 1980; Chapman, May 28, 1980; see also "Sam Rayburn: Using 42 Years."

96. For example, Beckham, December 17, 1980.

97. Peeler, February 25, 1981.

98. Bartley, January 6, 1982.

99. Ed Edmondson, "Mister Speaker," *Sam Rayburn Library Newsletter,* January 6, 1982, 46. Dulaney recalled that it was common for Rayburn to go early to a meeting and stay late; H. G. Dulaney comment to the author, March 31, 1982.

100. Bartley, January 6, 1982.

101. Freeman, January 6, 1982.

102. Dulaney, August 15, 1980.

103. Typewritten manuscript titled "Sam Rayburn's Fannin County Speech, 1947," 7, SRL Speeches File.

104. Peeler, February 25, 1981.

105. Quoted in Dulaney, Phillips, and Reese, *Speak Mr. Speaker,* 132.

106. G. C. Harris, one of Rayburn's most able and most influential county leaders considered rural electrification Rayburn's most important contribution to the people of Hunt County; Harris, May 21, 1980. Similar views can be found in Estes, February 13, 1981. See also Delbert Earl Tyler, "History of the Fannin County Rural Electric Cooperative" (M.A. thesis, East Texas State College, August 1964). Rayburn knew the great political value of rural electrification. That legislation could have been sent to the Agriculture Committee chaired by Marvin Jones, but Rayburn had had experience sponsoring very controversial legislation on securities and utilities, so Jones waived Agriculture's jurisdiction; see Judge Marvin Jones interview by Jerry N. Hess, April 3, April 20, April 24, May 8, and May 14, 1970, Harry S Truman Library. Caro thinks Rayburn took rural electrification from the Agriculture Committee because he considered Jones not tough enough to force the bill to passage. Rayburn demanded the bill be referred to his committee, saying to the House Parliamentarian, "Give it to me"; see Robert Caro, *The Years of Lyndon Johnson: The Path to Power* (New York: Knopf, 1982), 520.

107. Estes, February 13, 1981.

108. Tunnell, November 21, 1980.

109. Ibid.

110. Ibid.

111. Rayburn's strong support for soil conservation is detailed in Valton J. Young, *The Speaker's Agent* (New York: Vantage, 1957).

112. Inglish, March 13, 1981. There are reports of vast amounts spent by the holding companies to defeat Rayburn; Richard B. Henderson, *Maury Maverick* (Austin: University of Texas Press, 1970), 122.

113. Sam Rayburn speech before the Altrusa Club, Greenville, Texas, November 4, 1957, SRL Speeches File.

114. Richard Bolling, *House Out of Order* (New York: Dutton, 1965), 156–194.

115. Slagle, October 17, 1980.

116. Boyd, May 22, 1980.

117. Alben Barkley, *That Reminds Me* (New York: Doubleday, 1954), 165.

118. Comment made to the author by Oscar Lowry, June 13, 1981.

119. Aubrey McAlester interview, August 17, 1981.

120. Harold L. Ickes, *The Secret Diary of Harold L. Ickes: The First Thousand Days, 1933–1936* (New York: Simon & Schuster, 1953), 484–491.

121. Jimmy Dale Puett, "Sam Rayburn's Influence on Public Policy" (M.A. thesis, East Texas State University, August 1965), 89–90.

122. "Lavon Reservoir Groundbreaking Ceremonies," Dedication Book, December 27, 1947.

123. Boyd, May 22, 1980; Hardin, November 5, 1980.

124. Chapman, May 28, 1980.

125. Samuel Fenner Leslie interview by Wayne Little, July 26, 1965.

126. Hardin, November 5, 1980.

127. "Editorial," *McKinney Weekly Democrat Gazette*, July 15, 1948, 1; *The Handbook of Texas* (Austin: Texas State Historical Association, 1952), 2: 363. "Speaker Sam Rayburn Dedicates Latest Air Corps Training School at Bonham," *Paris News*, November 2, 1941, unpaginated, SRL clipping file titled "Scrapbook, September 15, 1940–December 9, 1941"; "Fourth Congressional District Have Opportunity Show Appreciation at Rayburn Home-coming Rally," *Bonham Daily Favorite*, June 13, 1948, 1.

128. "Tentative Staffing Plan for GM and S Hospital, Bonham, Texas," Domiciliary Information File, Sam Rayburn Papers.

129. "War Department Gives Its Approval for 1,500 Bed Army Hospital for McKinney; To Serve North Texas," *McKinney Daily Courier-Gazette*, September 4, 1942, 1.

130. Texas State Historical Association, *The Handbook of Texas* (Austin: Texas State Historical Association, 1952), 2: 838.

131. McAlester, August 17, 1981.

132. Ibid.; "Editorial," *McKinney Weekly Democrat Gazette*, July 15, 1948, 1.

133. Wilcox, August 22, 1980; Roberts, June 16, 1980.

134. Tunnell, November 21, 1980.

135. For example, McAlester, August 17, 1981.

136. Roger D. Greene, "Rayburn of Texas," *Houston Post*, December 12, 1954, v-3.

137. Irvin M. May, Jr., *Marvin Jones: The Public Life of an Agrarian Advocate* (College Station, Tex.: Texas A & M University Press, 1980), 62.

138. Steinberg, *Sam Rayburn*, 78–91; Dorough, *Mr. Sam*, 183–184.

139. Shanks, "Sam Rayburn and the New Deal," 18. Shanks cited a 1963 interview with D. B. Hardeman as his source.

140. Steinberg, *Sam Rayburn*, 80–81.

141. Dorough, *Mr. Sam*, 184.

142. Estes, February 13, 1981. Marvin Jones, asked about his sister's divorce from Rayburn, replied, "Yes, they were married about 1928, the early part of the year. They lived together about six months. They separated. No one knew exactly why. Neither of them ever talked about it. My sister married again and is the mother of two fine children and now has six grandchildren. She was a very attractive young lady in my book. I thought Sam was a great chap, but somehow they didn't get along. They parted as friends and she went by to see him in his last illness. He had asked me, oh, a year before he died saying, 'If Metze comes up here any time, I would like to see her.' And I said, 'I am sure she will come by to see you.' They never did really fall out. I never asked her and she didn't volunteer, said they just couldn't get along, and they couldn't and she respected him. That's about all she would say and he wouldn't say anything. Sam's sisters liked Metze. They remained friends. It all seemed rather strange, but strange things happen in law and in life. But that was merely an incident in our lives. Sam and I fished together for thirty years, all kinds of places, and I have been in his home both before and after that happened. His sisters admired my sister and they remained friends, and asked her to come to see them. One of them lived in Dallas. I have no further explanation." See Jones, April 3, April 20, April 24, May 8, and May 14, 1970. Metze's daughter from a second marriage contracted polio. Rayburn got the child into the Warm Springs polio treatment center in spite of a long list of people desiring admittance; Caro, *Years of Lyndon Johnson,* 331.

143. Leslie, July 2, 1965. Little, in "Political Leadership," 21, noted that the divorce was discreet and virtually unknown. "Rayburn might be referred to as a bachelor or unmarried, but never as divorced," says Kenneth Dewey Hairgrove, in "Sam Rayburn: Congressional Leader, 1940–1952" (Ph.D. diss., Texas Tech University, 1974), 218.

144. Dulaney, June 12, 1981.

145. "What's in the Air Isn't Romance," newspaper clipping without name of newspaper, August 30, 1957, unpaginated, "Scrapbook— Bascom Timmons Collection of Materials Concerning the Honorable

Sam Rayburn—Book 2." See also "Veep's Widow Denies Report of Romance," *St. Petersburg Florida Times,* August 30, 1957, 2A.

146. Freeman, January 6, 1982.

147. Dorough, *Mr. Sam,* 502.

148. Grover Sellers interview, October 6, 1979.

149. Steinberg, *Sam Rayburn,* 302. Little points to Miss Lou's death as the cause of Rayburn's turn to religion; Little, "Political Leadership," 320–321.

150. Freeman, January 6, 1982.

151. Sam Rayburn to Elder H. G. Ball, October 8, 1956.

152. The religious issue is explored in Lawrence H. Fuchs, *John F. Kennedy and American Catholicism* (New York: Meredith, 1967).

153. Theodore C. Sorensen, *Kennedy* (New York: Harper & Row, 1965), 164.

154. Ibid., 192–193.

155. Quoted in Dulaney, Phillips, and Reese, *Speak Mr. Speaker,* 405.

156. Ibid.

157. Ibid.

158. Kimbrough, November 23, 1980.

159. Harold Kimmerling, M.D., medical report on Sam Rayburn, October 2, 1961.

160. Dulaney, August 15, 1980.

161. For example, Kimbrough, November 23, 1980.

162. This personality trait is noted by Caro, "Years of Lyndon Johnson," 59.

163. Inglish, March 13, 1981.

164. Bentsen, June 18, 1980; Frank Ikard interview, June 14, 1980.

165. Dulaney, June 12, 1981.

166. Dale Miller interview, June 13, 1980.

167. Dulaney, August 15, 1980; Slagle, October 17, 1980.

168. For example, D. M. Tunnell interview, November 17, 1980.

169. Halberstam, *Powers That Be,* 3.

170. Burleson, December 18, 1979.

171. Kimbrough, November 23, 1980.

172. Little, "Political Leadership," 433.

173. Albert, December 6, 1979.

174. Kimbrough, November 23, 1980.

175. Dr. Joe Risser press conference, November 16, 1961.

176. Kimbrough, November 23, 1980.

177. Peeler, February 25, 1981.

178. Slagle, October 17, 1980.

179. Buster Cole interview, August 21, 1980.

180. Bolling, June 26, 1980.

181. Herbert S. Parmet, *The Democrats* (New York: Macmillan, 1976), 111.

182. Rayburn argued with Stevenson over the open-convention idea but could not sway him; Edward Lee McMillan, "Texas and the Eisenhower Campaigns" (Ph.D. diss., Texas Technological College, 1960), 391–392.

183. Hale Boggs interview by T. H. Baker, March 13, 1969, Lyndon Baines Johnson Library. Boggs noted that he was surprised by Rayburn's remark that he would like to be vice president. Rayburn offered no explanation for the statement. Lindy Boggs interview, June 12, 1980. Although Mrs. Boggs was not present when the remark was made and did not attend the convention, Mr. Boggs discussed it with her and expressed his great surprise. Mrs. Boggs noted that Mr. Boggs thought "that Mr. Sam really and truly wanted to have it [the vice presidency]."

184. Fenno, *Home Style,* 57–60; Roger H. Davidson and Walter J. Oleszek, *Congress and Its Members* (Washington, D.C.: Congressional Quarterly, 1981), 122.

185. Davidson and Oleszek, *Congress and Its Members,* 108.

Chapter 3

1. G. C. Harris interview, May 21, 1980.

2. W. M. Rodes letter to author, July 31, 1980.

3. H. G. Dulaney interview, August 15, 1980; Vernon Beckham interview, December 17, 1980; and Ray Peeler interview, February 25, 1981. The role of friendship in the political behavior of U.S. senators is explored in Ross K. Baker, *Friend and Foe in the U.S. Senate* (New York: Free Press, 1980). Baker, pp. 6–7, notes that friendship can take many forms: an institutional kinship arising out of professional pride, collegiality, and a satisfying business relationship; an alliance caused by political agreement; a mentor-protégé relationship that crosses generations and where there is great mutual solicitude and assistance; a social friendship caused by shared interests and social style. Friendship can also be a pure result of great affection and concern.

4. Buster Cole, "As Bonham Saw Him," *Sam Rayburn Library Newsletter,* January 6, 1982, 70.

5. Buster Cole interview, August 21, 1980.

6. Richard F. Fenno, Jr., *Home Style* (Boston: Little, Brown, 1978), 192–193.

7. Peeler, February 25, 1981.

8. Ibid.; Mrs. Lyndon Johnson interview, November 13, 1979; Aubrey McAlester interview, August 17, 1981.

9. Mrs. Gene Worley interview, June 20, 1980; Dale Miller interview, June 13, 1980; Johnson, November 13, 1979.

10. Rene Kimbrough interview, November 23, 1980; Cole, August 21, 1980.

11. Ray Peeler's interview (February 25, 1981) provides an exceptionally thoughtful treatment of Rayburn's power, his organization, and his assistance to friends.

12. Grover Sellers interview, October 6, 1979.

13. Peeler, February 25, 1981.

14. J. J. Pickle to Lyndon Johnson, February 23, 1954, Lyndon Baines Johnson Library.

15. BM [Booth Mooney] to Lyndon Johnson, memorandum attached to ibid.

16. "Record for Service Snapped by Rayburn," *Houston Post,* March 5, 1959, III-6.

17. Dwayne L. Little, "The Political Leadership of Speaker Sam Rayburn, 1940–1961" (Ph.D. diss., University of Cincinnati, 1970), 155.

18. R. C. Slagle interview, October 17, 1980; Stephenson, citing an interview with political activist Creekmore Fath, also states that Rayburn did not believe that Truman would win in 1948; see Charles W. Stephenson, "The Democrats of Texas and Texas Liberalism, 1944–1960: A Study in Political Frustration" (M.A. thesis, Southwest Texas State College, 1967), 14.

19. Told to the author by James McDade, January 5, 1982.

20. W. M. Rodes interview, May 9, 1980; Roland Boyd interview, May 22, 1980; E. B. Chapman interview, May 28, 1980; Truett Smith interview, May 16, 1980; Harris, May 21, 1980.

21. Chapman, May 28, 1980. Cong. Paul Kilday could not have been pleased with Rayburn's influence in reference to the Air Force Academy. Until Rayburn became interested in locating the academy in Sherman and Ft. Worth's Amon Carter became interested in a North Texas location, Kilday thought he had an agreement from the air force that the academy would be located in his district at San Antonio's Randolph Field. See Paul J. Kilday interview by H. W. Kamp, August 28, 1965, North Texas State University Oral History Collection.

22. Slagle, October 17, 1980.

23. Chapman, May 28, 1980; Lee Simmons, *Assignment Huntsville* (Austin: University of Texas Press, 1957).

24. Slagle, October 17, 1980.

25. Samuel Fenner Leslie interview by Wayne Little, July 26, 1965.

26. Cole, August 21, 1980.

27. Beckham, December 17, 1980.

28. Slagle, October 17, 1980.

29. For example, see Kate Reed Estes interview, February 13, 1981; Boyd, May 22, 1980.

30. Slagle, October 17, 1980.

31. Ibid.

32. Cole, August 21, 1980; Smith, May 16, 1980.

33. Buster Cole speech, Sam Rayburn Memorial Day, January 6, 1981.

34. Kimbrough, November 23, 1980.

35. Dulaney, August 15, 1980. Dorough notes that Rayburn's expenses in his early campaigns came to about fifteen hundred dollars a contested

primary, much of which came from Rayburn's personal funds; C. Dwight Dorough, *Mr. Sam* (New York: Random House, 1962), 139, 154–155.

36. Slagle, October 17, 1980.

37. H. G. Dulaney interview, October 16, 1981 (not available from the SRL).

38. Matt Sheley interview, March 3, 1981; McAlester, August 17, 1981.

39. Quoted in H. G. Dulaney, Edward Hake Phillips, and MacPhelan Reese, eds., *Speak Mr. Speaker* (Bonham, Tex.: Sam Rayburn Foundation, 1978), 211.

40. Slagle, October 17, 1980.

41. D. M. Tunnell interview, November 21, 1980.

42. Slagle, October 17, 1980.

43. Ed Nash interview, June 5, 1980.

44. Rodes, May 9, 1980.

45. Ibid.

46. Quoted in Dulaney, Phillips, and Reese, *Speak Mr. Speaker,* 52.

47. Rodes, May 9, 1980.

48. Carl Nall to Sam Rayburn, March 1, 1944.

49. James D. Buster to Sam Rayburn, undated, SRL 1948 Texas Politics File.

50. Charles Tune to Sam Rayburn, March 1, 1944.

51. Buster to Rayburn, undated.

52. Sam Rayburn to James D. Buster, March 19, 1948.

53. W. R. Dunn to Sam Rayburn, June 2, 1944.

54. Sam Rayburn to W. R. Dunn, June 7, 1944.

55. Leon Press to Sam Rayburn, undated, SRL 1948 Texas Politics File.

56. Sam Rayburn to Leon Press, April 17, 1948.

57. See, for example, Thomas P. Steger to Sam Rayburn, April 25, 1916; Sam Rayburn to F. M. Gibson, June 1, 1916.

58. Estes, February 13, 1981; Dan Inglish interview, March 13, 1981; Robert Bartley interview, January 6, 1982; Alfred Steinberg, *Sam Rayburn: A Biography* (New York: Hawthorn, 1975), 37.

59. Bartley, January 6, 1982.

60. Ibid.; Martha Rayburn Dye interview, December 2, 1980; Fred Conn interview, March 10, 1981; Cole, August 21, 1980.

61. Oscar Lowry interview, October 2, 1981; Dye, December 2, 1980; Bartley, January 6, 1982.

62. Bartley, January 6, 1982.

63. Elizabeth Carpenter interview, June 17, 1980. For Johnson's criticisms of the Rayburn staff, see Booth Mooney interview by Thomas H. Baker, April 8, 1969, Lyndon Baines Johnson Library.

64. Conn, March 10, 1981; Kimbrough, November 23, 1980; Dulaney, August 15, 1980; Robert Bradshaw interview, May 11, 1981.

65. Dulaney, August 15, 1980; Kimbrough, November 23, 1980; Martha Freeman interview, January 6, 1982.

66. Mooney, April 8, 1969.

67. Conn, March 10, 1981; Sheley, March 3, 1981.

68. Dulaney, August 15, 1980; Peeler, February 25, 1981.

69. Charles B. Brownson, ed., *Congressional Staff Directory* (Mt. Vernon, Va.: Congressional Staff Directory, 1980), 261, 326.

70. Inglish, March 13, 1981.

71. Dulaney, August 15, 1980; Kimbrough, November 23, 1980.

72. Sheley, March 3, 1981; Alla Clary interview by H. W. Kamp, August 12, 1969, North Texas State University Oral History Project; Inglish, March 13, 1981; Bill Wilcox interview, August 22, 1980; Ted Wright interview, March 11, 1981.

73. Dulaney, August 15, 1980; Kimbrough, November 23, 1980.

74. Clary, August 12, 1969.

75. Dulaney, August 15, 1980.

76. Wright, March 11, 1981; Robert Bradshaw interview, May 11, 1981.

77. Dulaney, August 15, 1980; Kimbrough, November 23, 1980.

78. Bradshaw, May 11, 1981.

79. Steinberg, *Sam Rayburn,* 199; Dulaney, August 15, 1980; Kimbrough, November 23, 1980; Wilcox, August 22, 1980; Bradshaw, May 11, 1981. It may have been part of the political folklore to pay special attention to handwritten letters. In 1937 Speaker Bankhead advised new members: "Answer those letters from constituents the day you get them. Reply first to those written in pencil on tablet paper. They come from somebody at the head of the creek who'll be your friend for life"; Walter Judson Heacock, "William Brockman Bankhead: A Biography" (Ph.D. diss., University of Wisconsin, 1952), ii.

80. Bradshaw, May 11, 1981; Alla Clary spoke of visitors from the district frequently being taken to lunch; Clary, August 12, 1969.

81. Told to the author by Karl Trever, January 5, 1982.

82. Freeman, January 6, 1982.

83. Nash, June 5, 1980.

84. Ray Roberts interview, June 16, 1980; Ray Roberts interview by Michael L. Gillette, June 9, 1975, Lyndon Baines Johnson Library.

85. Dulaney, August 15, 1980.

86. Ibid.

Chapter 4

1. Alfred Steinberg, *Sam Rayburn: A Biography* (New York: Hawthorn, 1975), 102.

2. Fiorina considers that "customarily, marginal districts are identified by victory percentages of 50–50 percent," a marginal district being one not firmly in the camp of a political party; Morris P. Fiorina, *Congress: Keystone of the Washington Establishment* (New Haven, Conn.: Yale University Press, 1977), 7. In a one-party state like Texas in the Rayburn era, fifty-five percent seems a reasonable cutoff point for primary votes close enough that defeat of the incumbent is a realistic possibility. If this measure is used, Rayburn's district was not always safe and secure. Using percentage of election vote rather than primary vote, however, Rayburn's district is at the extreme of safeness; see Barbara Hinckley, *The Seniority System in Congress* (Bloomington: Indiana University Press, 1971), 101–102.

3. Steinberg, *Sam Rayburn,* 53–55.

4. Ibid., 71–72.

5. Ibid., 100–103.

6. Friends-and-neighbors voting was common in southern states; see V. O. Key, *Southern Politics* (New York: Vintage, 1949), 302.

7. Sam Rayburn to N. A. Burton, February 23, 1916.

8. Steinberg, *Sam Rayburn*, 53–55.

9. Ibid., 54.

10. Sam Rayburn to Thomas Steger, February 28, 1916.

11. Thomas Steger to Sam Rayburn, February 24, 1916; Sam Rayburn to F. M. Gibson, June 1, 1916; Thomas Steger to Sam Rayburn, April 26, 1916.

12. See Sam Hanna Acheson, *Joe Bailey: The Last Democrat* (New York: Macmillan, 1932). A more objective treatment of Bailey is Bob Charles Holcomb, "Senator Joe Bailey, Two Decades of Controversy" (Ph.D. diss., Texas Technological College, 1968).

13. Rayburn's early ties to Bailey are described in C. Dwight Dorough, *Mr. Sam* (New York: Random House, 1962), 64–65, 96–97; see also Steinberg, *Sam Rayburn*, 8, 21. Bailey must have been an impressive person with his six-foot, three-inch stature and loud, booming voice. For many years he kept his hair long in the pre–Civil War style. He also wore clothing in the antebellum style—a large hat and Prince Albert coat. He is said to have had an explosive temper but also charismatic qualities he used in dealing with a crowd. He spoke with confidence. See Holcomb, "Senator Joe Bailey," 5, 9, 15. See also Joseph Alsop and Robert Kintner, "Never Leave Them Angry," *Saturday Evening Post*, January 18, 1941, 76–77. They note that Bailey supported Rayburn in his first congressional race.

14. Randell had announced against Bailey before Bailey's retirement, planning to run against Bailey on a progressive platform; see Holcomb, "Senator Joe Bailey," 498. Randell also challenged Bailey to debate in 1908 on the question of public officials accepting fees and gifts from corporations; of course Bailey did not accept. See ibid., 474.

15. Homer Thornberry interview, January 4, 1980.

16. Farming and politics occupied Rayburn's time when Congress was not in session; see Steinberg, *Sam Rayburn*, 200–209.

17. Sam Rayburn to J. T. Bizzell, February 22, 1916.

18. Sam Rayburn to H. E. Ellis, March 14, 1916.

19. Ibid.

20. Sam Rayburn to D. L. Dement, April 12, 1916.

21. Sam Rayburn to Ben Patterson, May 2, 1916; Sam Rayburn to W. H. Lankford, June 9, 1916.

22. Rayburn to Patterson, May 2, 1916.

23. N. A. Burton to Sam Rayburn, May 12, 1916.

24. Dorough, *Mr. Sam,* 90–97.

25. Ibid.

26. Sam Rayburn to J. W. Cannon, March 31, 1916. Lewis L. Gould's *Progressives and Prohibitionists* (Austin: University of Texas Press, 1973) is an excellent treatment of prohibition in Texas.

27. Burton to Rayburn, March 12, 1916.

28. Typewritten letter in SRL 1916 Texas Politics File, captioned Editorial, "Congressman Rayburn," *Bonham Daily Favorite,* July 4, 1916, unpaginated.

29. Typewritten letter in SRL 1916 Texas Politics File, captioned "What Rayburn has Done," *Bonham Daily Favorite,* July 18, 1916, unpaginated.

30. Typewritten letter in SRL 1916 Texas Politics File, captioned "Sam Rayburn's Labor and Other Votes," *Bonham Daily Favorite,* July 20, 1916, unpaginated.

31. Ibid.

32. Seth Sheppard McKay, *Texas Politics, 1906–1944* (Lubbock: Texas Tech Press, 1952), 326–327, 357–359.

33. Dorough, *Mr. Sam,* 325.

34. Lee Simmons to Sam Rayburn, June 19, 1944.

35. George Norris Green, *The Establishment in Texas Politics* (Westport, Conn.: Greenwood, 1979), 22–44.

36. Ibid., 49–50; idem, "The Far Right Wing in Texas Politics, 1930's–1960's" (Ph.D. diss., Florida State University, 1966), 52–53.

37. McKay, *Texas Politics,* 395–466.

38. Green, *Establishment in Texas Politics,* 50; idem, "Far Right Wing," 50.

39. Green, *Establishment in Texas Politics,* 46–47; idem, "Far Right Wing," 47. In spite of these difficulties, Roosevelt remained popular with Texas farmers. Patenaude wrote that rural Texans had a "blind, almost child-like devotion" to Roosevelt; Lionel V. Patenaude, "The New Deal in Texas" (Ph.D. diss., University of Texas, 1953), 279.

40. Dwayne L. Little, "The Political Leadership of Speaker Sam Rayburn, 1940–1961" (Ph.D. diss., University of Cincinnati, 1970), 84.

41. Fred Horton to Sam Rayburn, January 8, 1944.

42. G. C. Harris interview, May 21, 1980.

43. Sam Rayburn to Fred Horton, January 11, 1944.

44. Harris, May 21, 1980.

45. For example, Gus Hodges to Sam Rayburn, April 20, 1944. Rayburn said that he heard "from reliable sources that upwards of $200,000 was spent to beat me"; quoted in Dorough, *Mr. Sam,* 355. Most of the opposition funding must have gone to Morris; Green wrote that Rayburn was opposed by an anti–New Deal opponent "who represented oil, business and utility interests in Dallas"; Green, *Establishment in Texas Politics,* 48.

46. Jack McCullough to Sam Rayburn, January 13, 1944.

47. Leaflet titled "Teachers for G. C. Morris for Congress Club," SRL 1944 Texas and District Politics File.

48. Carl Nall to Sam Rayburn, March 1, 1944.

49. "Morris Voted against Farm Bills, Attorney Says in Radio Address," *Greenville Banner,* July 8, 1944, 1.

50. Gus Hodges to Sam Rayburn, February 4, 1944.

51. For opposition by utilities to rural electrification legislation, see Arthur M. Schlesinger, Jr., *The Politics of Upheaval* (Boston: Houghton Mifflin, 1960), 383; see also D. Clayton Brown, *Electricity for Rural America* (Westport, Conn.: Greenwood, 1980). For opposition by utilities to the Holding Company Act, see Robert Bartley interview, January 6, 1982; Steinberg, *Sam Rayburn,* 125–129.

52. David Batter, "Rayburn at Crossroads of Career in Hard Fight for Renomination," *Dallas News,* July 7, 1944, unpaginated; "Scrapbook 1939–1979 (extra)."

53. Typewritten letter in SRL 1944 Texas and District Politics File, captioned W. C. Poole, Jr., "Rayburn Fumbled the Ball," *Greenville Morning Herald,* undated, unpaginated.

54. Ibid. A political ad appeared in the Bonham paper, which reprinted this *Greenville Morning Herald* editorial; see, "Editorials Reprinted from the *Greenville Morning Herald*," *Bonham Daily Favorite*, July 17, 1944, unpaginated; "Scrapbook 1935–1954."

55. Little, "Political Leadership," 98.

56. W. A. Hawkins to Sam Rayburn, January 8, 1944; Sam Rayburn to Lewis Brown, January 21, 1944; Sam Rayburn to Miss Lou Arterberry, January 21, 1944; Sam Rayburn to John Large, January 21, 1944; Sam Rayburn to Wiley Hodges, January 21, 1944.

57. Sam Rayburn to H. A. Cunningham, May 22, 1944.

58. "Rayburn Ends Visit Here; Believes War to Last Long Time," *Bonham Daily Favorite*, January 9, 1944, 1.

59. Sam Rayburn to Charlie Tune, March 1, 1944.

60. Carl Nall to Sam Rayburn, March 4, 1944.

61. J. A. Benton to Sam Rayburn, June 10, 1944.

62. Sam Rayburn to Gus Hodges, March 20, 1944.

63. Lee Simmons to Sam Rayburn, February 14, 1944.

64. John McCormack interview, March 11, 1980.

65. R. C. Slagle interview, October 17, 1980.

66. John McCormack interview with Deward Brown, July 18, 1969.

67. Roland Boyd interview, May 22, 1980.

68. Edward L. Schapsmeier and Fredrich H. Schapsmeier, *Henry A. Wallace of Iowa* (Ames: Iowa State University Press, 1968), 264, 270. Sen. Tom Connally of Texas worked to get Rayburn the vice-presidential spot in 1940 until it was clear that Roosevelt wanted Henry Wallace; see Frank Herbert Smyrl, "Tom Connally and the New Deal" (Ph.D. diss., University of Oklahoma, 1968), 202. The Bonham paper reported that Sam Rayburn had a good chance for the vice presidency because he could be especially effective at attacking Wilkie's ties with the utility industry. He was also viewed as a candidate who could produce harmony between the Garner and Roosevelt forces in Texas. See "Sam Rayburn Boomed as Democratic Nominee for Vice President by Critics," *Bonham Daily Favorite*, July 10, 1940, 1, 4. Roosevelt, however, was hostile to Rayburn's friendliness toward Garner; see Robert A. Caro, *The Years of Lyndon Johnson: The Path to Power* (New York: Knopf, 1982), 586–594.

69. James MacGregor Burns, *Roosevelt: The Soldier of Freedom* (New York: Harcourt Brace Jovanovich, 1970), 504.

70. Harold F. Gosnell, *Truman's Crises: A Political Biography of Harry S Truman* (Westport, Conn.: Greenwood, 1980), 180–184. Little believes Rayburn was denied the vice-presidential place in 1944 because he was a southerner; Dwayne L. Little, "The Congressional Career of Sam Rayburn 1913–1961" (M.A. thesis, University of Cincinnati, 1963), 160–161. Former Congressman Gossett believes Rayburn would have been vice president were it not for the close race he had in the primary; Ed Gossett interview by H. W. Kamp, June 27, 1969 and August 1, 1969, North Texas State University Oral History Collection. Green has noted that some of the anti–New Dealers claimed the split Texas delegation at the Democratic convention kept Rayburn from getting the nomination for vice president; Green, *Establishment in Texas Politics,* 48.

71. Little, "Political Leadership," 81–82.

72. Green, *Establishment in Texas Politics,* 48.

73. Little, "Political Leadership," 81–82.

74. Charles Jones to Sam Rayburn, April 17, 1944.

75. Ibid.

76. Sam Rayburn to Charles Jones, April 25, 1944.

77. Sam Rayburn to H. A. Cunningham, April 25, 1944.

78. H. A. Cunningham to Sam Rayburn, May 13, 1944.

79. Gus Hodges to Sam Rayburn, July 25, 1944.

80. Nall to Rayburn, March 1, 1944.

81. For example, Charles Tune to Sam Rayburn, April 19, 1944; John Fitzgerald to Sam Rayburn, April 21, 1944.

82. For example, Gus Hodges to Rayburn, April 20, 1944; signature illegible to Sam Rayburn, June 16, 1944; B. S. Graham to Sam Rayburn, June 15, 1944.

83. M. H. Edmondson, sponsor of a leaflet titled "Congressman Sam Rayburn and Majors Army Air Field," July 17, 1944, SRL 1944 Texas Politics File.

84. Bourke Cartwright to Sam Rayburn, July 11, 1944.

85. Sam Rayburn to My dear Friend, June 28, 1944.

86. Sam Rayburn to Mrs. Pearl Seaton, July 1, 1944.

87. Transcripts of radio speeches by James Buster, July 4, 1944 and July 27 [sic], 1944, SRL 1944 Texas Politics File.

88. Quoted in Little, "Political Leadership," 92.

89. Gus Hodges to Rayburn, July 25, 1944.

90. Harris, May 21, 1980.

91. "Morris Voted against Farm Bills, Attorney Says in Radio Address."

92. Little, "Political Leadership," 90.

93. Little, "Congressional Career of Sam Rayburn," 160–161.

94. Campaign schedule, July 8, 1944, SRL 1944 Texas Politics File.

95. Campaign schedule, July 12, 1944, SRL 1944 Texas Politics File.

96. Sam Rayburn to Sterling Harte, June 19, 1944.

97. Quoted in H. G. Dulaney, Edward Hake Phillips, and MacPhelan Reese, eds., *Speak Mr. Speaker* (Bonham, Tex.: Sam Rayburn Foundation, 1978), 111.

98. Little, "Political Leadership," 146–147; Dorough, *Mr. Sam,* 383.

99. John W. Carpenter to Sam Rayburn, May 25, 1948. Nor was Carpenter the only political enemy of Rayburn's to have a change of heart. E. B. Germany, the ultraconservative oil and steel millionaire who had been a backer of the Texas Regulars (Green, *Establishment in Texas Politics,* 46, 49), wrote Rayburn's Fannin County leader in 1952: "In line with our telephone conversation today, if there is anything that you know of that I can do to promote the Speaker's welfare in his campaign for re-election in his district, I shall be happy to do it. As you know, I am out of the office a great deal and if you should happen to be coming to Dallas any time soon, I would appreciate your giving me a ring before you come so that I can make some time available to discuss the Speaker's situation with you"; E. B. Germany to Buster Cole, June 12, 1952. Germany discussed some of his political views and activities in an interview for the LBJ Library; E. B. Germany interview by Dorothy Pierce McSweeny, May 24, 1969, Lyndon Baines Johnson Library. In this interview Germany expressed opposition to Roosevelt but none to Rayburn.

100. See W. H. Kittrell, Jr., "Pay Tribute to Mr. Sam," *Longview News,* undated and unpaginated; scrapbook titled "Dedication of the Sam Rayburn Library, October 9, 1957."

101. Bartley, January 6, 1982. A good treatment of holding company practices is found in Rayburn's comments in *Congressional Record* 79 (June 27, 1935): 10315–10326. Treatments of holding company practices and the act are Clair Wilcox, *Public Policies toward Business* (Homewood, Ill.: Dorsey, 1960), 629–636; Alfred E. Kahn, *The Economics of Regulation: Principles and Institutions* (New York: Wiley, 1971), 70–77.

102. Quoted in Dulaney, Phillips, and Reese, *Speak Mr. Speaker,* 59.

103. R. B. Ridgway to Sam Rayburn, undated.

104. Slagle, October 17, 1980. Stephenson also claimed that Rayburn did not believe Truman would win in 1948, a statement he supported with an interview with Austin attorney and political activist Creekmore Fath; Charles W. Stephenson, "The Democrats of Texas and Texas Liberalism, 1944–1968: A Study in Political Frustration" (M.A. thesis, Southwest Texas State College, 1967), 14. There is little doubt that the odds against Truman in 1948 were overwhelming; see, for example, Gosnell, *Truman's Crises,* 391–412.

105. For example, Gosnell, *Truman's Crises,* 377–379.

106. Green, "Far Right Wing," 206–209.

107. G. C. Harris to Sam Rayburn, February 12, 1948.

108. G. C. Harris to Sam Rayburn, February 16, 1948.

109. Sam Rayburn to G. C. Harris, February 18, 1948.

110. Sam Rayburn to Mr. and Mrs. Norris Head, February 10, 1948.

111. G. C. Harris to Sam Rayburn, March 1, 1948.

112. Lee Simmons to Sam Rayburn, March 3, 1948.

113. Sam Rayburn to Lee Simmons, March 8, 1948.

114. "Rayburn Speaks in Commerce Saturday Night," *Bonham Daily Favorite,* July 19, 1948, unpaginated; "Scrapbook 1935–1954."

115. Slagle, October 17, 1980.

116. Buster Cole interview, August 21, 1980.

117. Sam Rayburn to Miss Ollie Coon, May 14, 1948.

118. Sam Rayburn to Fred Conn, March 19, 1948.

119. "David H. Brown Is Candidate for Congress," *Bonham Daily Favorite,* May 11, 1948, unpaginated; "Scrapbook 1935–1954."

120. Fred Conn to Sam Rayburn, March 15, 1948.

121. Sam Rayburn to L. E. Fuller, May 20, 1948.

122. William Cantrell, Jr., to Sam Rayburn, March 3, 1948.

123. Lester Loftice to Sam Rayburn, July 6, 1948.

124. Sam Rayburn to Ray Roberts, July 9, 1948.

125. G. C. Morris to Will Murphy, undated, SRL 1948 Texas Politics File.

126. Dick Rayburn, pencil notation on back of G. C. Morris to Will Murphy, undated, SRL 1948 Texas Politics File.

127. Charles Tune to Sam Rayburn, July 17, 1948.

128. For example, see Rene Kimbrough interview, November 23, 1980.

129. Ibid. Another aspect of this event is discussed in the Kate Reed Estes interview, February 13, 1981.

130. Boyd, May 22, 1980.

131. Ibid.

132. *Texas Almanac, 1980–1981* (Dallas: Dallas News, 1981), 131.

133. For the Morris campaign's denial, see the political ad titled, "A Self-explanatory Statement," *Bonham Daily Favorite,* July 21, 1948, unpaginated; "Scrapbook 1935–1954."

134. McKinney insurance agents, press release, July 22, 1948, SRL 1948 Texas Politics File.

135. Political leaflet, July 6, 1948, SRL 1948 Texas Politics File.

136. Press release, "Revolving Fund for Purchase of Natural Fiber Act," July 1948, SRL 1948 Texas Politics File.

137. Sam Rayburn to My dear Friends, July 19, 1948.

138. Handbill distributed in Royse City, undated, SRL 1948 Texas Politics File.

139. Sam Rayburn to Frank Johnston, June 3, 1948.

140. Cole, August 21, 1980.

141. For Rayburn's dislike of social occasions, see Dorough, *Mr. Sam,* 428–429; Alsop and Kitner, "Never Leave Them Angry," 23.

142. Cecil Dickson interview, June 29, 1980.

143. Skip Hollandsworth, "Reagan Brown," *Westward,* December 6, 1981, 11.

144. Robert E. Baskin, "Political Babe in Woods Challenging Sam Rayburn," *Dallas Morning News,* June 13, 1952, unpaginated; "Scrapbook 1939–1960 (extra)."

145. "Reagan Brown for Congress 4th District," *Bonham Daily Favorite,* June 25, 1952, unpaginated; "Scrapbook 1935–1954."

146. Boyd, May 22, 1980; Sam Rayburn to Fred Conn, May 24, 1952; Steinberg, *Sam Rayburn,* 276.

147. Rayburn to Conn, May 24, 1952.

148. Boyd, May 22, 1980.

149. Vernon Beckham to Sam Rayburn, June 5, 1952; Gus Hodges to Sam Rayburn, June 19, 1952.

150. Fred Conn to Fred Massengill, May 28, 1952; Ward Mayborn to Fred Massengill, May 22, 1952.

151. Fred Massengill to Sam Rayburn, May 23, 1952.

152. Sam Rayburn to G. C. Harris, May 29, 1952.

153. Gus Hodges to Fred Massengill, May 24, 1952.

154. W. M. (Pete) Rodes to Sam Rayburn, May 31, 1952.

155. Conn to Massengill, May 28, 1952.

156. Ibid.

157. Mayborn to Massengill, May 22, 1952.

158. Beckham to Rayburn, June 5, 1952.

159. Vernon Beckham to Sam Rayburn, June 26, 1952.

160. Beckham to Rayburn, June 5, 1952.

161. Don Davis to Sam Rayburn, June 24, 1952.

162. Fred Massengill to Sam Rayburn, June 16, 1952.

163. Fred Massengill to Sam Rayburn, June 23, 1952.

164. Fred Massengill to Sam Rayburn, June 27, 1952.

165. Charlton Griffith to Dear Sir, May 22, 1952.

166. Fred Massengill to Sam Rayburn, May 23, 1952.

167. Gus Hodges to Massengill, May 24, 1952.

168. Charles Tune to Sam Rayburn, June 12, 1952.

169. Lee Simmons to Buster Cole, June 11, 1952.

170. Sam Rayburn to Ray Cookston, June 29, 1952.

171. Gus Hodges to Rayburn, June 19, 1952.

172. Hollandsworth, "Reagan Brown."

173. Sam Rayburn to Roland Boyd, January 21, 1954. Finney did, however, announce in 1961 his plans to run against Rayburn in the 1962 primary. Rayburn, of course, died in late 1961, so the contest between the two never occurred. See Dorough, *Mr. Sam,* 469.

174. A. G. McRae telegram to Sam Rayburn, February 24, 1954.

175. Buster Cole to Sam Rayburn, February 6, 1954.

176. For an example of the belief that TP&L funded McRae, see M. B. Smith to Sam Rayburn, June 7, 1954.

177. Buster Cole to Sam Rayburn, February 19, 1954.

178. Ibid.; Sam Rayburn to Buster Cole, February 13, 1954.

179. Ibid.

180. A. G. McRae to Sam Rayburn, March 6, 1954.

181. Emmett Thompson to Sam Rayburn, May 26, 1954.

182. Sam Rayburn to Buster Cole, June 9, 1954.

183. Boyd, May 22, 1980; Slagle, October 17, 1980.

184. J. D. Wallace to Sam Rayburn, April 17, 1952.

185. See Dale Miller interview, June 13, 1980.

186. Green, *Establishment in Texas Politics,* 48.

187. John Davidson, "The Very Rich Life of Enrico Di Portanova," *Texas Monthly*, March 1982, 124.

188. Green, *Establishment in Texas Politics,* 49.

189. Judge Joe Ingraham and Jack Porter interviews by Dr. Maclyun Burg, November 9, 1972, Dwight D. Eisenhower Library.

190. Ray Roberts interview by Michael L. Gillette, June 9, 1975, Lyndon Baines Johnson Library.

191. "J. Howard Pew," *New York Times*, November 28, 1981, 73.

192. Frederick Rudolph, "The American Liberty League, 1934–1940," *American Historical Review* 56 (October 1950): 19–33.

193. Green, *Establishment in Texas Politics,* 49.

194. W. G. Hall interview, December 18, 1980.

195. Incredibly, even the 1981 ethics legislation, passed in the wake of Texas House Speaker Clayton's victory at his bribery trial, did not address the conversion of campaign funds for personal use.

Chapter 5

1. See generally Morris Fiorina, *Congress: Keystone of the Washington Establishment* (New Haven, Conn.: Yale University Press, 1977).

2. An example of an early congressman who better fits Fiorina's thesis is John Nance Garner, who was certainly policy-oriented and did not have much of a constituency orientation. Garner's biographer wrote that Garner did not canvass his district for thirty years and also "franked no speeches home"; Bascom N. Timmons, *Garner of Texas* (New York: Harper, 1948), 286.

3. Kate Reed Estes interview, February 13, 1981.

4. Truitt Smith interview, May 16, 1980.

5. Levis Hall interview, May 29, 1980.

6. Smith, May 16, 1980.

7. *Business Week* described Rayburn as never being far off center; "Sam Rayburn: Using 42 Years," *Business Week,* December 4, 1954, 167. Indeed, it is difficult to be a Democratic party leader unless one is a moderate; see Barbara Hinckley, *The Seniority System in Congress* (Bloomington: Indiana University Press, 1971), 104; Robert L. Peabody, *Leadership in Congress* (Boston: Little, Brown, 1976), 470.

8. Henry Jackson interview, June 12, 1960.

9. Richard F. Fenno, Jr., *Home Style* (Boston: Little, Brown, 1978), 136–170.

10. Jackson, June 12, 1980.

11. John Lyle interview, February 26, 1980; H. G. Dulaney interview, June 12, 1981 (not available from the SRL); Lindsy Escoe Pack, "The

Political Aspects of the Texas Tidelands Controversy" (Ph.D. diss., Texas A & M University, 1979), 143–144.

12. Sarah Hughes interview, February 5, 1980; see also Alfred Steinberg, *Sam Rayburn* (New York: Hawthorn, 1975), 83–84; C. Dwight Dorough, *Mr. Sam* (New York: Random House, 1962), 189–192.

13. For example, Robert A. Caro, "The Years of Lyndon Johnson: Lyndon and Mister Sam," *Atlantic,* November 1981, 43–44, 47, 51.

14. Hal Horton to Sam Rayburn, September 16, 1940.

15. Sam Rayburn to Thomas [Rayburn], February 18, 1922; see also Steinberg, *Sam Rayburn,* 69–70; Dorough, *Mr. Sam,* 170–171.

16. D. B. Hardeman, "Sam Rayburn and the House of Representatives," in William S. Livingston, Lawrence Dodd, and Richard Schatt, eds., *The Presidency and the Congress* (Austin: LBJ School, 1979), 242.

17. Roger D. Greene, "Rayburn of Texas," *Houston Post,* December 12, 1954, v-3.

18. Price Daniel interview, January 10, 1979.

19. For discussion of Shivers and his influence in Texas politics, see Sam Kinch and Stuart Long, *Allan Shivers: The Pied Piper of Texas Politics* (Austin: Shoal Creek, 1979); George Norris Green, *The Establishment in Texas Politics* (Westport, Conn.: Greenwood, 1979), 135–150; Jimmy Banks, *Money, Marbles and Chalk* (Austin: Texas Publishing, 1971), 113–129; D. B. Hardeman, "Shivers of Texas: A Tragedy in Three Acts," *Harper's,* November 1956, 50–56.

20. One of the most useful and comprehensive treatments of the politics of the tidelands controversy is Pack, "Texas Tidelands Controversy." See also David Rupert Murph, "Price Daniel: The Life of a Public Man, 1910–1956" (Ph.D. diss., Texas Christian University, 1975), especially 159–219. For a good treatment of the 1952 Presidential race in Texas, see O. Douglas Weeks, *Texas Presidential Politics in 1952* (Austin: University of Texas, Institute of Public Affairs, 1953).

21. Dwayne L. Little, "The Political Leadership of Speaker Sam Rayburn, 1940–1961" (Ph.D. diss., University of Cincinnati, 1970), 246; see also Green, *Establishment in Texas Politics,* 143–147; Pack, "Texas Tidelands Controversy," 222.

22. Little, "Political Leadership," 244–245.

23. W. G. Hall interview, December 18, 1980; Ronnie Dugger, *The Politician* (New York: Norton, 1982), 375.

24. Kinch and Long, *Allan Shivers,* 216.

25. Ibid.; W. G. Hall, December 18, 1980; Levis Hall, May 29, 1980; Green, *Establishment in Texas Politics,* 145.

26. Kinch and Long, *Allan Shivers,* 216; Allan Shivers interview by Joe B. Frantz, May 29, 1970, Lyndon Baines Johnson Library; Banks, *Money, Marbles and Chalk,* 114–117; Green, *Establishment in Texas Politics,* 145–146.

27. Byron Skelton interview, August 13, 1980; Byron Skelton interview by T. H. Baker, October 15, 1968, Lyndon Baines Johnson Library; Green, *Establishment in Texas Politics,* 143; Little, "Political Leadership," 235. The politics of the 1956 presidential election in Texas is examined in O. Douglas Weeks, *One Party Government in 1956* (Austin: University of Texas, Institute of Public Affairs, 1957).

28. Green, *Establishment in Texas Politics,* 143–145.

29. Ibid., 148–149; Banks, *Money, Marbles and Chalk,* 117–118.

30. Shivers, May 29, 1970.

31. Price Daniel interview by Joe B. Frantz, June 5, 1970, Lyndon Baines Johnson Library.

32. Pack, "Texas Tidelands Controversy," 142–143. Dugger wrote that Johnson told Sen. J. William Fulbright, "I'm sorry, but I can't campaign for Adlai in Texas. It would hurt my reelection chances"; Dugger, *Politician,* 376–377.

33. Joe Kilgore interview, January 24, 1980.

34. Ray Peeler interview, February 25, 1981; Herbert S. Parmet, *The Democrats* (New York: Macmillan, 1976), 110.

35. Ray Roberts interview, June 16, 1980; Ray Roberts interview by Michael L. Gillette, June 9, 1975, Lyndon Baines Johnson Library.

36. Daniel, January 10, 1979.

37. Hardeman, "Shivers of Texas," 50–56, 166–170.

38. Daniel, January 10, 1979; Green, *Establishment in Texas Politics,* 177–178; "Party Regulars on Top in Texas," *New York Times,* September 13, 1956, 27; Little, "Political Leadership," 328–330.

39. The charges of a "big steal" are from "Daniel's Forces Victors in Texas," *New York Times,* September 12, 1956, 21; see also Green, *Establishment in Texas Politics,* 178.

40. Little, "Political Leadership," 177.

41. Daniel, January 10, 1979; see also Price Daniel interview by Fred Gantt, February 25, 1967, May 6, 1967, and September 10, 1968, North Texas State University Oral History Collection.

42. Hardeman, "Shivers of Texas," 55.

43. The Senate was closely balanced, making Daniel an important force in making Johnson majority leader. Daniel was initially uncertain that he would align with the Democrats in the Senate because he feared poor treatment owing to his 1952 disloyalty, but Johnson made special efforts to insure Daniel's good treatment by Senate Democrats. See Daniel, February 25, 1967, May 6, 1967, and September 10, 1968; Daniel, June 5, 1970. The friendly relationship between Johnson and Daniel may be seen in letters between them that discuss visits, gifts, health, and political aid, for example, Price Daniel to Lyndon Johnson, November 11, 1955, Lyndon Baines Johnson Library; Price Daniel to Lyndon Johnson, November 14, 1955, Lyndon Baines Johnson Library; Lyndon Johnson to Price Daniel, November 18, 1955, Lyndon Baines Johnson Library.

44. The Johnson suggestion of an alliance is discussed in Daniel, January 10, 1979; Daniel, February 25, 1967, May 6, 1967, and September 10, 1968. Claims of a stolen election may be found in William G. Phillips, *Yarborough of Texas* (Washington, D.C.: Acropolis, 1969), 42–43.

45. Daniel, February 25, 1967, May 6, 1967, and September 10, 1968. Daniel noted that, whereas Johnson made every effort to be friendly toward him when he was a newly elected senator, "Mr. Rayburn had a little different attitude. He was peeved at me for several years, but he got over it finally"; Daniel, June 5, 1970.

46. Pack, "Texas Tidelands Controversy," 201–202. Rayburn claimed that Daniel privately told him at the Ft. Worth convention that he would support the Democratic nominees; Sam Rayburn to Harry Thom, September 19, 1956; Sam Rayburn to D. E. Box, September 19, 1956.

47. Daniel, February 25, 1967, May 6, 1967, and September 10, 1968.

48. Ibid.; Steinberg has suggested a far more inactive role for Rayburn than seems likely; Steinberg, *Sam Rayburn,* 309; cf. Green, *Establishment in Texas Politics,* 177–178.

49. W. G. Hall, December 18, 1980; J. R. Parten interview, January 19, 1980; Green, *Establishment in Texas Politics,* 174, 178, 181; Steinberg, *Sam Rayburn,* 303, 325.

50. For Rayburn's view that the liberals had no place to go, see W. G. Hall, December 18, 1980; Green, *Establishment in Texas Politics,* 177; Little, "Political Leadership," 329. That liberals could and have stayed home rather than vote is seen in Banks, *Money, Marbles and Chalk,* 48.

51. W. G. Hall, December 18, 1980.

52. Richard Bolling interview, June 26, 1980; see also Richard Bolling, *House Out of Order* (New York: Dutton, 1965), 174–194.

53. Harrell R. Rodgers and Charles S. Bullock, *Law and Social Change* (New York: McGraw-Hill, 1972), 2–27; Charles V. Hamilton, *The Bench and the Ballot* (New York: Oxford University Press, 1973), 41–61.

54. Hamilton, *Bench and the Ballot,* 50–59.

55. Carl Albert interview, December 6, 1979.

56. Kilgore, January 24, 1980; Dale Miller interview, June 13, 1980; cf. Frank Ikard interview, June 24, 1980.

57. John Bainbridge, *The Super-Americans* (Garden City, N.Y.: Doubleday, 1961), 78.

58. Ibid., 79–80.

59. For example, Kilgore, January 24, 1980.

60. W. G. Hall, December 18, 1980.

61. Bainbridge, *Super-Americans,* 218.

62. Ibid., 61–62.

63. Jackson, June 12, 1980.

64. Green, *Establishment in Texas Politics,* 147.

65. Banks, *Money, Marbles and Chalk,* 131–132; James W. Lamare, *Texas Politics: Economics, Power, and Policy* (St. Paul, Minn.: West, 1981), 59–60.

66. ELK [initials, but no name or signature] to Sam Rayburn, September 29, 1943, Lyndon Baines Johnson Library.

67. Little considered such fund raising to be a goal of Rayburn's involvement in Texas politics; Little, "Political Leadership," 73–74.

68. Dugger, *Politician,* 224–225. The letter Dugger cites has the following relevant text: "Paul has sent five. I had hoped he would send five times that amount but it isn't here and it may be that some of our folks

down there will get it to me Airmail"; Lyndon Johnson to Sam Rayburn, October 22, 1940, Lyndon Baines Johnson Library. A telegram is also relevant: "Careful check this morning shows we have 105 (One Hundred Five) men where help should be extended between now and Friday. Barrell has been scrapped. Our friends can be helpful now if they want to be by writing me Airmail Special Delivery 339 Munsey Building and directing me to apply as per attached list which I will make up. Hope when you talk to them today and Wednesday in Dallas you will impress importance doing this at once. Hope we can get total at least equivalent to amount I suggested to Paul because looks as if we have fallen down there"; Lyndon Johnson telegram to Sam Rayburn, October 22, 1940, Lyndon Baines Johnson Library; see also Robert Caro, *The Years of Lyndon Johnson: The Path to Power* (New York: Knopf, 1982), 606–664.

69. Bainbridge, *Super-Americans,* 65.

70. H. G. Dulaney, Edward Hake Phillips, and MacPhelan Reese, eds., *Speak Mr. Speaker* (Bonham, Tex.: Sam Rayburn Foundation, 1978), 119. In his effort to get Rayburn to use his friendship with Abercrombie on his behalf, Johnson wrote: "Last night you indicated you might call Myron [Blalock] and Jim Abercrombie. It is particularly important that I get Jim to be a little active and I don't believe I will unless you and Fred tell him what kind of Senator you think I will make"; Lyndon Johnson to Sam Rayburn, July 30, 1948, Lyndon Baines Johnson Library.

71. John Brademas interview, June 24, 1980; Dulaney, Phillips, and Reese, *Speak Mr. Speaker,* 228, 302, 416.

72. Little, "Political Leadership," 75.

73. Ibid., 416.

74. Peeler believed that Rayburn used wealthy oil men to get campaign money for congressmen he liked and who needed campaign funds; Peeler, February 25, 1981. When the money was mailed to the congressmen in 1960, the first batch of letters was sent by registered mail. The receipts show an October 6 mailing date. Caro, *Years of Lyndon Johnson,* 616–617, believed Rayburn was in 1940 unaware of his ability to raise money from independent oil men.

75. Ikard, June 24, 1980; see also Hardeman, "Sam Rayburn and the House," 245–246.

76. Hugh Scott interview, June 23, 1980; Jackson, June 12, 1980. See also Joseph Cooper and David W. Brady, "Institutional Context and Lead-

ership Style: The House from Cannon to Rayburn," *American Political Science Review* 75 (June 1981): 420; Bolling, *House Out of Order*, 65.

77. See Ross Baker, *Friend and Foe in the U.S. Senate* (New York: Free Press, 1980).

78. Grover Sellers interview, October 6, 1979; Peeler, February 25, 1981.

79. Albert, December 6, 1979.

80. Lindy Boggs interview, June 12, 1980. Lyndon Johnson commented, "If I am not as close to the Speaker as I once was, it is because I'm almost fifty years old. I'm too old for him—did you ever notice—he never has men his age around him—he always associates with people twenty and thirty years younger than himself"; Hardeman, "Sam Rayburn and the House," 241.

81. Bolling, June 2, 1980.

82. See Dorough, *Mr. Sam*, 96–97; Steinberg, *Sam Rayburn*, 14–15, 21. Job applicants might go through Senator Bailey to get a state job under Texas House Speaker Rayburn's patronage; see Virgie Turner to J. W. Bailey, November 5, 1912, Joseph W. Bailey Papers, Dallas Historical Society. Archie Parr even went through Bailey to get support from young Sam. He wrote Bailey about a political appointment and asked, "I wish you would write Sam Rayburn and all of your good friends to write Culberson and Sheppard to support me for this position. If we go at it right we can bring enough pressure to bear on them to get their help and win out"; A. Parr to J. W. Bailey, November 7, 1912, Joseph W. Bailey Papers, Dallas Historical Society. Rayburn was viewed as a Bailey lieutenant in the Texas House; see J. H. Collard to J. W. Bailey, April 25, 1913, Joseph W. Bailey Papers, Dallas Historical Society.

83. Bolling described Rayburn as Garner's "aide"; Bolling, *House Out of Order*, 150–151. Dies described his version of the mentor-protégé relationship between Garner and Rayburn: "He [Garner] was tough, wiry, and he taught politics to Sam Rayburn. Sam Rayburn was his boy Friday, and John Garner was very rough with his subordinates and very rough with Sam. I heard him dress Sam down one time before some eight or nine members and I don't think I could have taken it, perhaps I could, but I don't think I could have. But, at any rate, he trained Sam Rayburn—was responsible for Sam's advancement"; Martin Dies interview by A. Ray Stephens, April 23, 1966, North Texas State University Oral History Collection.

84. J. W. Bailey to Sam Rayburn, June 1, 1909.

85. Jim Wright interview, June 23, 1980.

86. Lyle, February 26, 1980; Cooper and Brady, "Institutional Context and Leadership Style," 420.

87. Scott, June 23, 1980.

88. Rene Kimbrough interview, November 23, 1980; Albert, December 6, 1979. In 1936 Smith had endorsed John O'Connor over Sam Rayburn in the race for majority leader. It therefore seems wrong to attribute a long-term bond between Rayburn and Smith. See the unsigned, undated letter on Smith's letterhead endorsing O'Connor, Hatton Sumners Papers, December 1936 File, Dallas Historical Society.

89. Kimbrough, November 23, 1980.

90. Omar Burleson interview, December 18, 1979.

91. Kilgore, January 24, 1980.

92. Vernon Beckham interview, December 17, 1980.

93. Compare W. M. Rodes interview, May 9, 1980 with Gus Hodges to Sam Rayburn, July 25, 1944.

94. Rodes, May 9, 1980.

95. Cecil Dickson interview, June 29, 1980.

96. Lyle, February 26, 1980.

97. Homer Thornberry interview, January 4, 1980; see also Neil MacNeil, *Forge of Democracy* (New York: McKay, 1963), 83.

98. Rayburn had a long-standing opposition to Fisher being seated on Ways and Means as shown in Jere Cooper to Sam Rayburn, November 19, 1948. Fisher was asked, "Did you become associated with Speaker Rayburn and the Board of Education. . . ?" He replied, "No, I would not say that I was included in that rather exclusive group"; O. C. Fisher interview by Dorothy McSweeny, May 8, 1969, Lyndon Baines Johnson Library.

99. Ikard, June 24, 1980; see also MacNeil, *Forge of Democracy,* 83.

100. Fenno, *Home Style,* 214, 248.

Chapter 6

1. Roger H. Davidson, *The Role of the Congressman* (New York: Pegasus, 1969), 180.

2. Ibid., 198.

3. Jim Wright interview, June 23, 1980; Richard Bolling, *House Out of Order* (New York: Dutton, 1965), 68.

4. Joseph Cooper and David W. Brady, "Institutional Context and Leadership Style: The House from Cannon to Rayburn," *American Political Science Review* 75 (June 1981): 420; Price Daniel interview, January 10, 1979.

5. Fred Schwengel interview, June 16, 1980; J. T. Rutherford interview, June 18, 1980.

6. Davidson, *Role of the Congressman*, 72–84.

7. Rayburn's district was not the smallest in population, but its small population was far less than most congressional districts; Neil MacNeil, *Forge of Democracy* (New York: McKay, 1963), 138–140.

8. High-budget campaigns are not new phenomena; see, for example, Caro's discussion of Lyndon Johnson's 1937 Congressional campaign, in which he reported that Ed Clark estimated Johnson's campaign costs between seventy-five thousand and one hundred thousand dollars; Robert A. Caro, "The Years of Lyndon Johnson: The First Campaign," *Atlantic,* April 1982, 75.

9. Robert H. Wiebe, *The Search for Order, 1877–1920* (New York: Hill & Wang, 1967), 133.

10. Ibid., 2.

11. Ibid., 164.

12. Ibid., 3.

13. Walter Dean Burnham, "Party Systems and the Political Process," in William Nisbet Chambers and Walter Dean Burnham, eds., *The American Party Systems* (New York: Oxford University Press, 1967), 227–307.

14. A good perspective on the diverse interests within the New Deal coalition is provided in William E. Leuchtenburg, *Franklin D. Roosevelt and the New Deal, 1932–1940* (New York: Harper & Row, 1963). MacNeil wrote: "Rayburn's Democratic party had long suffered major divisive splits on both economic and racial beliefs, and Rayburn concentrated on minimizing this divisiveness of his party. 'He is the glue that holds the Democrats together,' one House colleague said of him. 'The avoidance of open controversy,' said another, 'is his genius'"; MacNeil, *Forge of Democracy,* 107–108.

15. Roger H. Davidson and Walter J. Oleszek, *Congress and Its Members* (Washington, D.C.: Congressional Quarterly, 1981), 108.

16. Davidson and Oleszek point out the great difficulty in representing a diverse political district; the same difficulties are likely to occur with a Speaker representing a diverse political party; ibid., 117.

17. Bolling, *House Out of Order,* 157–158.

18. William S. White, "Labor Bill Voted by House, 320–79, Senate Acts Today; 35,000 Here Demand a Veto," *New York Times,* June 5, 1947, 1, 2.

19. Bolling, *House Out of Order,* 156–173.

20. Rayburn tried to avoid any break with Truman over civil rights. Reporter Hurd wrote: "The Southern representation seemed to be as solid as heretofore in its break with the White House over the civil rights program. The only exception appeared to be Representative Sam Rayburn of Texas, minority leader, whose floor position gives him special responsibility"; Charles Hurd, "President Ignores Revolts, Predicts Victory in Election," *New York Times,* March 26, 1948, 1, 16.

21. David Halberstam, *The Powers That Be* (New York: Knopf, 1979), 5–6.

22. For a discussion of some of the difficulties the modern congressman has in finding constituents, see Richard F. Fenno, Jr., *Home Style* (Boston: Little, Brown, 1978), 234–236.

23. Richard Bolling interview, June 26, 1980.

24. Ray Roberts has noted that Rayburn only visited his district two or three times a year, but those visits were often long. It generally was not until World War II that congressional sessions lengthened to nearly the entire year. See Ray Roberts interview, June 16, 1980; Davidson and Oleszek, *Congress and Its Members,* 123.

25. W. B. Ragsdale reporter's file on Sam Rayburn, undated.

26. Ibid.; see also W. B. Ragsdale interview, June 27, 1980.

Index